Lifestyle Drugs and the Neoliberal Family

Toby Miller
General Editor

Vol. 22

The Popular Culture and Everyday Life series
is part of the Peter Lang Media and Communication list.
Every volume is peer reviewed and meets
the highest quality standards for content and production.

PETER LANG
New York • Washington, D.C./Baltimore • Bern
Frankfurt • Berlin • Brussels • Vienna • Oxford

Kristin A. Swenson

Lifestyle Drugs and the Neoliberal Family

PETER LANG
New York • Washington, D.C./Baltimore • Bern
Frankfurt • Berlin • Brussels • Vienna • Oxford

Library of Congress Cataloging-in-Publication Data

Swenson, Kristin A.
Lifestyle drugs and the neoliberal family / Kristin A. Swenson.
pages cm. — (Popular culture and everyday life; vol. 22)
Includes bibliographical references and index.
1. Affective disorders—Chemotherapy—United States—History.
2. Psychotropic drugs—United States—History.
3. Work environment—Government policy—United States.
4. Capitalism—United States. I. Title.
RC537.S896 338.4'7615788—dc23 2012050309
ISBN 978-1-4331-1044-3 (hardcover)
ISBN 978-1-4539-1051-1 (e-book)
ISSN 1529-2428

Bibliographic information published by **Die Deutsche Nationalbibliothek**.
Die Deutsche Nationalbibliothek lists this publication in the "Deutsche Nationalbibliografie"; detailed bibliographic data is available on the Internet at http://dnb.d-nb.de/.

29 Broadway, 18th floor, New York, NY 10006
www.peterlang.com

for Brynnar

CONTENTS

ACKNOWLEDGMENTS

This book began as a dissertation at the University of Minnesota. I would like to thank my committee for their immense encouragement as the project morphed from an idea into a viable dissertation. My advisor, mentor, and dear friend, Ronald W. Greene, and my committee members Mary Vavrus, Margaret Werry, and Kirt Wilson, all offered guidance and encouragement throughout the dissertation process. I recognize my great fortune in having a committee of remarkable scholars, teachers, and, most importantly, friends that continue to be exemplars of living a full and meaning life inside and outside the academy.

I also want to thank my friends and colleagues at Butler University, especially my colleagues in the Media, Rhetoric and Culture program: Margaretha Geertsema-Sligh, Allison Harthcock, and Ann Savage, who literally cheered me on when I needed it most. Robin Turner and Terri Carney graciously sat next to me on writing dates. TC also taught me the invaluable skill of how to covertly change my son's diaper while sitting in a booth at our local coffee shop. I thank Tamara Leech for sharing her writing strategies and offering her encouragement. Susan Berger at Irwin Library was invaluable at locating resources. John Mugge provided helpful editorial comments. Thanks to Annette Lee and Melissa Friedman for their administrative support. I am grateful to my wonderful and smart students, especially Lauren Dunford, who offered her research assistance and organizational skills during the summer of 2011, and Mckeena Imholte, who proofread parts of this book.

I am indebted to Toby Miller for encouraging me to submit a proposal to this series. I am grateful to the staff at Peter Lang including Mary Savigar for her patience and for her assistance with the title; Phyllis Korper for her keen editorial eye; and Sophie Appel for formatting the manuscript and creating the fabulous cover design.

I want to graciously thank Megan Foley, Raymie McKerrow, and Greg Seigworth for their thoughtful comments to chapter 1 of this manuscript. Special thanks to Kristen Hoerl, Casey Kelly, and Jonathan Rossing for inviting me into their writing group and offering insightful feedback and continued encouragement. And a thank you to Rose Cherubin for her long distance support.

This book would not have come to fruition without the intellectual companionship and kindness of friends far and near. Meredith

Gill, Chani Marchiselli, and Cecily Marcus have been there for the long haul and have not waivered in their encouragement. I am grateful to J.D. Mininger for his invitation to present this work to his colleagues and students at Vytautas Magnus University. David Moscowitz and Leigh Moscowitz opened their hearts and porch to us upon our arrival to Indianapolis. Ageeth Sluis and Elise Edwards have proved that some friends do become family and without their love and support this project would not have been completed. Hilene Flanzbaum and Geoff Sharpless invited us into their family and have feed, nurtured, and cared for us so generously that there are no words to express my gratitude. I am grateful to Cesare Casarino for teaching me Spinoza, and to both Cesare and Jason Christenson for the many delicious meals and conversations about love, life, and theory. I am fortunate indeed.

Thanks to my mom, Karen Brown, for her headstrong belief in me and her unyielding love and encouragement.

I met Brynnar Swenson at a time when this project was still trying to find its theoretical voice. I fondly think back to those days in Minneapolis reading across the table from each other in one of the many coffee houses, and then sharing our thoughts over a night-cap in one of the many great bars that the twin-cities has to offer. He is my best reader and defender of my work. I am grateful for his wickedly smart mind and his intellectual companionship, his intensity of love, his ability to make me laugh, and for taking the brunt of the domestic responsibilities in order to give me time and space to write. I am most thankful that he wanted to "join forces," to make a life of love, a love that then made Aksel, which then made even more love. . . .

Permissions

A special thank you to the following presses for the permission to reprint chapter 1, and portions of chapter 2 and chapter 3.

Versita Press:

"Affective Labor and Governmental Policy: George W. Bush's New Freedom Commission on Mental Health," *Baltic Journal of Law and Politics,* 4 (2) (2011): 1-23.

SUNY Press:

"Productive Bodies: Women, Work, and Depression." In *Governing the Female Body: Health, Gender, and Networks of Power.* Lori Reed and Paula Saukko (Eds.). New York: State University of New York Press, (2010): 134-155.

International Communication Association and Wiley Blackwell Press:

"Capitalizing on affect: Viagra (in)action." *Communication, Culture, and Critique,* 1 (3) (2008): 311-328.

"It is then that you say, 'That's what it was, but I don't know if I really said it, or if I was convincing enough.' And you realize that having said it or been convincing hardly matters because, in any case, that is what it is now." —Gilles Deleuze and Félix Guattari

INTRODUCTION

Anxious Robots, Precarious Work, and Lifestyle Drugs

During the 2007 Super Bowl,[1] General Motors aired a controversial commercial in which a GM robot is fired from its union shop and then suffers the dreadful consequences of looking for work in an economic downturn. Demoralized by having no choice but to work in unsatisfying and low-paying service industry positions, the robot commits suicide. The commercial went something like this: The robot, working on the assembly line at the GM factory, suddenly drops a bolt. The factory and its workers become eerily silent. The other employees, both human and robot, stare at the robot in disbelief. The robot returns a panicked gaze. The robot is fired. We see the robot exit the garage door of the factory and wander the streets. Soon it passes a Help Wanted sign and begins the mindless work of a sign holder standing on the street advertising House for Sale. The robot's next job is to hold the intercom box at a fast-food drive-in. Finally, the robot stands on a bridge as the song "All by Myself" by Eric Carmen plays in the background. The robot jumps off the bridge into the dark and deep water below. As it is about to make contact with the water, the robot awakens from what was actually a nightmare to find itself back on the assembly line at the GM factory. The voice-over states, "At GM we are obsessed with quality" ("Robot," GM 2007).

How are we to make sense of this 60-second commercial in which a robot has work-related anxiety dreams? Is the anxiety due to the threat of losing its well-paying union job, the kind of job that is almost impossible to get today? How is it that even the robot finds service industry work unsatisfying and unrewarding? Is it because it is no longer producing anything material? Or is it because it is "all by itself," according to the background music, without the camaraderie of its former work colleagues? What we do know is that the robot represents workers from a variety of industries who are faced with the real possibility of losing their job.

The GM robot commercial is unnervingly useful in introducing the economic context that is the backdrop of this book. This commercial can easily be read as a precursor for the current recession that began in December 2007 as it illuminates the economic and work climate in which we now live.[2] For instance, the House for Sale sign certainly foreshadows the housing market crash. The fired robot expresses the failing economy's effect on workers and the precariousness of the workplace. The unsatisfying service industry jobs represent the low-paying and often only available option for many who have been either fired or laid off from their well-paying factory job. In just 60-seconds this commercial manages to express the precariousness of work in a failing economy.

The story is not unfamiliar. An employee loses his or her good union job at a U.S. car manufacturer. The only employment options available are lower paying and less personally satisfying than the union job at the factory. In complete despair, the fired employee attempts suicide. Although in the commercial the robot turns out to be "dreaming," this stress-related and anxiety-producing fear of losing one's jobs is certainly real for many. In fact, the reality is so pervasive that suicide prevention organizations were outraged by the commercial. The American Foundation for Suicide Prevention publicly criticized the ad and demanded that GM not air it again. It was subsequently aired without the suicide. We can wonder if our robot would have fared better had it been on antidepressants. And we certainly hope that the millions of Americans suffering from depression and anxiety do not experience the same fate as our robot in either their waking or sleeping life.[3]

At the time of the airing of the GM Super Bowl commercial, the antidepressant Lexapro was the fifth most dispensed drug in the United States (http://www.Rxlist.com), perhaps for the reasons suggested in that commercial: anxiety over losing one's job and fear of the consequences if one did lose his or her job. Statistically, as the economy declines depression increases, and as depression increases so too does the number of prescriptions written for antidepressants (see Chapter 2), especially in the age of direct-to-consumer (DTC) advertising.

Lifestyle Drugs and the Neoliberal Family weaves together the themes of drugs, work, and subjectivity in order to investigate the attributes that today's workers should emulate as articulated by the advertisements for and promotional materials of lifestyle drugs. Lifestyle drugs, especially for affective disorders like depression, offer hope as they chemically alter our moods to make us happier and more confident even in an economic downturn. Lifestyle drugs present us an opportunity to "feel good" (or, it is hoped, at least better) about our current life-work situations. To advance the discussion begun by the GM robot commercial, the remainder of this Introduction further explains what is meant by the term "precariousness" in reference to work, offers a brief definition of neoliberalism in order to define how this book defines our contemporary capitalist moment, and is followed by a few definitions of affect. But first, I offer a brief discussion on the marketing of lifestyle drugs.

The Marketing of Lifestyle Drugs

Just how are workers to deal with the anxiety and depression that stem from a precarious economy, a high unemployment rate, and a housing market crash, all of which make life increasingly difficult and worrisome? "The good life" is sold to us through the direct-to-consumer (DTC) advertising of lifestyle pharmaceuticals (Elliott 2003). "Lifestyle drugs," a term coined by the popular press, are not necessarily lifesaving drugs; rather, they promote an image of well-being, happiness, and the attainment of the good-life—the manufacturers of lifestyle drugs sell us the desired lifestyle for our current moment within contemporary capitalism. Like the GM robot, we may have good reason to be anxious and worried about job security, but an anti-anxiety pill allows us to feel better even if our material conditions do not change. As the "good life" moves farther and farther out of reach, the simple hope that some semblance of happiness and contentment can be derived from a "happy pill" becomes all the more appealing (Herzberg 2009). The attainment of personal happiness and economic security, or a comforting perception of such, is placed squarely into the hands of the consumer as the advertisements of lifestyle drugs sell us a version of the good life in the form of pills with friendly and soothing-sounding names such as Wellbutrin, Abilify, Concerta, Viagra, and Zoloft.

In the United States, advertisements for prescription medications and their attendant disorders pervade the television airwaves, print media, and Internet. Viewers are seduced into understanding their children's inability to focus as Attention Deficit Disorder, their worries as anxiety, their aching legs as restless legs syndrome, both incontinence and constipation as irritable bowel syndrome, and their lack of libido as sexual dysfunction. For each pharmaceutical, there is a corresponding disorder, and for each disorder there is an advertising campaign to show us a happier and more productive version of ourselves.

Lifestyle drugs differ from lifesaving medications in that lifestyle medications work to produce a more enhanced way of living, whereas lifesaving drugs seek to cure illnesses. As noted above, lifestyle drugs may treat ailments such as baldness, wrinkles, perspiration, erectile dysfunction, hot flashes, incontinence, insomnia, anxiety, adverse side effects of menstruation or menopause, irritable bowel syndrome, and any other bodily and affective imperfections that one desires to correct. Lifestyle drugs are centered more on style or quality of life, many taking the form of a technology of youth, rather than treating life-threatening medical conditions. For example, Viagra, a sexual performance-enhancing medication, may assist men in achieving an erection, whereas medications for cancer may prolong life itself.[4]

Interestingly, but not surprisingly, the growth industry of lifestyle medication coincided with the relaxation of DTC broadcast advertising regulations in August 1997. The United States is the only country besides New Zealand to allow the advertising of prescription drugs directly to consumers.[5] Since the relaxation of U.S. Food and Drug Administration (FDA) regulations on advertising, broadcast spending has significantly increased.[6] Today, the portion of marketing funds allocated for DTC advertising is the fastest-growing component of marketing budgets (Angell 2004: 123). In 1997, pharmaceutical companies spent $1.1 billion on direct-to-consumer advertising; by 2005, big pharma spent $4.2 billion (Donohue, Cevasco, & Rosenthal 2007). Every additional dollar that pharmaceutical companies paid toward DTC advertising in 2000 brought in an additional $4.20 in sales profit (Henry J. Kaiser Foundation 2003).

In the late 1960s, the FDA issued regulations to govern advertising of prescription medication to consumers. In 1981, the first advertisement for prescription medication appeared in *Reader's Digest* for a pneumonia vaccine. In 1983 FDA commissioner Arthur Hull Hayes Jr. declared a moratorium on direct-to-consumer advertising in order to allow the FDA to review regulations (Morrow 1998). The pharmaceutical companies waited in anticipation for two years while the FDA withheld any action until pressured by Congress. The FDA responded in 1985 by removing its moratorium and reinstating the original guidelines.

By the late 1980s television advertisements for Rogaine aired without any mention of the product's name and only the suggestion that consumers visit and talk to their doctors if they were concerned about thinning hair and hair loss. By 1997, the FDA's boundaries were tested as pharmaceutical companies pushed their advertisements to communicate their product to potential consumers. According to Morrow (1998), a commercial for Allegra, an allergy medication, showed people happily "surfing through wheat fields," without any mention of allergies (1). After discussion with the pharmaceutical executives of the makers of Allegra, the FDA allowed the Allegra advertisement to continue to air, initiating the relaxation of their guidelines. "Of the fifty drugs most heavily promoted in 1999 through direct-to-consumer advertising," stated Carl Elliot (2003) in his book *Better Than Well*, "thirteen were drugs that can be used for enhancement purposes," or what we would refer to as lifestyle medications. These were drugs for obesity, baldness, wrinkle control, acne, sexual dysfunction, contraception, social anxiety, and menopause side effects (119).

Pharmaceutical companies in the United States spend twice as much on drug advertising and marketing then they spend on drug research and development (Gagnon & Lexchin 2008). Many DTC television advertisements refer viewers to their online sites for more information, which has increased the spending for the online promotion of pharmaceuticals. In one report, big pharma spent $59 million on their online promotional sites (Choi & Lee 2007). As pharmaceutical companies increase their DTC spending, they reap their reward with an increase in consumers (Spake & Mathew 2007).[7]

Many DTC advertisements have enlisted popular political figures and sports heroes, such as Pfizer's endorsements from Bob Dole and Rafael Palmeiro in its Viagra commercials, to sell its wares. Now it is common practice for favorite celebrities to openly discuss their health issues. Remember Brooke Shields and Tom Cruise's public debate regarding the treatment of postpartum depression with antidepressants in 2005? On *The Today Show*, Cruise criticized Shields for her advocacy of antidepressants to treat post-partum depression. Shields retaliated with an op-ed piece in the *New York Times*. Cruise and Shields aren't the only celebrities to openly discuss their views and preferred medications. Melody Petersen (2002) reported the following in the *New York Times*:

> dozens of celebrities, from Ms. [Lauren] Bacall to Kathleen Turner to Rob Lowe, have been paid hefty fees to appear on television talk shows and morning news programs and to disclose intimate details of ailments that afflict them or people close to them. Often, they mention brand-name drugs without disclosing their financial ties to the medicine's maker. (1)

Drug manufacturers deny making payments for these product placements. Drug companies are able to sidestep FDA regulations as long as they describe these celebrity endorsements on television talk shows as educational campaigns (Petersen 2002).

Name-brand drugs are increasingly frequent on primetime dramas. For instance, the popular *Law & Order* included one plotline that revolved around a cancer drug, Gleevec, sold by Novartis. Actor Martin Sheen, as the president of the United States in NBC's *West Wing*, takes Betaserson, a drug to treat the character's multiple sclerosis. Bill Paxton plays the patriarch, Bill Henrickson, in HBO's *Big Love*, about a polygamous Mormon family. To sustain his masculine mojo and to perform his manly duties, Henrickson relies on a little help from his blue pill, Viagra. And the first season of the television hit *Glee*, a show about a high school glee club, depicts the benefits of pseudoephedrine. The school nurse doles out pseudoephedrine tablets under the guise of the drug being a "vitamin" in order to give the kids the extra bump they need to succeed in both school and glee club practice.

While the FDA may have relaxed regulations for television scripts that revolve around pharmaceuticals, the FDA does require that DTC prescription ads be approved by the governing agency; although, the guidelines do not require that the pharmaceutical companies receive approval prior to distributing their ads. For example, Viagra's (2004) advertisement "Wild Thing" aired for three whole months before its maker, Pfizer, received a letter from the FDA saying that the ad was inappropriate. In 2009, Bayer, the makers of Yaz birth control, spent $20 million to correct an advertising campaign that exaggerated the pill's benefits. The FDA argued that Yaz's advertising campaign overstated Bayer's claim that Yaz cured PMS and unwelcome blemishes. According to Jane Ridley (February 10, 2010) reporting for the *New York Daily News*, "There was no apology, but replacement TV commercials featured a voice-over saying, 'You may have seen some Yaz commercials recently that were not clear. The FDA wants us to correct a few points in the ads.'"[8]

The FDA submits letters to companies demanding that misleading or harmful information be removed, but with a staff of about 30 FDA reviewers and 34,000 DTC advertisements submitted in 2001 alone, by the time many pharmaceutical companies receive a problematic review, that ad cycle may have already been completed (Angell 2004: 124). Bayer's problems with Yaz continue. In April 2012, the FDA ordered Bayer and other drug makers of birth control pills to strengthen blood-clot warnings on their labels. To date, thousands of women have sued Bayer for blood-clotting issues. Bayer has paid out $402.6 million in settlements thus far (Feeley & Kresge 2012).

The FDA divides DTC advertisements into three categories. The first type is referred to as "help-seeking" ads. These advertisements state the symptoms of a treatable disease without mentioning the company's drug. The second category is termed "reminder ads," because they include the name of the product, but do not include the disease or its related ailments. The goal is to build brand-name recognition for the next encounter one has with his or her doctor. In the final category are ads that specify a product claim. These advertisements include the drug's name, its intended use, and the major side effects of the medication. FDA regulations contend that there must be a fair balance between a medication's risks and benefits. In addition, a contact for further information must be provided, such as a website or toll-free number (Weber 2006).

In November 2004, consumer groups gathered to argue to the FDA in favor of a moratorium on direct-to-consumer advertising of prescription drugs (Melillo 2005). Peter Luire, of the Public Citizen's Health Research Group, told the panel that the ads are usually "misleading or dangerous" and Gary Rusking, of Commercial Alert, claimed that the ads create a "culture of disease and fear" as they attempt to "convince people that they are ill" (as cited in Melillo 2005: 18). Many groups demonstrated outrage with the so-called help-seeking ads, arguing that they are merely product placements. One of the examples provided is that of an ad featuring actress Lorraine Bracco of the acclaimed TV show *The Sopranos*, in which she discusses her battle with depression and then sends viewers to the website http://www.depresionhelp.com, which just happens to be a website for the antidepressant medication Zoloft (Melillo 2005).

In response to consumer and governmental criticisms, in August 2005 Pharmaceutical Research and Manufacturers of America (PhRMA) issued voluntary guidelines for its members to follow in their DTC advertising practices (*Washington Drug Letter* August 8, 2005). These include the abolishment of "reminder ads," which, as discussed above, name the product without the conditions or disease it treats. The voluntary guidelines also called for a more balanced relationship between benefits and risks, and for presenting these in a consumer-friendly and easy-to-understand discourse, while maintaining a tone that conveys the seriousness of any and all medical conditions.

In response to criticisms of misleading advertisements, the FDA created the "Bad Ad" program in 2010. The "Bad Ad" program's goal is to "help healthcare providers recognize misleading prescription drug promotion and provide them with an easy way to report this activity to the agency" (http://www.fda.gov).[9] In its first year, 328 reports of false or misleading information were submitted to the FDA (2010–2011 Year End Report).

The aspect of DTC pharmaceuticals advertising that all can agree on is that much like other brand-name products of the past, from Xerox to Rollerblades, many lifestyle medications today have brand-name recognition. Ritalin, Prozac, and Viagra encapsulate not only their particular medicine, dysfunction, and cure, but they also are employed as umbrella terms for all generic medications that follow in their wake.

A closer look at the promotional material of DTC advertising of lifestyle drugs reveals a new understanding of a healthy subjectivity, a subjectivity that is considered healthy if it is medicated. An examination of the cultural representations of a "healthy" subjectivity, as presented in direct-to-consumer advertisements of pharmaceuticals, reveals the relationship between drugs and work. Following the organizational pattern of the heteronormative family—mother, father, and child—along with disorders and medications that primarily relate to these gendered subject positions, *Lifestyle Drugs and the Neoliberal Family* examines the relationship between women, work, and antidepressant medication; men, social potency, and erectile dysfunction medication; children, education, and attention deficit disorder medication; and even the family dog and separation anxiety medication in order to analyze and theorize the manner in which work, sex, and childhood are subsumed by the pharmaceutical industry. In each chapter, I argue that all of these lifestyle drugs present us with an affect of the successful contemporary worker in neoliberal capitalism. That is to say, these advertisements inform all of us as to what qualities are desired and required of workers today. More specifically, these advertisements inform us of the subjectivity that we are to embrace. *Lifestyle Drugs and the Neoliberal Family* argues that drugs do indeed work to put us back to work. In short, what follows is not an argument against the use of pharmaceuticals; rather, *Lifestyle Drugs and the Neoliberal Family* examines the ideal worker presented to us through the advertisements of lifestyle drugs.

Precarity of Work; Precarity of Life

Lifestyle drugs speak to the nation's current anxiety over economic security and stability. Our particular historical and cultural moment is one in which employment and, therefore, daily life itself has become precarious and unstable. No longer is an employee of a good American automaker guaranteed a middle-class wage and a job for the long term. According to the GM commercial, not even a robot can rely on job security. In the United States, basic social services such as health care and retirement are tied to employment; all the while, the ability to secure and keep a well-paying, benefit-inclusive job is more and more difficult. Contingent labor is on the rise while full-time and continuous work with benefits is on the decline (see Coy, Conlin, & Herbst 2010). Moreover, education and technical skills are no longer enough to secure and maintain employment. Now one must have the necessary communication and affective labor skills, which include the ability to get along well with others, and to offer the necessary "service with a smile" that at one time was demanded only of service workers. Affective labor has found its way into the most high tech of positions. While finding, securing, and keeping a good and stable job become more and more difficult and precarious, appropriate affective attributes are increasingly necessary. In other words, as work becomes more contingent and precarious, and the competition for even contingent and contractual labor grows increasingly intense, workers are required to demonstrate job-appropriate affective attributes such as confidence, competence, and communicative abilities regardless of the unstable and insecure situations in which they find themselves.

The term "precarity" is defined as the unstable and insecure work and life experience within contemporary capitalism. Just as the GM robot is threatened with being fired at any moment, everyday workers maintain a constant state of financial and economic instability and unease, as the only thing stable about job security is that it remains insecure. Millions of Americans find themselves in economic dire straits—over 8% of the workforce in the United States is unemployed (U.S. Bureau of Labor Statistics, Unemployment in August 2012) and "roughly four million families lost their homes to foreclosure between the beginning of 2007 and early 2012" (Foreclosures: *New York Times*).[10] These are indeed stressful times.

While work and life have become increasingly precarious, the burden of precarity is placed squarely on the worker. To maintain their viability for employment, workers must always be adaptable to a continuously altering work ground. This "flexible worker" is to be flexible both in mind and in body. She should be able to adapt to new tasks, situations, and communication skill sets quickly and easily (Lazzarato 1996; Martin 1995, 2000). The workplace itself must maintain a flexibility that speaks to the rapid changes in technologies, growing networks of communication, and an always shifting economic and political climate. While this flexibility has resulted, in some instances, in flexible work time, flexible work spaces, and flexible work tasks, all of this flexibility has led to an unnerving sense of anxiety in work-life (Gill & Pratt 2008; Gregg 2008).

Work-life was at one time experienced by some and imagined by others to be stable; continuous; unionized; and inclusive of health benefits, sick leave, vacation pay, set hours, retirement plans, and a known career trajectory. This model has essentially disappeared, to be replaced by part-time, contingent, and contractual labor that often lacks a benefit package, paid holidays, sick leave, maternity leave, a retirement plan, and any sense or semblance of permanence or security (Vosko, MacDonald, & Campbell 2009).

Rosalind Gill and Andy Pratt (2008) explain precarity this way:

> Transformations in advanced capitalism under the impact of globalization, information and communication technologies, and changing modes of political and economic governance have produced an apparently novel situation in which increasing numbers of workers in affluent societies

> are engaged in insecure, casualized or irregular labour. While capitalist labour has always been characterized by intermittency for lower-paid and lower-skilled workers, the recent departure is the addition of well-paid and high-status workers into this group of "precarious workers." (2)

As the global economy even in the affluent "West" becomes increasingly unstable, it directly affects the work-life of the population, from the already insecure laborers to now include those who find that their high-skilled and desirable attributes are hired on a contractual labor process. Precarity attaches equally to various forms of labor, from low-paid care labor to highly paid creative labor (see Gill & Pratt 2008). As Fudge and Owens (2006) note, "What is distinctive about the new employment relationships is the degree to which they are precarious" (11). They point to four trends in "precarious labor." The first is "the degree of certainty of continuing employment"; the second is "control over the labour process, which is linked to the presence or absence of trade unions and professional associations and relates to control over working conditions, wages, and the pace of work"; the third is "the degree of regulatory protection"; and fourth is "income level" (11). And there's the rub. As precarious work becomes increasingly dominant as a mode of work-life among the more affluent, a new form of subjectivity is rendered visible.

An important dimension of this emerging subjectivity is that the affect of the worker has become increasingly vital to the work-life of the worker. This has led to the use of the critical term "precariousness "as a way to describe both life and work. Lisa Adkins and Eeva Jokinen (2008) explain:

> The theorization of work, working, and of the relations of work to life are all currently undergoing substantial and radical revision. This revision strikes at the core not only of understandings of work and labour but also at some of the major themes and motifs of social and cultural theory. Ideas that capitalism now embraces Life, through suggestions that labour is now largely informational and communicative in character, to claims that capitalist political economy now involves the circulation and movement of non-quantifiable and non-measurable affects, represent perhaps some of the most significant lines of this revision. (139)

The subjectivity that is prevalent in a precarious economy is one in which the affects of the worker are subsumed and circulated within neoliberal capitalism.

Neoliberal capitalism, as I use it here, is derived from Michel Foucault (see Chapter 4). Neoliberal capitalism is understood as a mode within contemporary capitalism that directs individuals to overlook structural deficiencies such as high unemployment, expensive education, lack of affordable health care, few social welfare programs, and so on; instead, individuals are to focus their energies on self-improvement. This leads individuals to place the burden of economic and social success squarely on their own shoulders, regardless of the structural systems that negatively influence the lives and livelihood of many. One such manner in which individuals are directed to ensure their economic and social success is to invest in what Michel Foucault refers to as "abilities-machines." Foucault describes "abilities-machines" as the innate and acquired attributes an individual has that will aid or assist the individual in his or her earning potential now or in the future. As will become readily clear, lifestyle, or enhancement, medications are a means in which we can invest in our own human capital or abilities.

The precariousness of work and life is immanent to our currently practiced system of neoliberalism. Neoliberalism as a political economy is premised on the notion "that human well-being can best be advanced by liberating individual entrepreneurial freedoms and skills within an institutional framework characterized by strong private property rights, free markets, and free trade" (Harvey 2005: 2). The role of the state in neoliberal governing is to create and maintain an institutional framework that promotes free markets and protects the free market infrastructure regardless of the harm, such as the ever-widening divide between the haves and the have-nots, to real-life populations. The state, therefore, is useful to neoliberal economics only to the extent that its political interventions are to "secure private property rights and to guarantee, by force if need be, the proper functioning of markets" (Harvey 2005: 2). The role of the state is simply to allow the extensive and intensive reach of free market capitalism. The current practice of neoliberal political economy is attributed to further deregulation in industry including the continual privatization of public institutions and services such as prisons, schools, and utility companies.

What is of interest in *Lifestyle Drugs and the Neoliberal Family* is that this political-economic philosophy of thought informs a subjectivity that is valorized and productive for neoliberal capitalism. As Wendy Brown (2003) explains, "This rationality is emerging as governmentality—a mode of governance encompassing but not limited to the state, and one which produces subjects, forms of citizenship and behavior, and a new organization of the social" (2). Neoliberalism is more than an economic and political philosophy; rather, this philosophical rationality reconstitutes the social body. Neoliberalism traverses the market into the realm of social life. This rationality argues that each person is out to protect him- or herself and rejects any collective action by the body politic.

> The model neo-liberal citizen is one who strategizes for her/himself among various social, political, and economic options, not one who strives with others to alter or organize these options. A fully realized neo-liberal citizenry would be the opposite of public-minded, indeed it would barely exist as a public. The body politic ceases to be a body but is, rather, a group of individual entrepreneurs and consumers. (Brown 2003: 15)

This model neoliberal citizen is one who is directed to take as her own responsibility her economic and personal successes and failures. This rationality is premised on a business-oriented risk assessment of personal and daily life. For instance, the manner in which one decides whom to partner with, what neighborhood to reside in, where to send his children to school, and which health procedures to have and which to forgo are all to be decided on a risk-benefits analysis. That is to say, the rationality of thought today is premised on an economic model of accessing financial risk and economic gain in relation to life decisions that have formerly been considered as outside the economic realm. This "financialization of daily life" (Martin 2002) describes the way in which everyday decisions are premised on an economic rationality.

In this "financialization of daily life," everyday decisions are practiced on the premise that each one of us is an "active economic subject" (Foucault 2008: 223). Foucault (2008) articulates the manner in which in order to analyze work, we need to take into account that the worker is also an "active economic subject":

> The fundamental, essential problem, anyway the first problem which arises when one wants to analyze labor in economic terms, is how the person who works uses the means available to him. That is to say, to bring labor into the field of economic analysis, we must put ourselves in the position of the person who works; we will have to study work as an economic conduct practiced, implemented, rationalized, and calculated by the person who works. What does working mean for the person who

> works? What system of choice and rationality does the activity of work conform to? As a result, on the basis of this grid which projects a principle of strategic rationality on the activity of work, we will be able to see in what respects and how the qualitative differences of work may have an economic type of effect. So we adopt the point of view of the worker and, for the first time, ensure that the worker is not present in the economic analysis as an object—the object of supply and demand in the form of labor power-but as an active economic subject. (223)

In order to understand the worker we need to think of the worker not just as labor-power, one who sells his or her labor power for a wage in a supply/demand economic system; rather, we need to conceive of the worker as one who is an active agent of her own accumulation of capital. Foucault (2008) suggests that the "qualitative differences of work may have an economic type of effect" (223). The precarious quality of work today certainly has "an economic type of effect" on the subjectivity of the contemporary worker. This economic effect is one in which the worker recognizes herself as an "an active economic subject" (223). As an active economic subject it is her responsibility to invest in her own labor power as an investment in herself and her capital worth.

This "economic type of effect" that work has on the worker is one in which the worker employs himself as an active agent of his own making. He is an "entrepreneur of himself" as Foucault (2008: 226) remarks. As mentioned above, the investment in the self and the decisions that are made to make the self a more viable subject in contemporary capitalism is what Foucault refers to as an investment in oneself as an "abilities-machine" (2008: 224). As affective labor skills are now necessary for success in an unstable and precarious economy, the financial investment in one's affect is all the more vital to future long-term economic success. The following chapters argue that direct-to-consumer advertisements imply that successful neoliberal subjectivity can be bought through the consumption of a lifestyle drug. For instance, antidepressant advertisements sell women happiness through the consumption of a daily pill (see Chapter 2). The cause of depression is constructed in advertising discourse as a chemical imbalance in the brain and referred to as a medical condition, and not a condition of the instability and uncertainty of daily life within contemporary capitalism. The consumer is directed to think of herself as the cause of her depression. She is directed to care for herself and to invest in her "abilities-machine" by consuming antidepressants and altering her affect to more closely match the affect that is desirable in contemporary capitalism and, she hopes, to her own economic success.

Affect

Lifestyle Drugs and the Neoliberal Family, therefore, investigates affect in contemporary work and life. More specifically, it asks what the desired affective qualities are to contemporary capitalist subjectivity. To address this question this book understands affect in three ways. First, affect refers to the affect in "affective disorders." That is to say, affective disorders refer to the inappropriate presentation of one's attitude and behaviors as diagnosed by the American Psychiatric Association's *Diagnostic Statistical Manual* (*DSM*). Second, affect is at play in this book, as affective labor is the term used to describe the form of labor that requires the appropriate affective attributes of friendliness, communicating well with others, and the proverbial "service with a smile." And finally, affect in its Spinozian philosophical sense refers to the manner in which bodies (human and non-human) come together, each affecting the other, altering each in the process. I explain further each definition of affect below.

Affective disorders are defined by the *Oxford English Dictionary* (2012) as "designating forms of mental illness attributed to disturbance of the emotions or (in later use) characterized by disturbance of mood as the primary symptom (as in depression and bipolar disorder)."[11] The term "affective disorder" is now commonly replaced with "mood disorder" in the *DSM*. Mood disorders focus on the emotional state or how one feels, whereas affective disorders represents the outward expression of one's affect (Berrios 1985). The American Psychiatric Association's *Diagnostic and Statistical Manual of Mental Disorders* (3rd ed.) (*DSM-III*) (1980) defined affective disorders as

> a disturbance of mood, accompanied by a full or partial manic or depressive syndrome that is not due to any other physical or mental disorder. Mood refers to a prolonged emotion that colors the whole psychic life; it generally involves either depression or elation. The manic and depressive syndromes each consist of characteristic symptoms that tend to occur together. (205)

The footnote attached to "Affective Disorders" states, "The proper descriptive term for this group of disorders should be 'Mood

Disorders'; however, common usage and historical continuity favor retention of the term 'Affective Disorders'" (*DSM-III* 1980: 205). The American Psychiatric Association's *Diagnostic and Statistical Manual of Mental Disorders* (4th ed.) (*DSM-IV*) (1994) has opted for the designation "Mood Disorders" but this project employs "affective disorders" because advertisements for mood disorders are more concerned with external performance of affect rather than with the underlying causes of the disorder itself.

The second use of affect refers to affective labor. Affective and care labor is often defined as "labor in the bodily mode," to refer to work that requires human physical contact and care work. This form of work can include anything from domestic work and child rearing to sex work and nursing. While this form of work is generally gendered feminine and in the patriarchal division of labor is usually reserved for women, more recently, affective labor has entered the parlance of critical theory to describe the work that is required of many contemporary workers who rely on communication and information as their basic unit of production. That is to say, those involved in sales, service industries, information industries, teaching, life sciences, creative work, and so on are required to perform the appropriate affect that demonstrates competence, sociability, and communicative acumen. As Clough and Halley (2007) remind us, "While affective labor is not the primary form of labor worldwide (agriculture still is), there is nonetheless a worldwide meshing of biopolitics with an affective economy" (25). An affective economy is one in which affects circulate in order to produce more capital. Biopolitics functions in order to garner the affects that are most desirable for contemporary capitalism and to keep those affecting bodies in constant circulation. But in order to comprehend the power of affect and bodies, it is necessary to turn to a discussion of Spinoza and affect.

The third use of affect concerns the philosophical concept of affect that stems from the seventeenth-century philosopher Baruch Spinoza. At its most basic, affect is what is *absorbed* into the body; it is an experience (Deleuze 1988: 141). This definition of "affect" stems from Spinoza's *Ethics* (1678/2000) and was revived by Gilles Deleuze in his works *Expressionism in Philosophy: Spinoza* (1990) and *Spinoza: Practical Philosophy* (1988) in which he took as his task the correction of the translation of affect as "affection" or "emotion." "*Affectio*," explained Deleuze, "refers to a state of the affected body and implies the presence of the affecting body" (1988:

49). Or, in Spinoza's own words, "The human body can undergo many changes, and yet retain the impressions, i.e. the traces, of objects, and consequently the same images of things" (*Ethics*, part III, postulate 2). "*Affectus*," on the other hand, "refers to the passage from one state to another, taking into account the correlative variation of the affecting bodies" (Deleuze 1988: 49). Spinoza's definition of *affectus* is as follows: "I understand the affections of the body by which the body's power of acting is increased or diminished, helped or hindered" (*Ethics*, part III, definition 3). Thus, affect has a double meaning: the state of an affected body; and the transition from one state to another accompanied by activity or inactivity, speed or slowness, an increase or a decrease in power.

Affect, in this book, recognizes that lifestyle medication functions to produce a particular affect in those who consume it. For instance, an antidepressant is to function in such a manner as to alter the sad and listless affect of a depressed person into an affect of an active and content person. Therefore, affect, in its relation to its effect on the body through pharmaceutical medication, has the purpose to transform the affect of the one who consumes it. In Spinoza's formulation, a body, or what he refers to as a "mode," comes into contact with another body or mode. This interaction will either increase or decrease the body's power of action. This increase or decrease of power, for Spinoza, will either create joy or sadness. In the case of lifestyle medication, for example, antidepressant advertisements inform the viewer that when a depressed person consumes the drug her body is affected in such a manner as to increase her body's power of acting. She is literally no longer a listless body. She is now an active and laboring body (see Chapter 2).

Affect, therefore, refers to the affect and mood of the person, the affective labor required of many workers in contemporary capitalism, and also the transitioning from one affected state to another.

Conclusion

This Introduction contends that lifestyle drugs are significant to our contemporary cultural moment and our understanding of life and work. Through direct-to-consumer advertising of lifestyle drugs, consumers are presented with a view of how they should feel and act and the type of lifestyle that they should desire. These advertisements, and the disorders and drugs themselves, inform the consumer of the form of subjectivity that she should embody within her contemporary moment of neoliberal capitalism.

Each of the following chapters analyzes the subjectivity sold to us through direct-to-consumer advertising of drugs. The heart of this argument is that these lifestyle drugs inform us of the type of worker that we are to be, regardless of whether we have the particular disorder or not. The type of worker is one that relies on his or her affective and communication skills, ability to get along well with others, and the appearance of confidence and competence. Popular discourses surrounding these lifestyle drugs inform all of us of the affect and behavior that are required of work-life today.

The advertising of prescription pharmaceuticals directly to consumers presents an opportunity to explicate the promise of medicine in making a better-working body. The use of prescription pharmaceuticals in constructing working bodies is not limited to the pharmaceutical industry's advertising directly to consumers. In the following chapter, I examine the role that governmental policy has in this construction. Specifically, I examine George W. Bush's New Freedom Commission on Mental Health. I argue that the government employs multiple existing apparatuses to produce productive capitalist bodies. Borrowing Louis Althusser's (1971b) formulation of the "ideological state apparatus," I refer to this constellation of apparatuses as an affective state apparatus. An affective state apparatus coordinates various and sometimes competing constituents into a constellation that seeks to influence the affects of the body politic.

After the discussion of George W. Bush's New Freedom Commission on Mental Health and the theoretical explanation of an affective state apparatus, the remaining chapters offer a more nuanced reading of lifestyle drugs and their attending affective disorders as presented in advertising discourses and in the popular press. What is lurking behind each exploration is an affective state apparatus that promotes a particular affective subjectivity that is productive for our current mode of contemporary capitalism.

Through a critical analysis of print and television consumer advertisements of antidepressants, the second chapter explores the manner in which women are directed to alter their affect to meet contemporary demands of balancing both home life and professional work. The manner in which the affective state apparatus operates to direct women to govern themselves as productive bodies for capitalism is examined. Psychotropic advertisements for medications from Miltown, the tranquilizer of the 1950s, to the birth control pill Yaz, promise to maintain female bodies in a state of capitalist productivity and proper affective performance. Depression as an affective disorder is rhetorically explained through medical and pharmaceutical discourses as a chemical imbalance in the brain. Therefore, the cause of depression is rhetorically linked to the body and not to any societal pressures, social inequalities, or external circumstances. For example, Cymbalta's website contends that depression is caused by "chemical messengers" that fail to communicate with one another in the brain. The communication analogy is taken further, as those with depression are described as withholding from communicating with others and, in turn, antidepressants are described as putting one back into communicative circulation. What is revealed from the discourses of both Yaz and Cymbalta is that the female body is rhetorically constructed as a preexisting condition for depression, moodiness, anxiety, and irritability. In short, the relationship between contemporary work, women, and the use of pharmaceuticals in order to maintain current notions of gendered, affective labor both in and outside of the paid labor force is explored.

The third chapter examines the rise of erectile dysfunction (ED) medication. Specifically, the discourse of erectile dysfunction medication encourages men to maintain not only their physical or material bodies in circulation, but more significantly, to maintain and circulate the affects that coincide with youth, activity, and potency. I argue, through reading the advertisements and promotional materials of ED medications, that men are rhetorically constructed to circulate like capital itself. This chapter engages with the theories of Jacques Lacan in order to contend that the circulation of phallic power is a form of what Lacan refers to as phallic *jouissance* or a pleasure that once obtained, immediately reverts back to desire. Masculinity is subsumed into the circulation of capitalism via the pharmaceutical industry in order to produce a subjectivity that is forever sexually/socially potent. Ironically, this potency is premised on the fact that the male body is rhetorically directed to continually admit its own impotency.

The fourth chapter examines the use of Ritalin and other pharmaceutical drugs prescribed to children diagnosed with attention deficit disorder (ADD) and attention deficit with hyperactivity disorder (ADHD). Specifically, this chapter explores the intersections of the family, school, and medical discourses regarding the youthful body. An analysis of advertisements and cultural representations of children with ADD and ADHD is presented in order to argue that Ritalin and other ADD/ADHD drugs function to alter the affects, and heighten the communication skills, of those who consume them. This is important as it inextricably links communication, affect, and labor. In short, both the diagnosis and the pharmaceuticals prescribed for the diagnosis prepare young people to meet the demands of the contemporary labor force, a labor force that requires particular communication skills, the ability to build interpersonal relationships, and workplace adaptability.

The concluding chapter examines the increasing use of lifestyle medication prescribed to our closest friend: the family dog. "Who does depression hurt?" inquires Eli Lilly's "Depression Hurts" commercial. The answer: "Everyone." An image of the family dog, with a tennis ball in his mouth, looking longingly at the camera, illuminates that our companion species are affected by their human's depression. The final chapter spends some time with the family dog, which is now increasingly prescribed pharmaceutical treatments for affective illnesses such as depression, separation anxiety, and compulsive disorder. A reading of pharmaceutical advertisements and websites for "companion animal health" illuminates the growing concern with affect and the growing reach of the affective state apparatus.

Notes

1 Indianapolis beat Chicago on February 4, 2007, while an estimated 93,184,000 viewers watched ("Updated" 2009).

2 See Nadasan (2010) for a brief history.

3 For recent statistics on the number of Americans suffering from affective and mood disorders, see the National Institute of Mental Health's website: http://www.nimh.nih.gov/health/publications/the-numbers-count-mental-disorders-in-america/index.shtml#Dysthymic

4 In August 2011, Dr. Ezekiel Emanuel (August 6, 2011), oncologist and President Obama's former White House adviser, wrote an opinion piece for the *New York Times* in which he highlighted the crisis in cancer treatments due to a shortage of lifesaving medications. This shortage, he argues, is mostly due to "the consequences of corporate decisions to cease production, or interruptions in production caused by money or quality problems, which manufacturers do not appear to be in a rush to fix." The shortage of these lifesaving drugs puts many patients in peril, as they are unable to obtain the necessary medication to prolong their lives and treat their life-threatening illnesses.

Drugs had to be shipped from abroad in 2012. The *New York Times* reports that shipments of the cancer drug Doxil, used to treat ovarian cancer, and the drug methotrexate, used to treat childhood leukemia, had to be shipped in from India and Australia, respectively. "There is a years-long backlog of applications for new generic drugs at the FDA because the government does not have the money to hire enough reviewers to analyze the applications or inspectors to visit the facilities, many of them abroad" (Harris, Feb. 22, 2012, sec. A, National Desk, p. 13). In May 2012, "the Senate passed a major bipartisan bill to prevent drug shortages and to speed federal approval of lifesaving medicines, including lower-cost generic versions of biotechnology products" (Pear, *New York Times*, May 25, 2012, sec. A, National Desk, p. 22).

Curiously, it is not only lifesaving medications that are hard to obtain. In April 2011 medications that treat ADHD were reported to be in short supply as well. News reports across the media landscape were similar to this one from MSBC.com:

> Nationwide shortages of popular drugs used to treat ADD and ADHD are sending parents scrambling, with some combing multiple pharmacies for the Adderall and Ritalin that keep their kids calm.
>
> [....]
>
> In the past two weeks, federal Food and Drug Administration officials added the drugs methylphenidate hydrochloride and amphetamine mixed salts, the generic names for Ritalin and Adderall, to an expanding list of national drug shortages. Some distributors cite manufacturing delays and increased demand as the reasons; others offer no explanation for the shortages.
>
> But the American Society of Health-System Pharmacists, which tracks drug supply issues, has listed the products in short supply for nearly a month, and there have been regional reports of spotty shortages even before that. (Aleccia, NBCnews.com, April 14, 2011)

While lifesaving drugs are in short supply most likely due to the fact that drug companies make little profit on the generic cancer treatments, lifestyle drugs such as Adderall and Ritalin are reportedly in short supply because of their high demand. According to the *New York Times* (Harris, Dec. 31, 2011), "Medicines to treat attention deficit hyperactivity disorder are in such short supply that hundreds of patients complain daily to the Food and Drug Administration that they are unable to find a pharmacy with enough pills to fill their prescriptions." The *New York Times* explains the shortage as two-pronged: "Officials at the Food and Drug Administration say the shortages are a result of overly strict quotas set by the Drug Enforcement Administration, which, for its part, questions whether there really are shortages or whether manufacturers are simply choosing to make more of the expensive pills than the generics, creating supply and demand imbalances" (Harris, Dec. 31, 2011). Regardless of the cause of the shortage, patients are worrying about how to fill their prescriptions. Yet, unlike lifesaving drugs, those that do not have access to their Ritalin are usually not in threat of losing their life.

5 According to *Advertising Age* (Late News: 2005, September 5):

New Zealand...is seeking to ban the practice [DTC advertising] effective 2006. New Zealand's Ministry of Health, similar to the U.S.'s Food and Drug Administration, has had a voluntary moratorium on DTC advertising in place since December of 2004 but health minister Annette King said that on the advice of professional and consumer groups, she hopes to ban DTC advertising by next year. Much like consumer advocacy groups in the U.S. claim, Ms. King said her reasoning was that the benefits of DTC do not outweigh the risks.

To date, no legal ban has been placed on DTC advertising in New Zealand.

6 According to the *New York Times* (1998, June 7) article "Spending it: from lab to patient, by way of your den," the following increases in consumer advertising were reported:

For all of 1997, spending on consumer advertising for prescription drugs rose by 125 percent from the previous year, to $107 million, at Bristol-Myers Squibb; by 76 percent, to $122 million, at Merck; and by 57 percent, to $156.6 million, at GlaxoWellcome, the industry's biggest consumer advertiser. (1)

7 See Shaw (2008) "Direct-to-Consumer Advertising of Pharmaceuticals" for an overview of DTC advertising.

8 http://articles.nydailynews.com/2010-02-10/entertainment/27055888_1_toyotas-barbara-lippert-ads

9 http://www.fda.gov/Drugs/GuidanceComplianceRegulatoryInformation/Surveillance/DrugMarketingAdvertisingandCommunications/ucm209384.htm

10 http://topics.nytimes.com/top/reference/timestopics/subjects/f/foreclosures/index.html

11 "affective, adj.". *OED Online*. (2012, September). Oxford University Press. Retrieved from http://www.oed.com/view/Entry/3357?isAdvanced=false&result=1&rskey=Rmy2oX&.

ONE

Affective State Apparatus

Theorizing G. W. Bush's Policy on Mental Health

In the Introduction, the context of contemporary work-life was introduced. This chapter examines George W. Bush's policy initiative on mental health in order to reveal the economic interest that the government has in the mental well-being of the population. This governmental interest in mental health is driven by an interest in a healthy economy. One aspect of a healthy population is that it can meet the current requirements of labor. The government's current attention in constituting a subjectivity that is productive for contemporary labor is read through George W. Bush's New Freedom Commission on Mental Health.

Governmental policy reveals the form of subjectivity that the government desires of its population. George W. Bush's policy on mental health can be read to illuminate the affective behavior that is most productive for the government; in this case, it is a population that does not cost the government money or resources. A productive labor force is one that not only is able to work but that also possesses the attributes that are required of the worker within the system of neoliberal capitalism. Today, necessary attributes include the ability to communicate well, to have a positive and pro-social attitude, and to maintain a linguistic agility that keeps pace with the rapidly changing communication systems.

In order to constitute a healthy body politic, the government relies on current and new institutional structures and technologies. I refer to the deployment of these institutions and technologies that focus on the affective attributes of our subjectivity as an affective state apparatus. An affective state apparatus is concerned with constituting subjectivities that embody the appropriate affective skills that are a benefit to the government, capitalism, and often the worker herself.

Following this shift in the conceptualization of work-life from material production to immaterial production, cultural theorists and critics have turned toward the analysis of affective labor. The study of affective labor includes the analysis of human communication in the production of knowledge, care work, customer relations, social networks, and communities (Hardt & Negri 2000: 293). While many critics have analyzed various forms of affective labor, a growing body of scholars has sought to provide a theory of how affect is captured and exploited to meet the demands of work within contemporary capitalism (Gregg 2009, 2010; Hardt 1999; Hardt & Negri 2000; Lazzarato 1996). What remains under theorized is the way in which affect, capitalism, and the state intersect to constitute, capture, and circulate the affective attributes of the body politic. In the remainder of this chapter, I propose the concept of an affective state apparatus to describe the process by which the government is concerned with the population's mental health.

An increasing amount of labor in the "first world" has shifted from production-based to knowledge- and service-oriented labor. "The new competencies that employers value in the knowledge economy," explains the World Bank Group (2002), "have to do with oral and written communications, teamwork, peer teaching, creativity, envisioning skills, resourcefulness, and the ability to adjust to change" (30). The successful worker can no long rely on trade skills alone, but now must demonstrate competency in "creative thinking, problem solving, and interpersonal and communication skills" (81). This now dominant form of labor is referred to as affective labor because it requires deploying communicative affects for the production of relationships for professional growth. This, for example, takes the form of developing a client base, good customer relations, and the general ability to communicate knowledge and information. In the knowledge economies and service industries, employees are required to express the appropriate affective and attitudinal attributes necessary to fostering productive relationships with coworkers and customers alike.

Critics of the inequalities produced by global capitalism, such as Michael Hardt and Antonio Negri (2004), explain that in knowledge- and service-based economies, employers are apt to "highlight education, attitude, character, and 'prosocial behavior'" (108). Therefore, as labor becomes more affective, the employees' attitude or, as Maurizio Lazzarato (1996) refers to it, "personality," becomes a central location for value production (135). He describes the contemporary worker as someone who "*has* to express oneself…*has* to speak, communicate, cooperate, and so forth" (emphasis in the original, 134). The personality and attitude of capitalist subjectivity today requires the performance of communication competency and a "prosocial" attitude.

I use the term "affective state apparatus" to describe the "governing" of affect. I contend that the affective state apparatus operates through the very intimacies of the body in order to produce ever more efficient and productive capitalist subjects through the use of pharmaceutical enhancement. The concept of an affective state apparatus offers at once a critical and theoretical intervention into affect studies, as well as furthers the analysis of contemporary forms of subjectivity. I argue that the government has a vested interest in constructing affective attributes that enable the population to work.

The concept of an affective state apparatus offers a materialist intervention into affect studies by explicating the manner in which the material body is chemically altered through the consumption of pharmaceuticals in order to produce affective attributes that are productive for contemporary capitalism. I use George W. Bush's policy document, *Achieving the Promise: Transforming Mental Health Care in America*, as one case study to reveal the intersections of governmental policy, the pharmaceutical industry, the health sciences, and capitalism to demonstrate a constellation of institutions that converge on the body politic's affect. The concept of an affective state apparatus provides a means in which to understand a form of contemporary subjectivity that is premised on affective and "communicative labor" (Greene 2004: 188) and, in this instance, induced most prominently through the intersection of the state and psychopharmacology.

Affect, Louis Althusser, and Affective State Apparatus

The term "affective state apparatus" is a play on Louis Althusser's (1971b) formulation of the ideological state apparatuses in his well-known and often-discussed essay, "Ideology and Ideological State Apparatuses (Notes Towards an Investigation)." In that essay, Althusser dissects the traditional Marxist understanding of the state as the primary site of repression, and provides two distinct apparatuses that deploy its power: One apparatus functions through physical violence and the other apparatus functions through ideology. The "Repressive State Apparatuses" (RSAs) (142–143) consists of the government and its institutions, such as the police, courts, prisons, and the like. Althusser refers to these state apparatuses as repressive because, in the last instance, they have the power to act with violence, whether physical or symbolic. Conversely, the "Ideological State Apparatuses" (ISAs) consists of the cultural functionaries such as media institutions, the church, and the family, and operate primarily through ideology. Althusser refers to this process as a "double 'functioning,'" as one apparatus functions "predominately" and the other "secondarily"(145). Therefore, the repressive state apparatus functions predominantly by repression and secondarily by ideology; the ideological state apparatus works predominately through ideology and secondarily by repression. Both the repressive state apparatus and the ideological state apparatus illustrate the role of state power in subject formation.

To explain the state's role in constructing subject positions, Althusser advances a theory of interpellation. Althusser's theory of interpellation argues that individuals enter subjectivity through a process of linguistic hailing, which is the process of being addressed or called out. In Althusser's words, "the hail rings out: 'Hey, you there!'"(174). As soon as a representative of a state apparatus calls "you there," the individual is brought into a subject position defined by the call. Althusser describes the police officer's hailing as an example. At the moment when the police officer calls out, "Hey, you there," and an individual turns toward that call, he or she is interpellated into the subject position of a criminal, regardless of whether or not the individual committed a crime (174). Likewise, the ideological state apparatus hails individuals into a gendered subject position of either male or female, and all the associations with each position, as soon as one is declared a boy or a girl. As Althusser explains, the ideologies of gender precede the birth of any one individual (176). In both the RSA and the ISA, individuals, according to Althusser, are brought into a subject position through the process of interpellation.

Judith Butler revisits Althusser's theory of ideology and interpellation to examine the power of the linguistic hailing in subject formation and its subsequent subordination. Butler (1997a) reads Althusser's linguistic hailing and its accompanying ritualized performative act of turning toward the linguistic call to argue that it is "within the terms of language that a certain social existence of the body first becomes possible" (7). Likewise, Maurice Charland (1987) has appropriated Althusser's concept of interpellation to offer a constitutive rhetoric by explaining the process in which individuals insert themselves into subject positions offered by linguistic narratives. I offer an alternative story of Althusser's famous "hailing" in order to focus not on the linguistic call, but instead on the affective attributes that initiate the original call.

Warren Montag suggests that Althusser derived his concept of interpellation from a passage in Samuel Beckett's 1958 novel, *Molloy*. Montag (2003) explains the relevant scene: "Beckett's narrator can walk only with the aid of a crutch and then only with great difficulty. In spite of his handicap, he travels by bicycle....As he approaches a certain town he dismounts in compliance with town regulations" (66). Molloy labors through the town on his crutches, while at the same time pushing his bicycle; soon he must rest:

> But a little further on I heard myself hailed (*interpelle*). I raised my head and saw a policeman....What are you doing there, he said. Resting I said. Will you answer my question, he cried....I won't reconstruct the conversation in all its meanderings. It ended in my understanding that my way of resting, my attitude when at rest, astride the bicycle, my arms on my own handlebars, my head on my arms, was a violation of I don't know what, public order, public decency. Modestly, I pointed to my crutches and ventured one or two noises regarding my infirmity, which obliged me to rest as I could, rather than as I should. But there are not two laws, that was the next thing I thought I understood, one for the healthy, another for the sick, but one only to which all must bow, rich and poor, young and old, happy and sad. He was eloquent. I pointed out that I was not sad. That was a mistake. Your papers, he said. (Beckett, as cited in Montag 2003: 66, with French in parentheses)

As Montag explains, "Molloy is interpellated and finally subject to identification by the law, which endows him with absolutely free will, and then demands of him what he cannot do and then declares him a criminal for failing to do it" (66). Molloy is "hailed" by the law for his inability to *rest as he should*. Molloy explains "that my way of resting, my *attitude* [emphasis added] when at rest, astride the bicycle, my arms on my own handlebars, my head on my arms, was a violation" (Beckett, as cited in Montag 2003: 66) Montag neglects to note that Molloy's affect is what is in violation of the law. Molloy is stopped by the policeman (an officer of the state) because of his affect, or the way in which his posture and attitude while at rest is understood by the law as inappropriate. As Molloy notes, "That was a mistake" (66). His affective behavior, his attitude, was first recognized by the law, and then deemed to be in violation of the law. In a later passage, Molloy will attest to conforming, to the best of his ability, to what the laws deems as proper affective behavior. "What is certain is this, that I never rested in that way again, my feet obscenely resting on the earth, my arms on the handlebars and on my arms my head, rocking and abandoned....I only have to be told what good behavior is and I am well-behaved"(Beckett 1958: 24–25). Molloy's interpellation by the law reconstitutes his affective behavior so that his attitude while at rest can then be performed in accordance to the law. The process of interpellation may hail or capture an individual through the linguistic register into a subject position, but it does so based on the premise that individuals embody affective attributes, and it is the affective attributes themselves that may be in violation of the law. In this passage, we see that it is Molloy's affective attributes, his attitude and general way of being that initiated the officer's "call."

Althusser added his theory of ideology to the repressive state apparatus in order to account for the form of capitalism during his time. Likewise, the affective state apparatus accounts for the emphasis on affect within our contemporary capitalist moment. Brian Massumi (2002) argues that "affect holds a key to rethinking postmodern power after ideology," and continues by stating that "although ideology is still very much with us, often in the most virulent of forms, it is no longer encompassing. It no longer defines the global mode of functioning of power. It is now one mode of power in a larger field that is not defined, overall, by ideology" (42). This is not to say that ideology no longer matters, only that in contemporary capitalism, ideological transparency "enables ideology effectively to penetrate every pore of the social body," as Slavoj Žižek (1994) explains; therefore, "the weight of ideology as such is diminished" (14).

For Althusser both the ISA and the RSA function to reproduce the social relations that allow for their cultural moment's existing mode of capitalism. The affective state apparatus (ASA) is deployed to account for our contemporary mode of capitalism that increasingly relies on affective relationships and their reproduction. Following Spinoza's understanding of immanent causality, the relationship between the affective state apparatus and contemporary capitalism is not a linear one; rather, in Althusser's language it is "overdetermined" (1969: 233). Althusser's concept of overdetermination, as J. K. Gibson-Graham et al. (2000) note, "does not assign causal or constitutive privilege to any social instance or process"; rather, "each identity or event can be understood as constituted by the entire complex of natural, social, economic, cultural, political, and other processes that comprise its conditions or existence" (6–7). Similarly the affective state apparatus is not a determining apparatus, it is an overdetermined one. Althusser's overdetermination is important because it recognizes the contingency and historicity of subjectivities and events. An affective state apparatus speaks of a particular historical moment and a particular form of capitalist subjectivity.

When I employ the term the "state" in reference to an affective state apparatus, I am paying homage to Althusser, while referring to his student, Michel Foucault, who reconceptualizes the state into a conception of "governmentality."[1] Foucault (1991) claimed, "We live in the era of 'governmentality'" (103). He continues on to explain:

> This governmentalization of the state is a singularly paradoxical phenomenon, since if in fact the problems of governmentality and the techniques of government have become the only political issue, the only real space for political struggle and contestation, this is because the governmentalization of the state is what it is today, this is so precisely thanks to this governmentality, which is at once internal and external to the state, since it is the tactics of government which make possible the continual definition and redefinition of what is within the competence of the state and what is not, the public versus the private, and so on; thus the state can only be understood in its survival and its limits on the basis of the general tactic of governmentality. (103)

As Foucault explains, it is the tactics of government that function to constitute and reconstitute the state. In the case of Molloy, the police govern Molloy's affect in order to reconstitute it to the liking of the state, all of which renders the state visible. Thus affect becomes a technique of governmentality and therefore political.

While Samuel Beckett illustrates the manner in which Molloy's affect, while at rest, is singled out and then corrected by state law, the affective state apparatus reveals how the affect of the body politic is governed by the state to meet the contemporary demands of labor. As Althusser was a reader of Spinoza, it seems fitting to reiterate Spinoza's definition of affect. The seventeenth-century philosopher Baruch Spinoza (*Ethics* 1678/2000) explains that affect refers to the process by which one body affects another body as well as the transition from one affected state to another. Spinoza conceptualizes affect as "the idea of any mode, by which the human body is affected by external bodies." And for a body to be affected, it "must involve the nature of the human body and at the same time the nature of the external body" (*Ethics*, part II, proposition 16). A body that is affected by another body will result in the increase or decrease of the body's power to act (see *Ethics,* part III, definition 3). Spinoza's definition acknowledges the materiality of an affected body as well as the idea that a body contains within it that which alters the body's affect. This is referred to as immanent causality. By immanent causality, Spinoza means that "the knowledge of an effect depends on the knowledge of its cause, and involves it" (E1a4). Molloy rested as he could, rather than as he should, because his body is affected by his infirmity; Molloy's infirmity is revealed through the position of his body. For Spinoza, affect refers to the process by which a body is affected by an external body as well as "the transition in the body from one state to another" (Deleuze 1988: 49).

In the following, the functioning of an affective state apparatus is illuminated through a reading of President G. W. Bush's commissioned report *Achieving the Promise: Transforming Mental Health Care in America* (Hogan et al. 2003). A key component to the management of affect, as illuminated by *Achieving the Promise,* is the increasing role of psychopharmaceuticals. The report advocates a more efficient delivery system of mental health services and pharmaceutical treatments. This reveals a biopolitical management of subjectivity in which individual bodies are delivered to pharmaceutical companies in order to obtain the desired affective attributes. The document describes the desired affective behavior as a behavior that embodies a neoliberal form of productive capitalist subjectivity that advocates continual management of oneself and others.[2] In what follows, affect is at play on three distinct registers: 1) affective labor is used to define the functioning of the prosocial personality, which benefits contemporary capitalism and is a requirement for contemporary work; 2) affective disorders describe various mental disorders that alter moods, thoughts, and behaviors; 3) "affective state apparatus" is the term I use to describe the management of the population's affective health and capitalist (well-) being.

Achieving the Promise

In February 2001, 11 years after his father signed the Americans with Disabilities Act (ADA), President G. W. Bush announced the New Freedom Initiative, "to promote increased access to educational and employment opportunities for people with disabilities" (Hogan et al. 2003: 1). A year later, President Bush announced the creation of the New Freedom Commission on Mental Health as an offspring of the New Freedom Initiative. The commission was directed by an executive order "to conduct a comprehensive study of the *delivery* of mental health services" (emphasis added, Hogan et al. 2003: 16). The final report, *Achieving the Promise: Transforming Mental Health Care in America,* was released on July 22, 2003. "The recommendations we propose," states the commission, "can improve the lives of millions of our fellow citizens now living with mental illness." The commission continues, "The benefits will be felt across America in families, communities, schools and workplaces" (Hogan et al. 2003: cover letter). The commission's final report reveals the government's growing concern with *affective* illnesses such as depression, mania, attention deficit disorder, and other ailments that are regarded as hindering the productive capabilities of the citizenry.

The commission argues for six overarching goals: 1) to recognize that mental health is as important as physical health; 2) to make mental health care consumer driven; 3) to provide mental health services to everyone; 4) to allow access to mental health care early on; 5) to deliver evidence-based care; and 6) to use technology to manage mental health care. The report itself was met with both praise and criticism. The American Psychological Association (APA) applauded the commission's recommendations and released a press statement that includes a comment from Norman B. Anderson (July 23, 2002), CEO of the APA, that states, "Our Association looks forward to embarking on the journey with other stakeholders in mental health to breathe life and hope into the recommendations set forth by the Commission."[3]

Others were not as enthusiastic and demonstrated concern that pharmaceutical companies were becoming even more financially wedded to governmental programs. Jeanne Lenzer (2004b) reports for the *British Medical Journal* that "George Bush Sr. was a member of Lilly's board of directors and Bush Jr. appointed Lilly's chief executive officer, Sidney Taurel, to a seat on the

Homeland Security Council." And to solidify the entanglement, "Lilly made $1.6m in political contributions in 2000—82 percent of which went to Bush and the Republican Party" (1458). Other concerns focused on the reliance of medication for personal and social problems. "Concern that widespread screening will only increase the number of young people taking drugs," states Lenzer (2004a), "has triggered criticism of the plan," including comments from Dr. Daniel Fisher, one of the 22 commissioners. Dr. Fisher warns that with the implementation of the program "mental health will continue to be used as a substitute for addressing the social, cultural, and economic needs of children" (367). Indeed, the rise in prescription medication for children in the United States tripled during the 1990s.[4] Again, I do not argue against the policies within the document; rather, I offer an analysis in order to illuminate the government's vested interest in the nation's affect. *Achieving the Promise* provides a government document in which to explore the relationship between the state, capitalism, and affect as the document describes the manner in which the affect of the body politic is constituted through discourses of mental health, captured by state apparatuses, and circulated by new technologies in order to meet the "convenient ends" of both the state and capitalism.[5]

Constituting Affect

The affect of the population is constituted by the state in terms of mental health, while the "costs" of disability are described in terms of lost economic value and productivity, not in terms of social and personal loss. Those who are mentally ill cost the state billions of dollars. *Achieving the Promise* begins with startling statistics from the World Health Organization (WHO), which state that mental illness is the "leading cause of disability worldwide and suicide is the leading cause of violent death, outnumbering both death caused by war and homicide" (Hogan et al. 2003: 19). The report emphasizes the magnitude of the mental health crisis. In the United States, "suicide claims approximately 30,000 lives each year" and was the "11th leading cause of death among Americans in 2001" (21). Moreover, "In 1999, more than 152,000 hospital admissions and more than 700,000 visits to hospital emergency rooms were for self-harming behaviors" (21). The report states, "The vast majority of all people who die by suicide have a mental illness—often undiagnosed or untreated" (3). Mental illness is reported as the first cause of disability in the United States, Canada, and Western Europe, according to the 2000 WHO report (as cited in Hogan et al. 2003), followed by alcohol and drug use disorders. The highest disability rates are found in those with mental illness and the second in those who self-medicate. This information allows the commission to emphasize the urgency of the problem of mental health issues in the United States, as a vast number of the population are experiencing or will experience mental health distress.

The state defines mental health and affective disorders not in terms of humanism, or the concern over the needs and well-being of human life, but rather in terms of economic productivity. *Achieving the Promise* reads:

> In the U.S., the annual economic, indirect cost of mental illnesses is estimated to be $79 billion. Most of that amount—approximately $63 billion—reflects the loss of productivity as a result of illnesses. But indirect costs also include almost $12 billion in mortality costs (lost productivity resulting from premature death) and almost $4 billion in productivity losses for incarcerated individuals and for the time of those who provide family care. (Hogan et al. 2003: 3)

The reported statistics illuminate the economic cost of bodies that are unproductive for capitalism due to mental illness. Even those who commit suicide are retroactively valued through the measurement of their lost utility to the state's production of economic value. Those who "commit" other crimes against the state are more easily put to work through incarceration work programs.[6]

"Mental illness" is an open term that rhetorically allows for individuals to flow in and out of mental illness over time. According to *Achieving the Promise*, "Adults with a serious mental illness [are] persons age 18 and over, who currently or at any time during the past year, have had a diagnosable mental, behavioral, or emotional disorder…that has resulted in functional impairment which substantially interferes with or limits one or more major life activities" (Hogan et al. 2003: 2). For those under 18, the term "emotional disturbance" is used. The commission provides an example of the emotionally disturbed child whose "functional impairment…adversely affects educational performance"(2). Diagnostic factors include

> an inability to learn that cannot be explained by intellectual, sensory, or health factors; an inability to build or maintain satisfactory interper-

> sonal relationships with peers and teachers; inappropriate types of behavior or feelings under normal circumstances; a general pervasive mood of unhappiness or depression; or a tendency to develop physical symptoms or fears associated with personal or school problems. (Hogan et al. 2003: 2)

The description above avoids narratives of social and economic suffering that may reasonably cause mental or emotional distress. The affective behavior that children are expected to display as described above is one that coincides with the affective labor demands of the contemporary worker. Social well-being is once again transformed into economic value production and capitalist subjectivity. Children, like adults, should be flexible and adaptable to learning a vast array of subjects; they should be able to build and maintain interpersonal relationships with peers and superiors alike, display proper emotions, and deal with problems appropriately. Gordon Tait (2001) argues that basic personality traits are now reconstituted as affective disorders:

> Contemporary pupils are no longer simply too lively, they are reclassified first as hyperactive, and now as suffering from attention deficit disorder (ADD) or oppositional defiance disorder (ODD) or conduct disorder (CD). Pupils are no longer simply quiet or shy, they are reclassified as suffering from generalized social phobia or selective mutism or avoidant personality disorder. Pupils are no longer simply unpopular or obnoxious; they are reclassified as borderline personality disorder (BPD), or antisocial personality disorder (APD). (97)

What was once a personality trait is reconstituted as an affective disorder—an undesirable affective attribute—that does not meet the needs of the contemporary workplace, and that has often as its "cure" a corresponding pharmaceutical.

The definitions of mental illness and emotional disturbance provided by the New Freedom Commission are vague enough that it is easy to imagine that most children could, at some point, have a diagnosable "emotional disturbance"; likewise, most adults may easily experience some form of "mental illness." The affective state apparatus constitutes affect in a form that meets the contemporary demands of the labor force in contemporary capitalism by constituting what was once considered a personality trait into an affective disorder in order to treat the disorder and to alter the personality to be more "prosocial," adaptable, and communicative.

The subject's mental health and well-being are turned into a form of economic value. The affective state apparatus will continually monitor and access the affective attributes of the population in order to meet the economic ends of the state. As illustrated, the commission is primarily concerned with the loss of economic productivity from those who experience mental illness—in the form of disability, incarceration, and suicide—and it is clear that the government's main goal is to produce "healthy" individuals who manage their sickness in economically productive ways, in ways that promote the flexible and interpersonal affects necessary for labor in contemporary capitalism. As capitalism, the pharmaceutical corporation, and the state become ever more inextricably linked, the turn toward the biopolitical capture of affect becomes more visible.[7]

Capturing Affect

The concern for the mental health of a population arises when the welfare of the population affects the welfare of the economy. As Michel Foucault (1990) explains, "Biopolitics deals with the population, with the population as political problem that is at once scientific and political, as a biological problem and as power's problem" (138). Biopolitics works through the bodies of the population in order to govern by "taking control of life and the biological process" and of "ensuring that they are not disciplined, but regularized" (139). With the New Freedom Initiative Commission on Mental Health, the government proposes to employ both large-scale campaigns that "target public education initiatives to increase understanding of mental illnesses and to encourage help-seeking behaviors" (Hogan et al. 2003: 24). The affective state apparatus deploys already existing apparatuses to capture and compare the affective performance of individuals throughout their life span. Foucault (1991) explains that governmentality employs the family as "the privileged instrument for the government of the population" as whatever "information is required concerning the population[...], it has to be obtained through the family" (100). The New Freedom Commission solicited information from "more than 2,300 consumers," which are defined as "people who use or have used mental health services," as well as "family members, providers, administrators, researchers, [and] government officials..." (Hogan et al. 2003: 4). *Achieving the Promise* reveals that the state captures the affect of the population through already existing apparatuses including the family and the school. The commission found that mental illness affects "almost every American family" and explains that mental illness "can happen to a child, a brother, a grandparent, or a co-worker. It can happen to someone from any background..." and "it can occur at any stage of life, from childhood to old age" (2). The family is beckoned forth and employed in the capture of one another's affect. The report functions rhetorically to place the reader at the center of responsibility: a child must be taken care of; one must be my brother's keeper; grandparents, through age and infirmity, become infantilized and are the responsibility of the generations after them. The blurred lines between family and coworker imply that the relationships at work operate on the logic of familial relationships, and the sphere of the home is increasingly an extension of work, as relationships at work are increasingly coded as familial, intensifying affective labor. The worker is not only responsible for family members and coworkers, but also for him- or herself. Health is inversely defined as the ability to manage sickness, and this responsibility extends beyond the management of an individual's own health to include a whole social family. In short, the metaphor of the family signifies that workers are responsible for the production, value, and utility of an ever-expanding social network.

The mental health of children is of particular concern. The commission advocates for a "comprehensive, interagency system for early prevention services for children with disabilities from birth to 3 years old who have a developmental delay and physical, cognitive, communication, social or emotional, or adaptive development problem" (Hogan et al. 2002: 62). The concern for the "healthy" development of communicative and affective labor is made evident by the commission's concern that from birth, children must demonstrate a potential healthy subjectivity. The commission advocates "screening, assessment, early intervention, [and] treatment" (61). The commission writes, "New understanding of the brain indicates that early identification and intervention can sharply improve outcomes..." (57). The concern is centered on producing an end result: well-behaved children who will not disrupt a classroom, and who will become productive capitalist subjects. Toby Miller (2008) argues, "Children were the first targets for mandatory evaluation, because the Commission's pharmacorps members recognized schools as ideal testing venues for identifying

50 million potential customers" (24). And Nikolas Rose (2007) suggests, "One can foresee postconviction screening of petty criminals, with genetic testing and compliance with treatment made a condition of probation or parole" (249). The commission argues, "Since children develop rapidly, delivering mental health services and supports early and swiftly is necessary to avoid permanent consequences and to ensure that children are ready for school" (Hogan et al. 2003: 57). Most "emotional disturbances," or misbehaviors, appear to be cause for concern. "If the system does not appropriately screen and treat them early," states the commission, "these childhood disorders may persist and lead to a downward spiral of school failure, poor employment opportunities, and poverty in adulthood" (58). Purportedly, the failure to detect and treat emotional disturbances in children is a slippery slope that inevitably will lead to economically underperforming adults.

As the commission illustrates through its concern with the population beginning at birth, good behavior must be achieved prior to school. The commission reports that children under the age of 6, and as early as birth to 3 years of age, may be in need of mental health services. By assessing the affective behavior of children prior to school, the appropriate intervention can be made to ensure a certain type of behavior and emotional state once the child enters the school system. If a child has not developed the proper affective behaviors prior to school, the affective state apparatus will intervene in the school setting to ensure a normative state of behavior. By altering the affect of the child via diagnosing him or her with an affective disorder and then treating that disorder, the affective state apparatus strives to produce children that will be productive and prosocial while at school and as future workers.

In Bush's No Child Left Behind Act of 2001, which the New Freedom Commission says "is designed to help all children, including those with serious emotional disturbances reach their optimal potential and achievement," school funding is tied to students' test scores (Hogan et al. 2003: 63). The commission avers, "Growing evidence shows that school mental health programs improve educational outcomes by decreasing absences, decreasing discipline referrals, and improving test scores" (62). As Gordon Tait (2001) argues, "Schools have *always* sought to govern the behaviour of pupils, and the pathologisation of specific forms of conduct is simply a new tactic within a very old and familiar strategy" (95) (emphasis in the original). By "eliminating barriers to coverage," the commission seeks to make it easier to capture and compare the population's affect and to determine which treatment most efficiently alters the individual's affective performance.[8] "The apparatus of capture," explain Gilles Deleuze and Félix Guattari (1987), "constitutes a general space of comparison and a mobile center of appropriation" (444). In this instance, as in Althusser's theorization, the school becomes the epicenter of capturing the affect of future workers (see Chapter 4).

Circulating Affect

The New Freedom Commission advises that the state employ existing disciplinary apparatuses as places of mental health screening. Its members propose that early detection of mental illness should occur in public places such as schools, elder care facilities, and institutions and services that work with juvenile delinquents. This would allow for systemized screening, as well as continual screening throughout the life cycle of the citizen. There is also an implied threat for parents that do not comply with the state's demands. The commission states, "No longer will parents forgo the mental health services that their children desperately need. No longer will loving, responsible American parents face the dilemma of trading custody for care" (Hogan et al. 2003: 9). The use of the term "consumer" implies a sense of agency and freedom that locks the family in a cycle of pharmaceutical consumption, while blaming the family if its members fail as "free" agents and consumers.[9] The consumer is simultaneously an economic subject and a juridical subject in this discourse because the affective state apparatus functions in such a way as to conflate the historically distinct subject positions of the economic consumer with that of the juridical citizen.

The commission is concerned with providing an efficient drug delivery system. This is most evident in its extended discussion of the Texas Medication Algorithm Project (TMAP). The commission explains, "An algorithm is a step-by-step procedure in the form of a flow chart to help clinicians deliver quality care through the best choice of medications and brief assessment of their effectiveness"(Hogan et al. 2003: 69). In essence, the TMAP uses business technologies such as spreadsheets in the management of human/affective capital. The operational form of the TMAP mirrors the form of business procurement, management, and deployment as it functions in a smooth flow of resources in which its goal is to garner profits for the business. Here, the affective state apparatus functions to capture subjects through business, medical, and communication technologies in order to treat people not just as consumers but as objects and resources that are integral to the cycles of production and profit. They are circulated, following the procedure charted in the algorithm, throughout the business cycle and managed and deployed in the most fiscally efficient manner. The commission suggested coupling the TMAP with comprehensive screening of children for mental illness.[10] What becomes evident through this proposed coupling is the manner in which the state functions to capture the population, constitute its affect, and then, if need be, deliver it to the pharmaceutical companies, further solidifying the relationship between the state, capitalism, and the affect of the body politic.

In the commission's proposal, technology plays a vital role in the maintenance of mental health care. The report states, "Advanced communication and information technology will *empower* consumers and families and will be a tool for providers to deliver the best care" (emphasis added) (Hogan et al. 2003: 14). The commission states that "access to information will foster continuous, caring relationships between consumers and providers by providing a medical history, allowing for self-management of care, and electronically linking multiple service systems," effectively maintaining bodies in an expansive and intertwined system (14). Communication technology will work as an administrative apparatus to ensure self-management. Health records kept on electronic file will be available to various governing administrators. The use of computers will create a form of surveillance and administrative control beyond common current medical practices. To keep up with this newly forming mass communication networking system, the commission proposes to "improve and expand the workforce, providing evidence-based mental health services and supports" (13).

The affective state apparatus uses the efficiencies of new communication technologies in order to track individuals and their mental health throughout various governing apparatuses. In the name of technology, the site of mental health diagnosis is moved away from both the doctor and the doctor's office and into a growing network of communication technologies and community settings. These new locations provide a new type of mental health expert: a worker trained to administer treatments and prescriptions deemed as "evidence-based," as illustrated by the TMAP model.[11] This governmental streamlining of treatment illuminates the emergence of an affective power that is mediated by the capitalist marketplace, that is, the pharmaceutical industry.

The New Freedom Commission seeks to expand surveillance by employing technological advances such as "videoconferencing and telehealth" to penetrate "rural and less populated areas of the country" (Hogan et al. 2003: 10). Invoking a notion of community, members contend, "these technologies will be used to provide care at the same time they break down the sense of isolation often experienced by consumers" (10). The interconnection and cooperation between different state apparatuses allows "service providers across settings" to "routinely screen for co-occurring mental illness and substance use disorders" (11). Through the deployment of both repressive and ideological state apparatuses, "the Nation will have a more effective system to identify, disseminate, and apply proven treatments to mental health care delivery" (12). In short, the already existing state apparatuses are appropriated to function as a drug delivery system in order to extensively and intensively manage the bodies of the population to their proper affective ends.

An affective state apparatus gains its momentum and power by continually circulating bodies. The goal of the commission to "involve consumers and families fully in orienting the mental health system toward recovery" functions to induce families and consumers into self-governance and governance of one another (Hogan et al. 2003: 9). "The process of transforming mental health care in America drives the system toward a delivery structure that will give consumers broader direction in how care decisions are made," and will hold them responsible for choosing the best evidence-based practices (16). The result of the commission's recommendations is for government to stake a claim into the internal and affective workings of the brain as a site of conquest by both the state and capitalism.[12] This appropriation of the biological structure of the human body marks an emergent form of state power that illuminates the affective state apparatus.

The Affective State Apparatus

Just as Althusser recognized that we are not outside of ideology, Deleuze (1992) recognizes that "we belong to social apparatuses [*dispositifs*] and act within them" (164). The affective state apparatus is no exception. *Achieving the Promise* is just one example that reveals an affective state apparatus's functioning to constitute, capture, and circulate affect. We can readily think of other constellations that mobilize to center on the affect of the laboring body, including those that employ surveillance and technology to keep tabs on the laboring worker.[13]

In *Achieving the Promise*, the affective state apparatus functions primarily through the capturing of the population's affect via already existing institutions. The affective state apparatus accesses the affect of the population in order to alter it if necessary. (Like Molloy, we quickly learn which affect to affect or we too will be labeled and treated accordingly.) Once affect is captured and corrected, then it is circulated through various governmental and social apparatuses in order to continually monitor the affect throughout an individual's life span. This is not to say that the population is duped by the affective state apparatus. On the contrary, the benefits of receiving a diagnosis or even asking for a diagnosis of an affective disorder such as attention deficit with hyperactivity disorder (ADHD) may have benefits for the individual. For instance, a study reported by the *New York Times* (Parker-Pope 2009) compared students taking ADHD medication with students who were not taking medication and found that "taking ADHD medication was associated with gains in math scores that equated to about a fifth of a school year in extra learning." And scores in reading were even more impressive, "equating to progress of about a third of a school year." If there is a potential academic, social, economic, or interpersonal benefit to the treatments of affective disorders, individuals may find personal and social gain through active complicity with both the discourses and material practices of the affective state apparatus. (As Molloy explains, "I only have to be told what good behavior is and I am well-behaved" (Beckett 1958: 24–25). What I am highlighting is that today, the government actively engages with the populations' affect and new technologies such as those of psychopharmacology to produce a subjectivity that is productive for contemporary capitalism.

The state functions in constellation with other institutions and entities in comprising an affective state apparatus. In his discussion concerning the state, Foucault (2008) explains, "The state does not have an essence. The state is not a universal nor in itself an autonomous source of power" (77). The state functions with and through other institutions. This is evident in the affective state apparatus that combines with schools; juvenile centers; prisons; health-care facilities; and medical discourse, families, and public policy in order to converge on the body. Foucault continues to explain that "the state has no heart, as we well know, but not just in the sense that it has no feelings, either good or bad, but it has no heart in the sense that it has no interior." And this is key, the state has no interior, no heart, no essence because "the state is nothing else but the mobile effect of a regime of multiple governmentalities" (77). If we conceptualize the state as nothing else but the "mobile effect of a regime of multiple governmentalities," then we can understand the state through the organization of various entities that are deployed in governmentality.

The emphasis on affect is not to imply that ideology and repression are no longer present; on the contrary, an affective state apparatus may employ both repression and ideology. The New Freedom Commission alludes to a concrete example of this: The school is the primary site where young people may be singled out as emotionally disturbed because of their perceived inability to behave appropriately in the classroom. Once a student is singled out, parents of such a student will then be urged to comply with the recommendations of educational and medical professionals in the administering of pharmaceuticals to control their child's affect. In this example, both the repressive and ideological state apparatuses are present (the school may bring the law into the situation if parents refuse to medicate their child; and the school functions ideologically in that it is believed that school children should perform in a particular manner), but the site of conquest is the child's affect itself. Children are no longer disciplined physically; rather, they are medicated. This is not to say that the affective state apparatus is less physical. As Foucault has taught us, one form of discipline is not necessarily more or less gentle than the other. Whereas in the past, physical discipline may result in an obedient child who is being conditioned to be a productive subject for Fordist (factory) labor, the affective state apparatus functions to physically recode the brain in order to condition a productive subject for post-Fordist (affective) labor.[14] The affective state apparatus marks the chemical and biological appropriation of a population by governing affectively in order to allow for the further conditioning of both ideology and repression.

The New Freedom Commission's final report, *Achieving the Promise,* reveals the potential of an emergent affective state apparatus that functions to constitute, capture, and circulate the affect of the population. The affective state apparatus (ASA) functions by employing already existing repressive and ideological state apparatuses. These apparatuses capture, compare, and constitute a homogenized affect of the population. The affective state apparatus maintains bodies in a constant state of circulation, while inducing families and coworkers to continually monitor and regulate one another. To be clear, the ASA does not function in such a manner as to make us all the same. Althusser is correct in his explanation that state apparatuses function in order to "reproduce the relations of production." As he explains, "It is only within the processes of production and circulation that this reproduction is *realized*"(emphasis in the original) (Althusser 1971b: 183). At its most simple, the affective state apparatus functions to maintain the reproduction of the affective relations of production. In this case, the ASA regulates affect inside the body itself by affecting the body with pharmaceutical drugs that are manufactured to alter the affect of those who consume them, which assists the state in producing more economically productive laboring citizens. The subsequent chapters illumine further the subjective qualities of the laboring citizen.

In this chapter, I offer one example of how an affective state apparatus functions. The affective state apparatus as a concept is useful in theorizing contemporary subjectivity in contemporary capitalism. As Beckett illustrates in his story of Molloy, affective attributes are always linked to the capture and control of populations.[15] What *Achieving the Promise* reveals is the intensification in which the government colludes with capitalism (and, in this case, with the pharmaceutical industry) in such an overt manner as to materially transform the affect of the population. I have revealed the functioning of the affective state apparatus to illuminate that the government has a vested interest in creating subjectivities that are "prosocial" and that meet the current requirements for affective labor in contemporary capitalism. In the end, the affective state apparatus reveals the state's concern with governing the affect of the body politic to meet the convenient ends of capitalism, and to make certain that we are always performing the appropriate affect, while at work or at rest.

In the next chapter, the affect of feminized labor is explored through an analysis of antidepressant advertisements. Antidepressant advertisements reveal the relationship between women, work, and depression. Antidepressant advertisements and promotional materials promise a productive life regardless of external forces that may be the cause of depression.

Notes

1. Holden and Elden (2005) examine the relationship between the work of Althusser and that of Foucault. They point to writings in which Althusser claims Foucault as his student and Foucault claims Althusser as his teacher. Foucault "was a pupil of mine, and 'something' from my writings has passed into his, including certain of my formulations. But...under his pen and in his thought even the meanings he gives to formulations he has borrowed from me are transformed into another, quite different meaning than my own" (Althusser 1969: 257). Foucault put it in a similar way: "Having been his student and owing him much, I perhaps have a tendency to claim under his influence that which he might deny, although of course I cannot speak on his behalf. But I would say to everyone: open Althusser's books" (Foucault 1994: I, 587, cited in Holden & Elden 2005: 1).
2. Toby Miller (2008), borrowing from Foucault, refers to this as the "psy-function" (39).
3. American Psychological Association 2002.
4. Unfortunately, this does not mean that young people who are in serious need of medications are receiving them. A report by the President's Council on Bioethics cites a 2003 study that "found that the overall use of psychotropic drugs by children tripled during the 1990s, in many cases approaching adult rates of utilization" (Kass 2003: 72).
5. The term "convenient end" originates in a Foucault citation. Michel Foucault cites Guillaume de La Perrière, 'Government in the right disposition of things, arranged so as to lead to a convenient end' (Foucault 1991: 93).
6. While the cost of prison still far outweighs the profits that the state receives from inmate labor, the trend of putting inmates to work for private companies is an explicit example of the intersection between capital, the state, and regulatory policy.
7. Althusser (1971b) states that "the reproduction of the skills of labour power tends...decreasingly to be provided 'on the spot' (apprenticeship within production itself), but is achieved more and more outside production: by the capitalist education system, and by other instances and institutions" (132).
8. Many U.S. states fought laws requiring parents to comply with school administrators and doctors regarding medicating their children in order to allow them to return to school. Parents in Minnesota challenged such a requirement and worked to pass a state law that ensures that children who have been suspended from school are not required to take ADHD medication

as a condition of their readmission. At the national level, the Child Medication Safety Act of 2003 would not force parents to administer controlled substances to their children as a requisite for attending school. The APA opposed the bill and the bill never made it to the Senate for a vote. The strong resistance to medicating children for affective disorders is on point for recognizing the power of the ASA (Daly 2005: 10).

In 2004, President Bush did sign the Prohibition on Mandatory Medication Amendment, as part of the Individuals with Disabilities in Education Act (IDEA). The text reads:

Sec. 300.174 Prohibition on mandatory medication.

(a) General. The SEA must prohibit State and LEA personnel from requiring parents to obtain a prescription for substances identified under schedules I, II, III, IV, or V in section 202(c) of the Controlled Substances Act (21 U.S.C. 812(c)) for a child as a condition of attending school, receiving an evaluation under Sec. Sec. 300.300 through 300.311, or receiving services under this part. (b) Rule of construction. Nothing in paragraph (a) of this section shall be construed to create a Federal prohibition against teachers and other school personnel consulting or sharing classroom-based observations with parents or guardians regarding a student's academic and functional performance, or behavior in the classroom or school, or regarding the need for evaluation for special education or related services under Sec. 300.111 (related to child find).

(U.S. Department of Education, http://idea.ed.gov/explore/view/p/%2Croot%2Cregs%2C300%2CB%2C300 %252E174%2C)

9. *Mother Jones* reports on one such incident in which a child was institutionalized without the consent of her parents (Waters 2005). http://www.motherjones.com/ politics/2005/05/medicating-amanda?page=1
10. Miller 2008: 24; Rose 2007: 249.
11. Medication that is "evidenced-based" may be misleading due to pharmaceutical companies' desires for profits and the FDA's collusion with pharmaceutical companies. According to Moynihan and Cassels (2005), "More than 50 per cent of the FDA's work checking the safety and effectiveness of drugs was now paid for by the companies whose products were being reviewed" (159).
12. For a reading regarding the intersection of the brain, pharmaceuticals, the corporation, and Deleuze's control society, see Davi Johnson (2008) "Psychiatric Power: The Post-Museum as a Site of Rhetorical Alignment" (344–362).
13. I immediately think of call centers and the company's ability to listen in on workers to ensure "quality control."
14. Or what Gill and Pratt (2008) refer to as the "social factory."
15. As just one example, the United States has resorted to the use of stimulants in order to manage, modulate, and control the affect of the population since the colonial practice of providing natives with alcohol to induce cooperation. See, e.g., Peter C. Mancall (1997) *Deadly Medicine: Indians and Alcohol in Early America.*

TWO

Productive Bodies

Women, Work, and Depression

> Depression is a serious medical condition that can take so much out of you. I feel like I have to wind myself up just to get out of bed and, well, I have to keep winding myself up to deal with the sadness, the loss of interest, trouble concentrating, lack of energy.—Pristiq advertisement

> Depression hurts.—Cymbalta advertisement

> Depression and the Recession: Cymbalta Sales Are on the Rise—*The Washington Post* 2009[1]

The female body has long been considered a site of disorder, disease, and, ultimately, conquest. This chapter explores the female body and its relationship to both depression and work. Specifically, the predominance of depression in women and their use of antidepressants link the female body, work, and affective personal and social relations to the requirements of productivity in a service and knowledge economy. The confluence of these factors allows us a glimpse into contemporary cultural, social, and economic production. This chapter argues that the relationships among women, work, and depression reveal the changing status of work; the process by which women have been incorporated into wage labor; how labor has altered to reflect feminine characteristics; and the form of self-governance required to participate in today's labor force.

As a modern phenomenon, depression is culturally constructed primarily as a feminine malady. According to the *Diagnostic Statistical Manual* (*DSM-IV*) a person is depressed if she experiences two or more of the following "for more days than not, as indicated by subjective account or observation by others, for at least 2 years": "poor appetite or overeating; insomnia or hypersomina; low energy or fatigue; low self-esteem; poor concentration or difficulty making decisions; feelings of hopelessness" (349). As the economy recedes, prescriptions for antidepressants steadily increase, as noted by the *Washington Post*'s (2009) headline above: "Depression and the Recession: Cymbalta Sales Are on the Rise." Cymbalta sales are indeed on the rise as antidepressants are among the most dispensed prescription pharmaceutical, signifying that antidepressants are now as common as the commercials that advertise them.

Recent data from the Intercontinental Marketing Services (IMS HEALTH 2011) report that in the United States antidepressant prescriptions have steadily increased from 2006 (231.1 million) to 2010 (253.6 million). Antidepressants were the most consumed drug in 2007–2008 in adults (NCHS Data Brief, no. 42, Sept. 2010) and the fourth largest class of drugs prescribed in 2009, earning the pharmaceutical companies $9.9 billion (IMS HEALTH 2010). In 2008 antidepressants were the third most prescribed pharmaceutical and by 2010 they had steadily climbed to the second most prescribed type of pharmaceutical in the United States, topped only by cholesterol-reducing medication (IMS HEALTH 2011; McDevitt 2009). Although Americans may be physically unhealthy and depressed about it, the popular discourses on depression point to other factors.

According to Prozac's website, one of the most well known antidepressants, the prime risk factors for depression include having low self-esteem and anxiety, and feeling that life is out of control.[2] Another risk factor for depression, according to Prozac's website, is the biological workings of the female body itself, including menstruation, pregnancy, childbirth, and menopause. This gendering of depression—the female body as a preexisting condition as well as the multiple roles that many women embody as parent, spouse, employee, and homemaker—is often used to explain that women are twice as likely as men to experience clinical depression (American Psychiatric Association, *DSM-IV-TR* 2000: 372).

This gendering of depression is revealed in the direct-to-consumer advertisements for antidepressants whose primary target audience is women. For instance, Pfizer's (2009) commercial for its antidepressant, Pristiq, explains, "Depression is a serious medical condition that can take so much out of you. I feel like I have to wind myself up just to get out of bed and, well, I have to keep winding myself up to deal with the sadness, the loss of interest, trouble concentrating, lack of energy." The visual that accompanies this commercial is of a wind-up toy modeled after the female speaker. This is interesting in that women are directed to think of themselves as their own object, in this case an object that is not functioning properly. As Nikolas Rose (2007) suggests, "Drugs do not so much seek to normalize a deviant but to correct anomalies, to adjust the individual and restore and maintain his or her capacity to enter the circuits of everyday life" (210). Pristiq becomes a battery to replay the mechanical device of winding. The commercial places the agency into the consumption of the drug, constructing the woman as "whole" again, a woman who is her own subject and is no longer alienated from herself. This allows her to re-enter the "circuits of everyday life." For instance, in one version of the commercial, an African American woman now on Pristiq is able to get through her day of work at an antiques store. In another version, a white woman is able to participate in playing at the park with her husband and children. This Pristiq commercial suggests that depression is common and that many women experience depression. Once the antidepressant is consumed, then the daily tasks of both work and family time, which occupy many women's lives, are more bearable. Eli Lilly's print, television, and web advertising campaign for the drug Cymbalta is more direct: Depression Hurts.

These scripts that advocate that drugs work and that they work to get you back to work are prevalent in direct-to-consumer advertisements of antidepressants (Gardner 2003). Take, for example, Eli Lilly's 2010 ad campaign Depression Hurts, which offers a depression (and depressing) narrative. Just as in Pfizer's Pristiq commercial, the viewer of the Cymbalta ad is informed of the symptoms of depression, including the pain suffered emotionally and physically. The cause of depression is attributed to faulty chemical messengers located in the brain that affect the levels of serotonin and norepinephrine. While depression is purportedly caused by a chemical mishap, the commercials' visual images tell us a different story. For instance, one commercial presents us with a woman in her early 30s who lives alone in a drab apartment and waits tables at the local diner. The same commercial then flashes us an image of a middle-aged woman all alone except for her canine companion as company in her urban apartment. Reading these images together reveals that depression is more than faulty chemicals in the brain; rather, it is loneliness, alienation from other people, unsatisfying jobs, and feeling that one has not reached one's true potential in life. The voice-over informs the viewer: "Depression hurts, but you don't have to." The remedy offered for the feelings of depression is a pharmaceutical drug—a chemical alteration in the brain—and not a change of job, a better apartment, or a love affair.

Although there are external causes for depression, a depressed person need not *feel* depressed. These commercials advertise that there is a drug to make life more bearable, to relieve the pain of loneliness and alienation. These commercials argue that taking a drug will allow us to feel better even as our material circumstances remain the same. These women remain lonely, single, stuck in unsatisfying jobs, and in a lower socioeconomic class than they reasonably desire. There are concrete reasons that each of the women experiences depression. The pharmaceutical remedy offered does not change the material circumstances of the depressed person's life; rather, it alters the chemicals in the brain in order to temper the symptoms of depression. The commercial concludes with the following images: The waitress appears a little more content when she opens the curtains to her apartment and serves pie at the diner; the middle-aged woman appears more satisfied as she leaves her apartment building to walk her dog. The discourse of these advertisements reveals that antidepressants are not a cure for what ails us, but rather a remedy for making bearable the lives we live within contemporary capitalism.

Makers of antidepressants such as Prozac and Cymbalta claim these drugs regulate the chemical makeup of the brain to alter the depressed person's affective being.[3] Reversing the symptoms of lethargy, Prozac is often described as a "productivity" drug that transforms the medicated depressed person into an energetic, enthusiastic, and productive subject (see Metzl 2003). Prozac and other antidepressants are prescribed to aid women in keeping pace with their multiple roles. The traditional roles of married women have included housework and primary child-rearing responsibilities, as well as lesser-acknowledged affective roles, such as the maintenance of interpersonal and social relationships. Since the last century, married women's roles have expanded to include not only an active social and family life, but also the demands of balancing wage and home labor.

Women, Work, and Psychotropic Medication

The mass movement of women into wage labor coincides with the onslaught of modern psychotropic medication. In the early 1950s, antidepressants were developed after serotonin was linked to emotional function. In 1952, the American Psychiatric Association published the first *Diagnostic and Statistical Manual* (*DSM*) (1952).

In 1955, Miltown, the first mass-marketed tranquilizer, became widely available and prescribed (see Metzl 2003; Solomon 2001). Simultaneously, in the 1950s a significant increase of white, married, and older women entered the paid labor force as part-time workers.[4] This confluence of events altered the entire terrain of work: who was working, where they worked, the length of the workday, and the forms of socialization occurring inside and outside the workplace.

The first generation of psychotropic medication treated symptoms of anxiety in women whose primary role was that of housewife. As more women moved into paid labor, both the symptoms and treatment of depression changed to reflect the shifting affective and daily experiences of women. Depression, previously dominated by symptoms of anxiety and restlessness, was later redefined by symptoms of listlessness, sadness, and melancholy. In early advertisements of psychotropic medications, prior to direct-to-consumer advertisements, women appeared angry, aggressive, and agitated. A 1965 advertisement for Valium presents a close-up of an aggressive woman with her jaw clamped shut, her teeth exposed, her eyes squinting with hostility, and her brow furrowed in obvious agitation. Under the heading "Reduce psychic tension," the text proclaims, "Symptoms of psychic tension, anxiety or depression are often intermingled and rarely appear as separate, distinct elements" (*American Journal of Psychiatry* 1965: xii–xiii, reprinted in Metzl 2003: 16). In this historical moment, women's symptoms of depression comprised both anxiety and melancholy. In the first *DSM* (1952) under the heading "Depressive Reaction," anxiety is the first symptom mentioned prior to connecting it with other symptoms of depression (33–34). In contrast, a 2005 ad for the dual anti-anxiety and antidepressant drug Zoloft portrays a crying, egglike figure with a rain cloud overhead. Affirming feelings of depression, the text reads, "You know when you feel the weight of sadness. You may feel exhausted, hopeless, and anxious. Whatever you do, you feel lonely and don't enjoy the things you once loved." This ad demonstrates that the symptoms of anxiety are subordinated to those of depression. This inversion suggests an alteration not only in a shift of affective symptoms but also a historical transformation in the experience of the depressed. With tranquilizers such as Miltown and later Valium, the agitated, threatening, and discontented woman was sedated to keep her in the proper role of mother, homemaker, and wife. With antidepressants, the depressed woman is uplifted and energized to maintain her productivity in all her roles from wage earner to caretaker.

The medical treatment of depression was transformed by the social changes in the labor force, essentially targeting women workers as the main market for antidepressants. As the workplace incorporated women, and the responsibilities of work were not just to perform job tasks, but also to fulfill requirements that previously existed only in the social sphere, the workplace benefited from a subjectivity embodied in the medicated, depressed woman. As a result, depression can be understood as productive for capital in two ways at once: first, through the pharmaceutical industry, in the production and consumption of chemical treatments; and second, through the production of new forms of subjectivity. The depressive, by caring for the self through medication, has become the ideal productive worker in the now feminized sphere of paid work.

Biopower and the Affect of Contemporary Work

The process by which women in the United States entered the paid labor force in the post–World War II era can be described theoretically through Foucault's (1990) notion of biopower. The control of life through an intensified form of power and politics is defined in two ways: first, through the formation of "the body as a machine" that is disciplined accordingly to produce certain results; and second, the body is formed and understood as a biological entity that can be organized through the control of life, death, health, and "all the conditions that can cause these to vary" (139). The first is concerned with the body at the level of capital (biopower) and the second with the body at the level of the state (biopolitics).[5] Foucault's disciplinary society locates sites of discipline in various institutions including the family, the school, the factory, the hospital, and the prison, each with its own set of rules and organization of time, space, and movement. Foucault recognizes that capitalism "would not have been possible without the controlled insertion of bodies into the machinery of production and the adjustment of the phenomena of populations to economic process" (141). This is evident in the feminization of the labor force in which the movement of the female population into wage labor both produces, and is the result of, new forms of discipline that correspond to this historical transformation.

With the increase of rapid technological advances beginning after World War II, the world saw a shift in emphasis from a society of discipline to a society of control. Deleuze (1995) articulates the difference between discipline and control as the difference between *molds* and *modulations* (178). In a disciplinary society the factory disciplines the individual; in a control society, there is no mass mold, but rather a process of continual "remolding" without a set or static pattern. The difference is a change from *quantity* to *quality* and from *effect* to *affect*. Discipline works on the body to effectuate a particular model of being, while control works *through* the body by modulating affectations. As Deleuze explains, "Disciplinary man [*sic*] produced energy in discrete amounts, while control man [*sic*] undulates, moving among a continuous range of different orbits" (180). This alteration in the primary formulation of work leads to a shift in the forms of self-governance. The primary requirement of flexibility—the ability to adapt to constant and continual changes in the workplace—in the contemporary workforce reflects how a system of control relies on affective relations rather than explicit commands to organize behavior in both the social and economic realm. Italian Marxist theorist Antonio Negri (1992) argues that transformations in the mode of production occur in response to large-scale collective movements. Each transformation is a result of a process whereby social relations and cooperation create new forms of experience and existence that capital responds to by creating new processes of valuation. Negri's argument is this: Capital never changes on its own. History is always a relation between labor and capital where capital reflects new movements in the labor force. In response to the events of May 1968, he argues that "capital has followed this revolutionary force, it has repressed it, it has sought to close it off in new technical dimensions of production and command" (157). Negri is arguing that the events of May 1968 in France, as well as corresponding movements throughout Europe and the United States, reflect a qualitative change in the relation between labor and capital. As a result of the social movements of the late 1960s, the form of value, or the formal way in which capital is capable of producing surplus value, has changed to include functions that previously existed primarily in social relations. This form of response to a social movement, as opposed to a workers' movement, represents Negri's account of the rise of biopower as the subsumption of social relations and specifically the affective experiences of individuals into capitalist production and exploitation.

The formulation that Negri (1992) explains, that is, that capital subsumed the revolutionary social movements of 1968 with the creation of a new form of production, helps to explain how a social and personal experience such as the change in the quality of depression in women can be made productive for capital during this time. Negri's account overemphasizes the importance of collectively organized social movements and neglects the "subtle revolution"[6] such as the everyday experiences of women at work. In either case, the workings of capital have arguably changed to incorporate these mundane social relations into the new and quickly advancing forms of technological production. This is the process that Negri, following Marx, refers to as real subsumption. Even with his inclusion of the social revolutions of the 1960s, Negri's Marxism privileges the proletariat as the prime movers of history. This type of Marxism, while privileging the relations of human labor, systematically neglects the mundane aspects of everyday life, especially the feminine sphere of social labor.[7] For example, capital subsumed social relations in the 1950s as employers opened their doors to women as part-time laborers, not because of a revolutionary movement, but rather because of the banal existence of consumer demand, which had increased dramatically following World War II.

The Feminization of Labor

The decrease in the labor force preceding World War II is the condition that permitted older and married women to enter into wage labor (Weiss 2000). The low birthrates during the Great Depression resulted in a decreased labor supply by the 1950s when industries were ramping up their output and needs for employees. The labor force was further affected as women began to marry earlier than in previous decades and left paid labor for unpaid, domestic, and child-rearing labor (Hesse-Biber & Carter 2000: 38). In response, employers, in need of workers, relaxed their policy of hiring single women only and began to employ married women. Employers were willing to make part-time work available, accommodating married women with school-age children. As women entered the paid labor force and as the need for laborers increased after World War II, hiring requirements changed to include the female worker and capitalism accommodated the lifestyles of married women to benefit the ends of production.

Capitalism accommodated life to meet the needs of production by subsuming human relations into its fold. In this sense, employers "cooperated" with the lives of married women in the form of part-time labor, allowing women to continue their social roles as mother and spouse. "In every moment of the development of the capitalist mode of production," argues Negri (1992), "capital has always proposed the form of cooperation" (154). However, to produce productive labor, Negri continues, "this form had to be functional with the form of exploitation" (154). Hiring married women as part-time workers exploited their labor with substandard pay and an absence of benefits. Corporations cooperated with the existing social relations of women's primary roles as mothers and wives by offering the flexibility of part-time labor to accommodate management needs while maintaining traditional forms of exploitation including unpaid labor at home. Capital does not only respond to collective social movements; but more important, capital is always responding to the real social experiences of living labor.

As the services sector increased in economic importance along with the availability of part-time work, more employment opportunities were made available for women and, in response, many middle-class married women became active participants in wage labor (Jenson, Hagen, & Reddy 1988: 5–6). Women's participation in the labor force and their relation to work was different from that of the traditional male worker. Women moved into and out of the paid labor force throughout their life cycle because most middle-class women quit work when they married and reentered the workforce when their children were school age or when the family desired additional income to purchase consumer items (including new technological household appliances) (Weiss 2000).

At the 1957 National Manpower Council meeting, labor analyst Howard Kaltenborn explained the rationale behind hiring married women:

> These older women, as a group, constitute the least effectively utilized sector of our working population. [We] will [have] to employ them in increasing numbers in business, industry, and government in order to meet the nation's manpower needs and to insure the continued prosperity and growth of our national economy. (As cited in Blackwelder 1997: 161)

Kaltenborn recognized that married women were an untapped labor force and could be subsumed readily into paid labor and exploited as part-time wage earners. The recognition that this previously untapped source for wage labor was ripe for exploitation was not lost on employers. As the National Manpower Council advocated the hiring of female laborers for part-time work, its members touted the benefits of hiring married part-time workers by explaining that they could easily be laid off during an economic downturn and rehired during growth periods. Part-time work and flexible work schedules exploited the previously untapped female labor force while saving employers a significant amount in wages and benefits (see Blackwelder 1997: 162–163).[8] This progressive move is significant in that it *presupposes* the feminist movement of the 1960s and 1970s. Regardless of the success or failure of this particular equal rights agenda, the movement of women entering the labor force, and capital's response to this movement, demonstrates that as early as the 1950s, with regard to white, middle-class, married women, capital was already recognizing the productive aspects of progressive movements. Far from resisting what will become the feminist movement, capital, by responding to the "subtle revolution" of the transformation in women's daily experiences, is able to exploit the newly skilled yet inexpensive female laborer. During the 1960s the number of wage-earning women increased from "23 million to well over 31 million, and female labor force participation increased from 37.7% to 43.3%" (Blackwelder 1997: 177). Women entered the wage-earning labor force in increasing numbers, but unlike the 1950s, middle-class and working-class mothers maintained a constant relationship to wage labor, and many, including mothers with infants and toddlers, accepted full-time employment (see Blackwelder 1997; Jenson et al. 1988). During the 1960s and 1970s, labor demand increased and women continued to fill the needs of the growing service industries. The number of women working in the service industries doubled between the mid-1930s and the mid-1990s (Hesse-Biber & Carter 2000: 126; U.S. Bureau of Labor Statistics 2001). Regardless of class and family status, more women were seeking employment out of economic need as the cost of living continued to rise. By the 1970s, the service industry surpassed manufacturing and by the 1980s service-sector jobs accounted for 65% of the national income (Blackwelder 1997: 6). The labor market was in continual need of service-sector employees such as retail clerks, waitstaff and food preparers, nurses, dental assistants, maids, child-care workers, and hairdressers, and because service positions were traditionally segregated as women's work and as women's financial status required the necessity to earn a wage to support themselves and to contribute to their families, women were further integrated into the labor force.

In the 1980s, the economic downturn affected the labor force in its entirety. As Jenson et al. (1988) explain, the expanse of global capital on the world market shifted the economic structures of advanced industrialized countries. "The link between mass production and stable demand collapsed in the face of a process of increasing internalization of capitalism and interpenetration of domestic economies by one another" (9). The effects of the ebbs and flows within global capital resulted in a significantly altered labor force. In the face of recession, businesses responded by downsizing, cutting costs by turning full-time labor into part-time labor, stagnating wages, and replacing human bodies with new technologies. Businesses drastically altered their structure by shortening product production time and increasing flexibility in response to an unpredictable global market (see Blackwelder 1997: 260; Jenson et al. 1988: 9–10).

In the unstable economy of the 1980s, temporary work began to replace full-time and part-time work. Although the proportion of female laborers had remained constant since the late 1970s, "the part-time employment of women [became] increasingly involuntary" (Albin & Appelbaum 1988: 148) as women who had previously held full-time positions were now redirected to part-time work. Moreover, "involuntary part-time employment of women, which accounted for 12% of part-time workers in 1970, counted for 22% by 1986" (148). Although part-time employment paralleled "the expansion of traditional service industries, the growth of temporary employment . . . outpaced the American economy as a whole" by the late 1980s (148). In addition, with the prevalence of computers and newly developing rapid communication systems, the labor force altered as large companies that at one time employed a significant number of full-time employees, began maintaining a "core" of full-time employees, supplemented with temporary laborers (149). Not unlike the part-time female laborers of the 1950s, at the sight of an economic downturn, these temporary laborers were readily let go.

During the 1990s and the first decade of the new millennium countries across the globe have seen their economies rise and fall. In the early 1990s, the U.S. economy fell into a recession but rebounded a few years later. Workers that produced goods continued to lose their jobs throughout the decade, while those in the service and technology industries began to gain employment. Ninety percent of the job growth in the 1990s was in the service sector (Hatch & Clinton 2000: 3). The growth of service-sector employment was greatest in temporary and contract employment (Hatch & Clinton 2000). The recession of the late 2000s resulted in more layoffs in all sectors with, once again, the goods-producing sectors suffering the most. Due to the intense loss of jobs in manufacturing and goods-producing industries, and the more secure employment for those who worked in education, government, and health care, for the first time women momentarily outnumbered men in paid labor (Rampell 2010). Simultaneously, "chronic joblessness" increased as more and more unemployed workers found it difficult to secure employment. For those who found employment, the jobs secured were often temporary and part-time as employers in all sectors shifted to a more contingent workforce (Goodman 2010).

In this precarious and volatile economy, the laborers who possessed traditionally feminine characteristics including interpersonal and relationship-building skills are the most likely to survive. An employable employee needs to be flexible, responsive to change, and able to keep pace with rapidly altering communication technologies, while navigating the rocky terrain of global capital. Emily Martin (1994, 1995) articulates that the physical body of the worker and the organizational system of the corporation must both be "flexible." She writes, "The successful and ideal organization is no longer a monolithic, hierarchical bureaucracy but a fleeting, fluid network of alliances with great organizational flexibility" (1995: 225). The worker must be "innovative, flexible, whole in mind and body, nimbly managing a multitude of relationships and circumstances to maintain a vigorous state of health" (225). Women's traditional ebbing and flowing in and out of the labor force, their ability to multitask and manage wage labor while managing the "second shift" at home, along with their agility in riding the waves of employment opportunities by accepting part-time and temporary labor, positioned them as the most qualified employee. They are, in short, "flexible survivors" (Martin 2000: 512). The labor force has further subsumed women, their qualities, characteristics, and social relations while deepening their relation to capital and intensifying their exploitation.

Donna Haraway (1991) explains the restructuring of work "as both literally female and feminized, whether performed by men or women" (166). Haraway explains:

> To be feminized means to be made extremely vulnerable; able to be disassembled, reassembled, exploited as a reserve labor force; seen less as workers than servers; subjected to time arrangements on and off the paid job that make a mockery of a limited work day; leading an existence that always borders on being obscene, out of place, and reducible to sex. (166)

This feminization of the contemporary professional worker is reminiscent of the traditionally feminine roles of mother, wife, homemaker, and caretaker, only now this intensification of feminization applies to work itself. The feminization of labor does not result in better working conditions for women, but rather new working conditions for everyone. The effects of a feminized labor force—a labor force that is unstable, flexible, amorphous, ungrounded, and based on service and social relationships—is a labor force in which new sentiments appear as workers strive to maintain some footing on ground that is continually slipping away.

In the new millennium, with the rise of affordable portable communication technologies and a wireless connection that allows many to work anytime from anywhere, flexibility has taken on an increased intensity (Gregg 2008). On the commuter train, in the airplane, at the coffee shop, at a kid's game, and even from bed at night, workers are able to remain in constant and continual contact with work. Today's worker now has the "freedom" to work from anywhere, which on the surface suggests a truly flexible work-life schedule. Work time is potentially all the time now. "The concept of overtime is blurred," states Riikka Kivimaki (2004), "when, instead of measuring working by the hours on the clock, it is measured by work periods during which a certain task is completed" (189). Moreover, workers are becoming more contractual and contingent as they are hired for short-term, project-specific employment.

In January 2010, *Bloomberg Businessweek* featured an article titled "The Disposable Worker." The cover art presents an image of the contemporary iconic employee. She is a professional woman; her name badge identifies her as a "contractor." On one arm she totes a bag that holds her clock and cough syrup, while in the other she transports her potted plant. The corresponding text explains that 26% of the U.S. workforce is temporary or contingent workers. "With the economy expanding again, and employers loath to add permanent workers, temp employment is one of the few sectors of the labor market that is growing rapidly" (Coy, Conlin, & Herbst 2010: 36). Temporary and contingent workers have higher rates of depression and anxiety because of "a lack of job security and healthcare benefits, as well as social ties to the rest of the workforce, increase stress levels for temps and contractors" (38). In addition, temporary workers have zero paid sick days, and no paid vacation or retirement plan, leaving the contingent employee increasingly vulnerable and the corporation able to operate more cost effectively, as it does not have to pay for costly health benefits, vacation days, and employee training (Coy et al. 2010). Putting the image of a female worker on the cover is not incidental as it speaks to the required entrepreneurial spirit of flexible feminized labor that is required of all workers today while subtly suggesting "women's 'natural' preference for flexible labor" in a precarious working environment (Gregg 2008: 287).

Maintaining a flexible mind and body is necessary in all areas of life as "we are required to be flexible, to be in continuous training, to participate in life-long learning and perpetual assessment; we are faced with continual incitement to buy and to improve ourselves, urged to engage in constant monitoring of our health and never-ending risk management" (Rose 2003: 430). When work-life is precarious and contingent, the worker must always be working on her self-improvement in order to maintain viability in the labor force. As Martin (2000) explains, "Workers and managers are 'evolving' with the aid of self-study, corporate training sessions and an insistence on self-management when they are lucky enough to be employed inside a corporation, and then aggressive entrepreneurialism during the frequent periods they are now expected to spend outside" (513). The worker must never rest. This neoliberal form of self-governance requires that the worker "engage in a constant process of modulation, adjustment, and improvement in response to the changing requirements of the practices of his or her mode of everyday life" (Rose 2007: 223). This "mode of everyday life" is the sphere of an always and everywhere work-life, regardless if one is employed or not.

The characteristics of work today are described by social researchers and cultural theorists as "precarious." The precarious characteristics of work embrace the entire spectrum of the working-life. Workplace characteristics of precariousness include a temporal dimension in which length, duration, and possible termination of employment are uncertain or known to be only temporary, as demonstrated by the iconic employee on the cover of *Bloomberg* with her "contractor" nametag. The social dimension of work-life are increasingly precarious and instable as workers rights' and safety nets are weak or uncertain. There is an economic dimension in which income and benefits are insecure because they are doled out at the whim of multiple forces including the economy, personal relationships, and other unknown forces. Additionally, the length of the workday, the pace of work, and the space of work, are continually shifting. And finally, professional and traditional career paths and economic wages are precarious and uncertain as workers are never certain as to how long their job will last or whether or not there will be another job (Rodgers 1989; Laparra et al. 2004; Vosko et al. 2009). This places workers in the position of thinking of themselves as always in search of a job; therefore, they must continually hone and develop their abilities and personal and professional relationships. These conditions certainly require that workers remain flexible and always self-motivated and socially present, as they never know where the next job may come from.[9] This precarious work environment as well as the affective relations and flexibility of the worker are examined below in the hyperbolic example of Donald Trump's first season of *The Apprentice.*

Ironically, the first season of Donald Trump's reality show *The Apprentice*, with its dreaded signature "You're fired!" was rated the number one show during the start of our most recent economic downturn.[10] *The Apprentice* presented a hyperbolic example of the demands on the contemporary workforce along with the flexibility required of today's professional worker. In each episode, two teams were given a task to complete; the team that completed the task most successfully won for the week and the team members were thereby temporarily relieved of the possibility of being "fired" (the winning teams also received rewards that included traveling in Trump's private jet and other glimpses at the moneyed life). Mirroring the structure of the professional workforce, with its use of organized teams rather than individual job positions, each team named its mini corporation: Versacorp and Protégé. For each task, the team elected a project manager who both directed the team and was held responsible for its success or failure. The project manager of the losing team selected two team members to accompany him or her into the "boardroom" for possible termination. In the boardroom, the team members had to defend their performance and respond to Trump's and his two associates' scathing comments. Trump would then fire one of the three team members present. The show proceeded accordingly for 13 weeks until a winner was selected. The "winner" was then awarded the opportunity to work for one year as president of one of Trump's companies. The tagline, "This isn't a game. This is a 13-week job interview," is all the more salient.

These 13 weeks of work and competition were organized for the sake of entertainment in the form of reality television. Nonetheless, the "real-life" outcome—the opportunity to work—differed from the outcome of most other reality competitions in which the winner leaves with a cash payment and ostensibly the possibility of *not* having to work.[11] This show exhibited both the active participation in work tasks as they exist in contemporary corporate America and, because of its competitive component, made a statement about the form and quality of contemporary professional work and the form and quality required of the worker who is to succeed in today's economy. Each week the contestants were required to perform divergent tasks that ran the gamut from selling lemonade on the streets of New York City, to negotiating with known celebrities for a fund-raising event, to renovating and renting a New York apartment. Notably, the tasks were not representative of the job position for which the candidates would be "applying"; rather, the tasks themselves were immaterial. The team and candidates that succeeded were those that best demonstrated the qualities of the postindustrial worker. That is to say, it is not that a candidate can *do any particular thing,* but rather that the candidate is flexible enough to *do anything.* Particular skills were not required; instead, what was necessary was the ability to develop affective relationships both inside and outside of work. In the case of *The Apprentice*, the social adeptness or ineptness of the candidates was illustrated not only during the workday, but also in their interactions with other contestants in the context of communal living arrangements. For the contemporary capitalist worker, work does not end.

The teams were initially divided by gender. Choosing their corporate name was the first task of each team. The name Protégé Corporation recognized the objective and role of each candidate in her relationship to Donald Trump. The name Versacorp recognized the versatility and flexibility that both corporations and their employees must embody. The teams and their members were required to move easily from one set of tasks to the next, from one skill set to another, and were to adapt quickly to unpredictable changes and opportunities. This quick adaptation required the potential employees to use all of their resources, including their material bodies. Although their choices were depicted as presenting ethical concerns to both the teams and the audience, the contestants readily sexualized and racialized their bodies in order to complete the job tasks. Whether taking the opportunity to use one's sexual qualities to sell alcohol at Planet Hollywood, as the women were accused of doing, or to capitalize on one's sex and race by presenting oneself as a famous athlete, as an African American male was accused of doing, the strategy was similar in kind: The candidates employed the resources they had available, including their material bodies, and the opportunities to exploit them.

The candidates also had to quickly shift language codes. In one task, the teams had to sell their choice of goods at a flea market, while the following week's task required them to negotiate with celebrities. One candidate misread the codes of conduct in her celebrity meeting, insisting that the celebrity spend four days with the highest auction bidder, which mortified her team and led one member to accuse her of being a "loose cannon." When the candidates had been whittled down to the four "survivors," they were each formally interviewed by four of Trump's high-level employees and most trusted advisers. The conclusions they reached of each candidate were telling: Kwame's perceived low energy was a concern; Nick had charisma and could sell a product but it wasn't believed that he had anything more to contribute to the corporation; Bill was well liked and successfully defended his lack of an MBA; Amy, the sole woman who had made it to the final four, was reported by one adviser as "boring to talk to" and a "Stepford wife."[12] Importantly, just because work requires feminine characteristics, this does not imply that "women win." In this new feminized sphere, a show such as *The Apprentice* demonstrated that although work is feminized, feminine characteristics, when exhibited by women, may still carry a negative connotation. This was exemplified by the numerous moments in which the socialization of women was portrayed as "cattiness," "bitchiness," and "competitiveness," while similar traits exhibited by men were characterized positively as leadership qualities.

In the final week of competition, Bill and Kwame each put together teams of former candidates to work under their supervision. Bill was given the task of successfully executing a national golf tournament. Kwame was challenged with the task of successfully managing and executing a pop concert event. While both candidates and their teams succeeded in their projects, Bill was ultimately selected as the Apprentice. Although both candidates were definitely qualified, their differences are significant. Kwame represented the traditional, Ivy League MBA candidate; he was the quintessential "corporate man" in the best sense.[13] In contrast, Bill had what he referred to as "entrepreneurial blood," and was openly enthused and flexible. Kwame, conversely, was not perceived as taking opportunities when they arose. This was demonstrated when Kwame did not break what he thought were the rules, and therefore made the "mistake" of not taking the opportunity to terminate a team member who was sabotaging his performance and frustrating other team members. Kwame was perceived as being too hands off, whereas Bill, whose overt enthusiasm may have at times annoyed his team, was reviewed positively and completed the tasks with fewer mishaps and fewer significant teammate problems.

This section illustrates the feminization of labor and the fact that qualities associated with the social realm have become prerequisites for paid labor. The following section examines more closely how these traditionally feminine qualities are "put to work." As qualities required for work are no longer differentiated from those required in one's personal life, the affective state apparatus apprehends our affect—via the intersection of work, life, and medicine—to modulate our bodies for the purpose of producing appropriately motivated workers both at home and at work. Having examined the shift in the nature of work from material-based production to service-oriented work and feminized labor and from permanent employment to contingent and temporary employment, I now make a closer examination of the qualities and sentiments of contemporary workers and the corresponding ailment of depression along with its corrective psychotropic medication.

Feminine Qualities Put to Work

The primary qualities of the wage laborer today include the ability to be habitually multitasking: the capability to keep pace with rapid conversations (e.g., communication technologies and their software updates); the skill of adaptability in every enterprise; the flexibility of shifting from one set of rules to another; the facility for a multiplicity of language games; a command of the rapid flow of information and communication; and, finally, the dexterity to navigate successfully within the realm of "limited possible alternatives" (Virno 1996: 14). Importantly, as Virno notes, "these qualifications are not products of industrial discipline as much as results of a socialization that has its center of gravity *outside of the workplace*" (emphasis in the original, 14). Job candidates are not hired necessarily because of particular expertise in a field, but instead because of general social skills that are acquired prior to specific professional training. This is evidenced by the fact that employers continually rank communication skills as the most desirable skills they seek in job candidates. For instance, *Job Outlook 2010* ranked the top three desirable attributes in job seekers as follows: 1) communication skills, 2) analytical skills, and 3) teamwork skills (see Job Outlook 2010, *National Association of Colleges and Employers*). All of these are learned prior to entering the workforce.

On the one hand, the process of socialization, the process of experiencing the self and the world, "appears independent of production outside the initiatory rituals of the factory and the office" (Virno 1996: 14–15). On the other hand, the "continuous change in the organization of labor *has subsumed* the complex of inclinations, dispositions, emotions, vices, and virtues that mature precisely in a socialization outside of the workplace" (emphasis in the original, 15). The workplace no longer "molds" the body into performance; rather, the workplace itself has mutated to absorb the affectations of social skills that mature prior to work.

The subjectivity of today's wage earner is constituted by the ambivalence generated through the blurring of work and life, and then by the deteriorating ability of work to ground the subject and provide a sense of a stable identity. Because work now occupies the entire field of social relations and because the subjectivities productive for capital are characteristically feminine, then it follows that the sicknesses traditionally associated with femininity will be absorbed by capital as well. Stated simply, those aspects of life that are traditionally experienced outside and prior to work are now a requirement for work itself, including the worker's affective responses. The relation between women, depression, antidepressant medications, and work reveals tensions between the dominant form of subjectivity—the neoliberal, flexible, feminized worker—and the contemporary form of value in capitalism.

Antidepressant Advertisements

Jonathan Michel Metzl (2003) explores the proliferation of psychotropic medication and its relation to traditional gender roles in print advertisements and psychological journals from 1955 through 2002. He aptly notes, "The process whereby—unlike most other types of medication—psychotropic medications become connected with both curing disease and maintaining certain specific notions of gender roles is a mechanism of action that evolved over the latter half of the twentieth century" (12). Significantly, as the number of women entering the labor force after World War II increased, the use of psychotropic drugs became more common. Metzl argues that with the shift toward psychotropic drugs and away from psychoanalysis, "women were assumed to be the source of an epidemic of 'cultural anxiety,'" and with psychotropic drugs such as Miltown, "culture found its restorative cure" (27). With psychotropic drugs women could consume a prescription medication to make life more bearable and to be content in their traditional roles of mother and spouse regardless of their new responsibilities as wage earners.

In the 1960s and 1970s, as women were gaining more power in the workforce and fought to alter the patriarchal social structure, psychotropic pharmaceuticals were advertised to calm down angry and irate feminists who would rock the social boat by demanding equality in wages and opportunity. A 1965 ad in the *American Journal of Psychiatry* offered Valium as a panacea for women who were tense and frustrated: "With adjunctive support from Valium, ...patients generally find life more bearable despite continued situational problems." The advertisement also claimed that Valium was found "effective in controlling tensions associated with symptoms such as insomnia, restlessness, and other psychic and somatic complaints" while also aiding the patient's ability to "withstand the stress and strain of environmental pressure" (ad reprinted in Metzl 2003: 16). Similar to the advertisements discussed earlier, although social injustice may have been the cause of women's frustrations and anxieties, women's condition was articulated as pathological, and psychotropic medication was the remedy prescribed to cure their restlessness and agitation.

Early psychotropic drugs such as Miltown and Valium were sedatives and attempted to produce sedate women who did not complain about their social or work roles. Drugs such as Valium were advertised as calming tonics with the purpose to soothe and quiet the unsettled, restless, and discontented woman. In a 1970 Valium advertisement, a single woman of 35 was diagnosed as "psychoneurotic." Jan, the "35, single and psychoneurotic" female in the advertisement, is described as one of the many "unmarrieds with low self-esteem." Valium was the prescribed cure for the "problem" of singleness and helped to relieve the "emotional 'storms' of psychoneurotic tensions and the depressive symptoms that can go hand-in-hand with it" (ad reprinted in Metzl 2003: 148).

This hypothetical Jan crossed the traditional expectations of femininity by not getting married, but more important for not being marriageable, and would come to realize that her dissatisfaction is her fault and her fault alone. Jan would be drugged into submission to conform to the traditional standards of her day, not only the social relations of heterosexual coupling, but we can also imagine that Jan, without a husband and as a mature single woman, works for a living. It follows that Jan takes her depression into the workplace, and while depression, like other sicknesses, would be understood as a detriment to productivity, with psychotropic medication, Jan is able to go to work and also to be productive and content with her constricted role while there. Even at this historical moment, Jan's diagnosis as being "sick" places the blame squarely onto herself rather than on external social and economic limitations. She is culturally constructed as pathological because of her deviance from the prescribed social roles of her time. Jan is given Valium to calm her discontent, to maintain the status quo, and importantly, to keep her quiet, productive, and cooperative at work. To be clear, even as Jan is being calmed of her anxiety and the agitation, which has a clear, material cause in a historical set of social relations, her new affective self also allows her to meet the needs of the workplace. As society and the economy shift and change over time so will the symptoms, narratives, and "cures" of women's depression. In each case, women who are treated for depression are also treated for life as a woman in capitalism.

Depression has been linked to one's ability to be productive since Nietzsche wrote about it in 1887. Depression, unlike other illnesses, is rhetorically constructed to turn the subject against herself. In Friedrich Nietzsche's (1887/1996) *On the Genealogy of Morals*, he eloquently describes depression as "a feeling of physiological inhibition" (109). This definition describes the inability of the body to move, to produce, to be of use. The depressed body is "listless" and experiences a "certain fatigue and inertia" (108–109). Depression differs, notes Nietzsche, from other illnesses in that the depressed are directed toward self-blame and the burden of healing is placed on them. Whereas in other forms of sickness one may blame an external force, with depression "you alone are to blame," states Nietzsche; "you alone are to blame for yourself!" (104). This self-blame leads to feelings of guilt and shame, which in turn directs the depressed toward the self in "an introspective turn to their *resentiment*."[14] This turn toward self-resentment and blame is used, argues Nietzsche, in order to "*exploit* the bad instincts of all the suffering to the end of self-discipline, self-surveillance, self-overcoming" (emphasis in original, 107). Hence, the instinct toward self-resentment is fallacious in that it leads to disciplining one's own behavior and actions; it produces self-monitoring and self-assessment; and encourages that one "get over" one's self, that the depressed are responsible for de-pressing or inflating their listless, physiologically inhibited bodies. Blaming oneself is an important component of the definitions and experiences of depression: First, the depressed are responsible for their illness and its cure, turning the depressed subject into its own object. Second, this move ignores external and structural forces that may be the cause of depression. Mourning the loss of a loved one, grappling with a miserable job or financial worries, and trying to mend a broken heart are all left out of the equation explaining why we may experience depression. In sum, the depressed are the reason for their illness and the agent of its "cure." There is no external blame directed outward toward social conditions or forces; rather, the self is the originator of sickness and as such, the depressed must discipline and govern herself appropriately as even then external causes of depression are obscured in treatment of the depressed.

Ironically, work was often the cure prescribed for depression. One form of self-discipline that the depressed were encouraged to perform is labor, and specifically, mechanical labor. "There is absolutely no doubt," states Nietzsche (1887/1996), "that it brings considerable relief to a life of suffering: this state of affairs is nowadays called, somewhat dishonestly, the 'blessing of work'" (112). Mechanical labor and all of its attendants provide "absolute regularity, absolute and unconscious obedience, a way of life which has been determined once and for all, time which is fully occupied, a permitted degree of 'impersonality,' even a disciplining with a view towards impersonality, towards the forgetting of the self" (112).

This form of depression and its cure are directly linked to the dominant form of work in a disciplinary society. Work is the prescribed remedy for the listless body. Mechanical labor disciplines the body through external forces and produces the body as a cog in the wheel of production. This is most reminiscent of a disciplinary society in an industrial economy; work is mechanical work and the remedy for depression is to "lose oneself" in work. While work has changed in its requirements of affective labor, and as women have become wage-workers, the relationship between depression and work still persists. Work, the discourse still claims, will cure you. Thus, depression itself *works* to discipline and govern the self in the production of work. Capital is served on two fronts at once: The working subject is produced through a disciplining of the self, and the working subject views work as a means of becoming healthy through the loss of the self.

While the incidence of depression has increased since 1955 for both sexes, modern forms of labor that developed during the same period no longer provided relief from depression in the manner that Nietzsche (1887/1966) describes. This new form of labor replaced "absolute regulatory" with the management of fluid relations, and as such, depression symptoms reflected the change in both the economy and social relations. In 1992 the *New York Times* reported on the first international study of major depression. The study found that the possibility of experiencing depression is three times higher for people born after 1955 than their grandparents' generation (Goleman 1992). This depression is described as not just feelings of sadness, "but a paralyzing listlessness, dejection and self-deprecation, as well as an overwhelming sense of hopelessness" (C1). This increase in depression is consistent with the increase of work-related disability claims attributed to depression. According to an analysis of MetLife's database of disability claims, depression accounted for 55% of psychiatric claims, as reported in *Mental Health Weekly* ("Depression, Stress" 2003). The report noted that white-collar employees were more than twice as likely as other working populations to submit a psychiatric claim. Regardless of the cause of depression, more people are reporting that they have the symptoms of a depressed person and those who seek medical assistance are being prescribed antidepressants.

Not surprisingly, the narratives associated with the iconic antidepressant Prozac read as liberatory text. Prozac is the productivity drug that inflates the once physically inhibited body. Peter Kramer (1994) describes those on Prozac as "optimistic, decisive, quick of thought, charismatic, energetic, and confident" (16–17), all qualities required of today's wage earner. As the qualities of work are now primarily feminine and as work occupies the entire field of social relations, Jacquelyn Zita's (1998) contention that "the higher prevalence rates of depression among women can be read as a gendered function of women's over socialization into relational and interpersonal orientations" (75) is congruent with the process whereby social relations are integrated into the sphere of work. Likewise, Blum and Stracuzzi's (2004) suggest that "women with the greatest status vulnerability mark distinction through the body with discipline, restraint, and 'elective asceticism'" (281) and that Prozac is a way in which women can continue to modulate the body in order to keep pace with shifting codes of professionalism in the workplace. They are, indeed, flexible survivors.

As workplaces increasingly operate on a more feminized model of flexibility and multitasking, and function through the management of social relationships, the increase of depression is more and more likely. Depressed people still blame themselves for their depression, but in the age of pharmacology and advanced biology, the depressed person can also blame his or her biological makeup and consume antidepressants to regulate this chemical aberration. Changes in our understanding of depression also correspond to changes in advertisements, and as depression becomes more pervasive, advertisements for depression may include both sexes, but remain quite definitely gendered (see, e.g., Blum & Stracuzzi 2004; Gardner 2007).[15] In the Zoloft advertisement described earlier, the image presented is not a human image, but rather an egg-shaped blob that has a tear escaping from an eye. A rain cloud follows the depressed egg. The text informs us that depression "affects over 20 million Americans" and that "while the cause is not known, depression may be related to an imbalance of natural chemicals between nerve cells in the brain." The ad presents depression as sexless and locates the cause of depression in the physical body. While the egg itself appears sexless, eggs connote femaleness in their relation to reproduction. Perhaps this sexless egg is the apt expression of depression today. First it demonstrates that depression is biological and that it is primarily centered in the femaleness of the body. Second, because female eggs are necessary for the reproduction of the species, we can begin to see that depression is now necessary for the "reproduction of the conditions of production," to appropriate Althusser's (1971) phraseology (127).[16] That is to say, as work has appropriated feminine affectivity and its attendant depression, the egg aptly expresses that the ability to reproduce symptoms of depression occurs because the affect of depression has become productive. In Nietzsche's time, the depressed person was simply directed to perform physical and manual labor in order to work through his depression; today, the affect of the medicated depressive is the model worker as she embodies the necessary affective and communicative qualities for success in contemporary capitalism.

Communication

The discourses of depression and antidepressants articulate health and productivity in the form of communication. "Communicative labor" (Greene 2007: 328) is the necessary requirement for success as a feminized and flexible worker in a precarious work environment. For example, Cymbalta's (2007) promotional campaign Depression Hurts articulates depression as faulty communication and antidepressants as a remedy to aid in better communication. By remedying this faulty communication, antidepressants assist in maintaining the body and mind within capitalist circulation. Cymbalta's website includes four "real-life" narrative testimonials, each from a white, middle-class woman (Mary, 44; Karen, 37; Barbara, 41; and Nancy, 56).[17] The first three narratives are from single women, which harkens back to Jan in the Prozac advertisement discussed earlier. In each of the following narratives, depression is constructed rhetorically as a "cure" to faulty communication.

Each woman provides a narrative of her depression: Mary describes how she is overworked and exhausted; Karen explains that she had no life outside of her children and her troubled marriage; Barbara tries to keep it all together as a working, single parent; and Nancy is weighed down by the burden of working full time and her responsibility as the main caregiver to her ill husband. Mary describes her depression as "endless days of feeling no emotion," "thoughts of suicide," and spending "a lot of time alone." Echoing a Zoloft ad, Karen describes her depression as "a constant cloud that hung over everything every day." In more specific language, the women describe depression as a lack of communication with others. Mary states, "I spent a lot of time alone, avoiding family and friends." Karen notes that she had difficulty "relating to other people" and was not "good at communicating or expressing how I felt." Barbara describes that she was a "recluse," and found little time for herself. She explains that she didn't realize that "what I didn't do was a red flag to depression." And Nancy describes herself as depressed as she is "easily irritated," has a "short fuse," and is tired at work. These narratives reveal a failure in communicating and connecting with others. This failure to communicate and to connect to others produces an "alienated affect," an affect that alienates the self from others.[18]

Each woman then explains how Cymbalta has helped her to get back into circulation. Mary describes that she now enjoys time with family and friends and is looking for a job. Karen explains that she and her husband did get a divorce but now their "communication is much better," better even than when they were married. She continues to explain that her motivation has improved and that she is a different parent now: more "active," "involved," and "caring." Barbara didn't realize that she was depressed. When she complained to her doctor of being tired and unable to concentrate at work, he suggested that she try Cymbalta. Barbara shares that Cymbalta changed the way she functions at work and assisted her with her daughter's departure to college. She explains that she "now handles stress a whole lot better." While Cymbalta helped Mary reach out to her friends and family and look for a job, it helped Karen become a better homemaker. Barbara became more accessible at work and at home and Nancy is less irritated. In each narrative, the material circumstances remain troubled: Mary is unemployed and single; Karen is divorced and raising her children; Barbara is still a working, single parent; and Nancy remains the primary caregiver for her spouse. After consuming Cymbalta, each woman's narrative illuminates that her affect has altered, making her more pleasant, social, and less irritated and moody, even though her material circumstances, once again, remain the same.

Communication becomes a metaphor for describing the manner in which antidepressants remedy the symptoms of depression. The Cymbalta website claims that "there are many theories about the cause of depression," and "one of the most commonly accepted theories suggest that two naturally occurring chemicals, serotonin and norepinephrine, are believed to affect core mood and pain symptoms of depression." Paula Gardner (2003) contends, "Though cause is not investigated, the most important cause is *assumed* to be the neurotransmitter, leaving other possible causes out of the scenario" (emphasis in the original, 122). The Cymbalta text continues by explaining that these chemicals function as "messengers" that "communicate between many areas of the brain and spinal cord that affect emotional aspects of a person's nature." Moreover, these chemical messengers "are also important in 'controlling the volume' of messages about pain between the body and the brain" (Cymbalta.com-Understanding Depression). This suggests that Cymbalta increases the messenger's performance, correcting the chemical imbalance. Antidepressants improve communication between chemicals and this, in turn, makes one less depressed and, simultaneously, a better communicator. Antidepressants aid in the performance of communicative labor, as the depressed are now able to circulate their material and affective bodies to garner surplus value in the form of better social relationships.

Life without communicative circulation embodies not only emotional pain but physical pain as well. Cymbalta advertises depression as an emotional ailment, but also a physical ailment that depresses the entire body and withholds the body from circulation. The physical symptoms of depression make it more visible and work to shift it from the discourse of mental health to one of physical health. For example, Cymbalta's Depression Hurts (2010) ad campaign features a commercial that moves from the emotional symptoms of depression into the physical ones. The commercial begins with a tight close-up of a white middle-aged woman looking tired and fatigued while the female voice-over states, "I don't want to feel depressed." Another close-up of another white middle-aged woman appears while the voice-over states, "I'd like to enjoy things again." A white woman sits on her stairs alone, rubbing her neck as the voice-over explains, "I feel those aches and pains." The next image is of a white mother and son. The boy is alone while the mother rests her weary head on the doorframe and the voice-over informs us of "the guilt." A middle-aged white man is shown and the voice-over informs us, "My sleep just isn't right." A woman stares out while we learn, "I'm so anxious." A middle-aged black man rests his head against a pillow while the voice-over states, "I need to focus." Depression includes not only general feelings of depression, lack of joy, and guilt, but also the physical symptoms of lack of sleep, inability to focus, and physical aches and pains. Not uncommonly, physical symptoms are mostly represented by the men featured in depression advertisements while emotional symptoms are usually represented by women, a schism that functions to maintain gender stereotyping.

This commercial concludes with the following images. The "anxious" woman stands up and stares out the window, and smiles. The woman with "aches and pains" walks her dog as he affectionately licks her face. The man who couldn't sleep embraces his wife as they cross the finish line after a race in the park. The woman who would "like to enjoy things again" strolls down the street, window-shopping for new shoes. The man lacking "focus" encouragingly takes his wife's hand as they walk along the rocky coast. Last, the mother experiencing "guilt" snuggles with her son, rubs noses with him as he gently touches her face. She kisses him and smiles. Similar to the other advertisements discussed at the beginning of this chapter, the material cause for depression is left unaltered. What is argued in these commercials is that with antidepressants one accepts his or her situation more easily. While most of these images show that the opposite of depression and alienation is to engage and circulate with others, the lone woman who would like to enjoy things again is not socializing with others but rather is circulating in consumerism as she shops for shoes. As Gardner (2003) explains, "Antidepressant marketing schemes sell the idea that depression is an illness, antidepressants work, while authorizing the larger depression script and paradigm" (124). The script presented in the Cymbalta commercial is one that suggests that antidepressants will make you *feel* better and make you more social, regardless of the material conditions of your depression.

The metaphor of communication also functions in Cymbalta's commercials to suggest that it is not only the depressed who suffer, but also those around the depressed, as illustrated in the commercial above and made explicit in Cymbalta's commercial "Who Does Depression Hurt?" (2010), which illustrates that the alienated affect of the depressed alienates those closest to the depressed, including children, pets, spouses, and friends. The voice-over inquires, "Where does depression hurt? Everywhere." "Who does depression hurt? Everyone." To support that depression hurts more than just the depressed, various images pass across the screen: two children playing together while the mother sits separately on the stairs alone; a dog sits longingly at the door; a middle-aged couple sits at a distance across the dining room table until the wife walks away without a word; a man in his pajamas hunches over his bathroom sink; a man sits at his work desk and rubs his shoulders; and a woman alone cuts vegetables in her kitchen. Each image argues that the affect of depression alienates the depressed from others. The "cure" for depression is pharmaceutically induced communication. The commercial shows Cymbalta at work as it travels down the spine of a female silhouette while the voice-over explains that Cymbalta increases the body's natural production of serotonin and norepinephrine. The result of this chemical interaction is a less alienating affect and better communication and relationships with others. The commercial then presents us with the following images: The woman who was watching television in the dark draws the curtains open; the dog sitting alone at the door is now walked and played with by his owner; the uncommunicative couple is now happily socializing with others on an outdoor deck; the woman is now cooking and laughing with her female friends instead of being alone in her kitchen; the mother is seen talking to her two children as they happily eat their ice-cream cones; the businessman is no longer rubbing his shoulders but is outside chatting happily with his colleagues; the man who was in his pajamas and hunched over the bathroom sink is now outside with his arm around his female companion. This commercial argues that depression alienates one from communicating properly, and in order for the depressed not to alienate oneself from others, he or she must enact the appropriate affect and communication with others. Not only is the depressed the cause of her depression, but she is now also responsible for alienating and affecting others with her depression. Even as work and life become more precarious, the depressed is responsible for her depression and its effect on others.

Sara Ahmed (2004) argues that “affect does not reside positively in the sign or commodity, but is produced only as an effect of its circulation” (120). But what we see with the rhetoric of antidepressants is the attempt to fix sadness and depression as a sign that resides in the body of the sad and depressed. Ahmed rightly notes that “it is…movement that intensifies affect” (127), but with depression it is precisely the lack of movement and circulation that intensifies sadness and depression, and limits communication with others. Depression works to restrict the circulation of communication and antidepressants work to redress this situation by circulating the chemicals in the brain in order to circulate the body into communicative labor. But if the rhetoric of depression works to locate and fix the sign of depression in the body, how is it that we are to understand the body? I argue that we are to understand the body, and the female body in particular, as a preexisting condition that leads to faulty and dysfunctional communication, a preexisting condition that renders women as always flexible to whichever mechanism of survival corresponds to the demands of contemporary capitalism. To support this point further, I turn to discuss Yaz briefly, a birth control pill that includes within it an antidepressant.

The Female Body as Preexisting Condition

In 2009, the National Women's Law Center ran the campaign Denied: Being a Woman Is Not a Pre-existing Condition to fight for equal health-care protection on Capitol Hill. The campaign argues against unequal and discriminatory practices toward women's health care, including charging more money for the same health coverage as men, denying health-care coverage to women who survived sexual assault and domestic violence, charging women more for health-care coverage if they had previously had a cesarean section.[19] While arguing that just because a woman is a woman is not reason to charge her more for health-care coverage, the female body itself is often advertised as inherently flawed. While it is not new that the female body is pathologized, the traditional feminine characteristics that are often associated with the female body continue to get deployed in advertisements that point directly to the female body for its disorder.

The promotional material for the birth control pill Yaz is a case in point. Yaz advertises itself as “the only birth control approved to treat emotional and physical premenstrual symptoms” including the emotional symptoms of irritability, moodiness, depression, and sensitivity along with the physical symptoms of fatigue, breast tenderness, and increased appetite. What we learn from reading the rhetoric of both Yaz and antidepressant medication is that the female body is rhetorically constructed as a preexisting condition for depression, moodiness, anxiety, and irritability. The illness of the female body resides and is fixed directly *in* the female body. Yaz is a particularly interesting site of inquiry because of its "bundling," like communication software, of various remedies including those for anxiety, depression, moodiness, and acne, along with its overshadowed primary purpose as birth control.

Thus, lifestyle drugs such as antidepressant medication and birth control pills that promise to cure irritability and moodiness work primarily to aid our communication skills in order to exploit the affective labor of the worker. By reading these ads and their lists of symptoms we quickly discern what it is to be a good communicator. A good communicator is not "moody," "irritable," "anxious," or closed off and reclusive. A good worker must be an adept communicator, not just for her sake or happiness, but also for the sake of her children, family, coworkers, and capitalism itself. This is not to suggest that consumers do not have agency or that they do not benefit from the rhetoric of depression. Consumers smartly engage in the discourses around them that can assist in their management of the self. As Fullagar (2009) states, "In relation to health, 'patients' are no longer passive recipients of expertise, they are urged to become active responsible consumers of medical services, products and pharmaceuticals" (391–392). And direct-to-consumer advertising provides a discourse for consumers to enter in order to manage their situations. Perhaps antidepressants are among the top dispensed drugs because we are all searching for assistance in becoming better communicators, having more significant social relationships, and having more surplus value in the form of "happiness." The discourses of antidepressant advertisements illuminate that by employing the rhetoric of depression, the consumer is able to perform the communication skills necessary for successful social and work relationships.

Conclusion

The use of antidepressants is on the rise.[20] In what today seems like an ironic telling, the *DSM-IV-TR* (2000) presents a work-related example of depression: "a Realtor may become preoccupied with self-blame for failing to make sales even when the market has collapsed generally and other Realtors are equally unable to make sales" (350). While this example focuses on an objective condition, the ability to reach a goal, the model presented can be extended to understand the affective condition of the depressed worker today. That is to say, while a depressed person may blame herself for the objective conditions such as the lack of making sales, this chapter argues that the process of self-blame is often extended beyond objective conditions to include the inability to manipulate or control fully the amorphous and precarious condition in which the worker is required to survive. The depressed takes on as his or her own fault the mutable, unstable status of his or her own subjectivity. This subjectivity mirrors expectations for postindustrial labor under contemporary capitalism. Both the environment of work and the essential condition of the subject within it lack stability and are defined by their fluidity, mutability, and essential lack of a grounding force. While this condition of subjectivity in work is dominant today, the depressed blames the self for his or her lack of ground or stability in all areas of life. Therefore, the example in the *DSM-IV-TR* is already dated because it suggests a concrete objective relation as the site for self-blame. This would assume that if one did get the sales or attain the goal, then one would not be depressed. Thus, the only stability the depressed person has is the internalization of the unstable relations in which he or she lives.[21] The condition allows for a particularly intense form of self-governance; whereas the depressed is diagnosed as "sick," because of the self-blame for her own instability, she is, nevertheless, arguably, the most able worker in the economy.

This pervasive form of depression can be understood as literally objectless, and the proposed *DSM-V* capitalizes on this with the suggested removal of a concrete loss object as reason for depression. The loss of a loved one or "bereavement" will no longer be excluded from a "major depressive episode." The mention of bereavement is removed altogether (see http://www.dsm5.org/ProposedRevisions for Major Depressive Episode).[22] What remains are the symptoms of depression, regardless of the cause (except for physiological conditions such as medical illness or substance abuse) to diagnose one as clinically depressed. Therefore, although advertisers can readily point to the external causes of depression, and as they mostly focus on the daily life patterns of living within contemporary capitalism, the proposed *DSM-V* focuses solely on the symptoms of depression. What is interesting is that the advertisements and the *DSM* are at odds with one another. While the advertisements often point to a clear external cause of depression, the *DSM-V* is absent of external causes and concerned only with symptoms. Ironically, this move follows Freud's distinction between mourning (depression with an external cause) and melancholia (depression in which an external cause has been internalized). What remains when the symptoms dissipate is the material causes of depression. In the argument presented here, the material causes of depression reside in the experienced exploitation of living and working in contemporary capitalism.

Antidepressants in the age of a feminized labor force produce a feminine subjectivity that is productive for capital. The depressed subject is still directed toward the self—today by mass-mediated institutions—but the remedy that the self is directed toward is that offered by psychotropic pharmaceuticals. The blame for depression still lies within the individual. There is no external object to blame, and because this blame is directed toward the self, it becomes a form of self-resentment, requiring the individual to seek her own treatment and to "overcome" herself: literally, to become someone else at the level of one's affective being. The shift to biopower produces a different form of governance that works through the body to alter its biological functions to produce the affects that correspond to the qualifications necessary for work. Antidepressants assist in the production and performance of affective qualities that are necessary for today's model worker, suggesting that depression can be productive, and perhaps necessary, within contemporary models of work.

The relation between depression and work continues to intensify. In a disciplinary society, the depressed were encouraged to seek refuge in mechanical labor as a means to forget one's self and, therefore, one's depression. Now, little difference exists between the relationships at work and those in the social sphere. The ability to escape one's depression becomes nearly impossible. No longer is refuge found in forgetting that one is depressed. Through the management of depression, one is never able to forget that one is depressed. In both social and work relations, the process of continually monitoring, managing, altering, and becoming that constitutes the medicated depressed person's relationship with the self mirrors the process in which contemporary life is lived.[23]

This chapter articulated the relationship between affect, women, and work and the use of psychotropic medication to enhance one's affect to meet the shifting conditions of work and life. The affective state apparatus functions through the intersections of labor, the body, and medicine in such a manner as to capture us affectively, while maintaining a cooperative, and not an antagonistic, relationship between capital and social relationships.

While this chapter was concerned with feminine qualities that are put to work, in the following chapter the relationship between men and Viagra is explored through an analysis of Viagra's promotional materials. I argue that not only does capital cooperate with our social relationships, but that affect, in an analogous relationship to capital, also circulates our bodies and its pleasures in the form of phallic power. This phallic power, however, is a misrecognition of actual power and forecloses our actual potential for action and joy. In sum, I have examined the role of the state in the affective state apparatus, and the cooperation of capital in capturing and employing feminine affects for the ends of work. Next, the pressure placed on men to continually circulate their potency in order to maintain their social and economic capital is explored. To complete the heteronormative, familial relationship, the chapter succeeding the next explores the relationship between kids, school, and medicine to illustrate the workings of pharmaceuticals in the construction of our future laboring citizens.

Notes

1 This was the headline in the financial section of the *Washington Post* on August 30, 2009. In times of recession and economic downturn, an increase in feelings of depression does not seem unreasonable.

2 The Prozac website, http://www.prozac.com, expresses these symptoms as a sign of depression. This chapter is in no way a critique of those of us who have experienced depression or have used medication to ease our depression. Rather, this chapter seeks to understand the affect or attitude women are required to display in order to be productive capitalist subjects.

3 Other disorders that are primarily associated with women, including bulimia, panic disorders, and irritable bowel syndrome, are considered affective disorders and, as such, suggest that the female body is dysfunctional at the level of its affect. These affective disorders are illustrative of the point that affect, as I use it here, is not reducible to emotion. Brian Massumi (1996), in "The Autonomy of Affect," explains that affect differs from emotion and that "affect

is intensity," and "follows different logics and pertains to different orders" (221) than does emotion.

4 Women have always been part of the labor force. Black and poor women have always worked, in both paid and unpaid labor, and have long experienced the exploitation of capitalism. Middle-class women have been historically called on as a paid labor force during times of economic and national crisis, such as during the two world wars. The significance of the post–World War II labor force is that married and predominately white women were still needed to meet the demands of the economic recovery.

5 I thank Brynnar Swenson for pointing out this distinction.

6 "Subtle revolutions" is a term appropriated from Ralph Smith and colleagues' (1979) book, *The Subtle Revolution: Women at Work.*

7 For an account of why economics and gender exist in "different economies," and why Marxism is structurally blind to the economy of gender relations, see Gail Rubin's (1975) work, "The Traffic in Women: Notes on the 'Political Economy' of Sex."

8 This progressive move is significant in that it *presupposes* the feminist movement of the 1960s and 1970s. Regardless of the success or failure of this particular equal rights agenda, the movement of women entering the labor force, and capital's response to this movement, demonstrates that as early as the 1950s, with regard to white, middle-class, married women, capital was already recognizing the productive aspects of progressive movements. Far from resisting what will become the feminist movement, capital, by responding to the "subtle revolution"(Smith 1979) of the transformation in women's daily experiences, is able to exploit the newly skilled yet inexpensive female laborer.

9 Precarious work conditions are arguably not unknown or new, especially to working-women. Rather, as Mitropoulous states, "On a global scale and in its privatized and/or unpaid versions, precarity is and always has been the standard experience of work in capitalism" (Mitropoulous 2005: 5, as cited in Gill & Pratt 2008: 10).

10 The first season of *The Apprentice*, produced by Mark Burnett and Donald Trump, aired on NBC in the United States in 2004.

11 Interestingly, the number of applicants for the first season of *The Apprentice* exceeded those of any previous reality show, according to Trump. On *Larry King Live* (2004, February 27), Trump reported that 215,000 people had applied for the first season of *The Apprentice* and 500,000 for the second season.

12 The website http://www.nbc.com/The_Apprentice/ provides episode summaries as well as a dossier of each week's task and objectives.

13 Kwame's status as a young African American male and Bill's status as a young Caucasian male complicate a simple correlation between race and the reception of the two performances.

14 *Resentiment* is the term that Nietzsche (1887/1996) used to describe how the weak construct themselves through negating the strong. What is significant about this turn toward depression is that the "direction of resentment" (106)

is changed from negating an external entity and redirected toward a self-negation.

15 For a discussion regarding the gendering of depression advertisements, see Paula Gardner's (2007) essay "Re-gendering Depression: Risk, Web Health Campaigns, and the Feminized Pharmaco-Subject."

16 For an understanding of the process of "the reproduction of the conditions of production," see Althusser's (1971) essay, "Ideology and Ideological State Apparatuses (Notes Towards an Investigation)." Althusser argues that production is always already dependent on the material practices of reproduction and, like Virno (1996), these practices occur prior to work through what he coined "the ideological state apparatus." In this book, I argue that we now can recognize an "affective state apparatus" that works not only through ideology but also through the control of our biological affective being through such things as lifestyle drugs.

17 http://www.cymbalta.com/depression/dep_real_stories.jsp

18 I thank Michael Dorland for this term.

19 See the National Women's Law Center campaign Being a Woman Is Not a Pre-exiting Condition at http://awomanisnotapreexistingcondition.com.

20 "Antidepressants Use Skyrockets 400% in Two Decades," announces a *USA Today* headline (Lloyd, October 20, 2011).

21 While this form of depression has become dominant, its symptoms have always existed, often understood as melancholy (see Freud's [1963] essay, "Mourning and Melancholia," in *General Psychological Theory*). The loss of a stable subjectivity is both made into an object and internalized in the depressed person. Judith Butler (1997b) reflects on the incorporation of a lost object when she states, "If the object can no longer exist in the external world, it will then exist internally, and the internalization will be a way to... postpone the recognition and suffering of loss" (134). Julia Kristeva (1989) put it this way: "My depression points to my not knowing how to lose—I have perhaps been unable to find a valid compensation for the loss? It follows that any loss entails the loss of my being—and of Being itself" (5).

22 The rationale provided states, "The exclusion of symptoms judged better accounted for by Bereavement is removed because evidence does not support separation of loss of loved one from other stressors" (http://www.dsm5.org/ProposedRevisions/Pages/proposedrevision.aspx?rid=427#).

23 The goal of this chapter is to understand our current sociocultural condition. This is what Foucault and others have done in their work. This is what I believe Fredric Jameson (2004) suggests when he states, "I think it is only in the light of the study of late capitalism as a system and a mode of production that we can understand the things going on around us today . . . and understanding cultural production today is not the worst way of trying to understand that system and the possibilities it may offer for radical or even moderate change" (presented at the "End of Theory" conference at the University of Chicago and reprinted in *Critical Inquiry* 2004).

THREE

Impotent Bodies

Viagra, Masculinity, and Potency

> The possibility of using our bodies as a possible source of very numerous pleasures is something that is very important. For instance, if you look at the traditional construction of pleasure, you see that bodily pleasure, or pleasures of the flesh, are always drinking, eating, and fucking. And that seems to be the limit of the understanding of our body, our pleasures. What frustrates me, for instance, is the fact that the problem of drugs is always envisaged only as a problem of freedom and prohibition. I think that drugs must become a part of our culture.—Michel Foucault (1997: 165)

> Twelve years ago, Pfizer launched Viagra and changed the way America—and the rest of the world—thinks about sex. The changes have been cultural as much as medical. No longer do men need to assume that sometime in middle age their sex lives will go gently into that good night (as Dylan Thomas may have put it). Most people don't remember that the condition was universally referred to as "impotence" before Viagra came along, and therapists routinely told men that only by overcoming their issues would their former vigor return. Viagra taught us that this simply wasn't true: Almost all the time, "erectile dysfunction" (as Pfizer rebranded it) is a medical condition caused by too little nitric oxide in the blood.—"Viagra, Like Its Fans, Faces Old Age" (2010)

Viagra clearly positions masculinity as sexual prowess. This chapter examines Viagra's promotional materials in relation to male economic and social potency in order to argue that men are instructed to maintain their masculine potency. As Viagra is coming to the end of its life span and about to be reincarnated in its generic form, Viagra's promotional materials offer a particularly interesting site in which to explore the selling of masculine potency. The selling of potency shifts with the changes in the economy. For instance, in the earlier promotional material of Viagra the appearance of strength and virility is premised on the ability to circulate confidently among others and to be recognized as socially and economically potent, regardless of one's personal economic and social status. In contrast, as Viagra is about to sing its swan song, its advertising campaign, "Anthem," speaks to the current economic moment in which unemployment remains worrisome, work is precarious, and neoliberalism reigns. The commercials in the Anthem campaign are premised on individual self-reliance and a pull-yourself-up-by-the-bootstraps mentality.

Lifestyle advertisements do not neglect their male audience. Rather, they strike where it hurts most at the heart of masculinity. Viagra is a lifestyle drug unlike any other. Sold for the treatment of "erectile dysfunction," Viagra is a drug whose sole purpose is to induce an erection in a man so that he can have old-fashioned sex via penetration and perhaps, most important, an orgasm. Oddly enough, Viagra is not sold as a fertility treatment and any discussion of procreation is absent from its promotional materials. Viagra is about pleasure, sexual and social, for all ages.

Just as Viagra is about to embrace its teen years and hit its horny stride with its raging hormones in full effect, it is slated to retire and be replaced by cheaper, generic brands of itself. "Viagra, Like Its Fans, Faces Old Age," states the headline of *Media Week*.

> It's too bad that Viagra's glory days are probably behind it. Much like many of the men who use it, Viagra is facing its looming enfeeblement. In 2012, the blue diamonds [Viagra pills] lose their market exclusivity and for the first time will face competition from cheap generic versions of the drug that can be made by any company. That won't just decimate Viagra's sales, it will negatively impact both Cialis and Levitra as well, as consumers flock to the new, low cost options. (23)

Viagra is the go-to, can-do staple of treatments for erectile dysfunction, and it has forever altered the landscape of impotence and its treatment. Now part of our cultural parlance, Viagra no longer seems to carry any stigma and erectile dysfunction now seems as common as aging actively. But Viagra has had its controversies.

Viagra is undeniably a drug to be used in order to have sex; it garnered national debate in regard to whether it should be paid for by federal insurance, especially in comparison to the first lifestyle drug, the Pill. In 2005 representative Steve King, a Republican from Iowa, argued against Medicare coverage of Viagra:

> We are promoting abstinence for young people with raging hormones, and yet we are going to ask them to pay taxes for sex-enhancing drugs for seniors? In good conscience, I cannot support that. We have only a finite amount of money. When Medicare covers Viagra pills, you are, in effect, taking money away from someone else's life saving drugs. (As cited in Pear 2005)[1]

Disputes regarding insurance coverage for Viagra intensified after the Associated Press reported that "nearly 800 convicted sex offenders in 14 states got Medicaid-funded prescriptions for Viagra and other impotence drugs" (Freking 2005). The dispute over what is and isn't covered by insurance brings to the forefront definitions of lifestyle and lifesaving medication. Dr. Richard Atkins, chief executive officer of the National Prostate Cancer Coalition, contends that "states that have imposed a ban on coverage of erectile dysfunction are effectively lumping thousands of victims of crippling disease in with criminals," and that, for the former group, Viagra is treatment for a medical condition, rather than a lifestyle drug (as cited in Freking 2005). And as President Obama's health-care initiative has received resistance from religious and conservative groups because of its inclusion of birth control coverage, the opposition to Viagra seems to be concerned only with covering criminals.[2]

The economic component of Viagra speaks not just to issues of insurance coverage of lifestyle drugs like Viagra, but also to the need to ensure masculine social viability through active social potency. Viagra advertisements sell a masculine form of self-assurance, individualism, and active and social potency, regardless of age.

Cultural criticisms of Viagra's advertisements and promotional materials have argued that rhetorical constructions of Viagra users reestablish a hegemonic masculinity premised on heterosexual standards of traditional gender norms (Baglia 2005; Bordo 2000; Loe 2004). This is readily seen in many Viagra commercials that feature attractive middle-aged men and their wives in the prelude to sex. For instance, in one commercial in the Viva Viagra advertising campaign, an attractive affluent husband and wife are sitting on the sofa together, she skimming women's magazines, he channel surfing. Soon they start throwing remote controls and golf clubs and magazines out the window and begin dancing to a tango-infused soundtrack all the way to the bedroom. The heterosexual normative relationship is clearly established. Viagra's earlier use of sports figures, such as Texas Rangers first baseman Rafael Palmeiro, established Viagra as a drug for strong, masculine men who represent hegemonic masculinity. Cultural critics have also noted that Viagra's promotional materials allow "for alternative readings by potential users who do not fall into the category of the 'traditional/ideal' Viagra user" including women and homosexual men (Mamo & Fishman 2001: 14). Mamo and Fishman (2001) argue that the use of the word "partner" in many of Viagra's print and television campaigns offers a space in which women and gay men can read themselves into the discourse. What most criticisms fail to take into account is that Viagra, like other lifestyle drugs, does not only reestablish cultural constructs of the contemporary gendered body and its subversions, but that Viagra's advertisements also provide a rhetorical site in which to investigate the cultural body's relationship to contemporary capitalism.

In an economy based on the circulation of intimate and personal relationships, the manner in which our affect is appropriated and circulated is important to the study of contemporary forms of subjectivity.[3] The importance of interpersonal relationships in the contemporary workplace relies on "communicative labor" (Greene 2004), the work of building and sustaining personal relationships for the sake of business. As Emily Martin (1995) explained, the contemporary worker must be "innovative, flexible, whole in mind and body, nimbly managing a multitude of relationships and circumstances to maintain a vigorous state of health" (225).[4] The contemporary worker needs to manage not only his or her physical body to meet the desired standards of health, but with the advent of lifestyle drugs, he or she must also manage the affects of the body in order to induce the proper communicative responses necessary for the management of "a multitude of relationships and circumstances" (Martin 1995: 225). Therefore, contemporary workers must not only be flexible and competent, but also be likeable and confident. Prescription drugs, along with their attendant advertisements, have altered our cultural understanding of "illness" and the definition of a medicinal "cure" by suggesting that ailments such as depression, anxiety, and even impotence are aberrations within the physical body and not effects caused by social factors outside the body. With the use of lifestyle drugs, we are told any person may now attain likeability and confidence.

The advent of direct-to-consumer advertising in the United States allows for pharmaceutical companies to market the qualities deemed desirable in today's precarious and competitive labor force directly to consumers.[5] These advertisements sell the "good life."[6] This is described by Sut Jhally (2003) as "personal autonomy and control over one's life, self-esteem, a happy family life, loving relations, a relaxed, tension-free leisure time, and good friendships" (251). The advertisements for lifestyle drugs promise an altered affect. By alleviating our depression, shyness, anxiety, and impotence, and revealing our "true selves," it will be possible to "regain" a self that is desirable, confident, likeable, and potent. Advertisements have always been a form of "social communication" that reaches into "the domain of interpersonal relations, a domain of nonmaterial goods" (Leiss, Kline, & Jhally 1986: 252). The advertising of lifestyle drugs to consumers takes this beyond persuasion and into the physical body. Advertisements for lifestyle drugs mark a qualitative difference because the commodity being sold is capable of altering the makeup of the physical body for the purpose of attaining the affective qualities that are requirements for the "good life." As consumers are encouraged to be the agents of their own health-care needs, pharmaceutical marketers use this direct access to sell symptoms as illness and medicine as cure (Gardner 2003), and the good life to all of us.[7]

The theoretical underpinning of this chapter resides in Spinoza's understanding of "affect," Karl Marx's concept of circulation, and Jacques Lacan's conceptualization of phallic *jouissance* (pleasure).[8] Spinoza formulated a theory of affect that includes both the material and immaterial alterations that occur when two bodies come into contact. For example, Pfizer's advertisements claim that Viagra positively affects the material and immaterial body of its user because it produces more than an erection: It produces the confidence that stems from sexual prowess. In addition, Marxist thought is employed for the purpose of understanding how these advertisements rely on the rhetoric of capital and, in particular, on the relationship between circulation and the "health" of capital: That is to say, just as "money" becomes capital only when it is circulated, the body becomes "healthy" only when it too is in circulation. An examination of Viagra's promotional materials reveals the manner in which social capital and affective health are garnered through the circulation of the body. Moreover, as Viagra is a drug premised on a heteronormative standard of sex as penetration, its advertisements open themselves up for a Lacanian analysis of phallic *jouissance* (pleasure). Lacan's conceptualization of phallic *jouissance* illuminates the fact that desire is never fully satisfied, even when one attains that which is desired. Because Viagra's promotional material relies on both the rise and fall of desire, the concept of *jouissance* is particularly useful for this analysis. In the following, I join together theoretical formulations borrowed from Spinoza, Marx, and Lacan in order to argue that media representations of Viagra express the manner in which social potency, or cultural capital, is garnered through the circulation of bodies in an analogous relationship to the circulation of financial capital.

This chapter proceeds in the following manner. I begin with a discussion of Viagra's emergence in the United States. I then analyze the Viagra commercials "Bob" and "Joe," as each commercial reveals the role of affect in late capitalism. I argue that affective potency is required for success in both personal and professional life, and that Viagra's promotional materials reveal that a body must continually be in circulation in order to remain potent. The "success" of Viagra, then, is premised on a prior recognition of one's own impotency and the loss of social potency. Only when a consumer recognizes that he is impotent, is he then able to momentarily suspend his impotency by consuming Viagra. This chapter concludes with Viagra's recent advertisements from its The Age of Taking Action ad campaign to argue that Viagra has responded to the recent recession with a stronger representation of neoliberal subjectivity and the expectation of self-reliance.

Cultural Context of Viagra's Emergence

Viagra, the first and most profitable pharmaceutical remedy for impotence available in pill form, was approved by the FDA in 1998 and introduced to television viewers in 1999 when Pfizer aired a commercial that featured the former presidential candidate Bob Dole, who spoke openly about his prostate cancer and his subsequent erectile dysfunction (ED) (Loe 2004: 56).[9] Dole urged his fellow Americans to speak to their doctors about their concerns with their sexual performance.[10] While Viagra was never named in the advertisement, Pfizer's name did appear in the bottom right-hand corner of the television screen. After the initial Dole advertisement, Viagra commercials featured younger and more masculine men including NASCAR driver Mark Martin in 2001 and professional baseball player Rafael Palmeiro the following year (see Baglia 2005; Loe 2004).[11]

It is significant that the aging former presidential candidate and senator Bob Dole was Viagra's first spokesperson. The relationship between politics, power, and the body has become almost inextricable. In 1997 it was estimated that 52% of men worldwide aged 40 to 70 experience ED (Horvits 1997b) and that between 10 million and 20 million U.S. men suffer from erectile dysfunction at some point in their life. This concern has been alleviated with the advent of Viagra, whose timing couldn't have been better if it had been orchestrated: Viagra emerged against a backdrop in which sex became headline fodder and the penis reared its head in public and political discourse, most prominently in the Monica Lewinsky and Bill Clinton scandal.[12] During this sex scandal, mainstream journalism kicked where it hurt most, below the belt, with public discussions of the president and his penis and its performance. Sex was a topic that was widely discussed and the aging baby boomers were readily aroused when, in March 1998, Viagra received FDA approval and became the first oral treatment for erectile dysfunction.

In an article for *Newsweek*, John Leland (1998) noted that 1998 was the year of sex: "In 1998," wrote Leland, "it seemed, Americans wanted to talk about nothing else: if it wasn't sexual, it wasn't intercourse" (62). Sex and politics converged on the national scene with the Starr Report, and as Leland noted, "The Starr Report brought a fetish for thongs, Altoids and cigars into polite conversation, Viagra emboldened the pen as well as the sword" (62). Leland reminds us that "Bob Dole, so modest he once balked at touting his war record, declared on national television that he was an early Viagra popper" (62). What we have then, at least in the popular press, is the intersection of sex and our political representatives brought front and center to the public's attention. When former presidential candidate and senator Bob Dole became the poster-elder for the blue wonder pill, sex and politics once again conflated with the penis, illuminating the anxiety of aging and the fear of political and social impotence among upper- and middle-class heterosexual men. Of course Bob Dole had lost the presidential race in 1996 to the younger and, as we learned, more virile Bill Clinton.

As the baby boomers age, the United States will experience the largest population of aged persons in its history.[13] In 1998, baby boomers found the ideal aged male body in John H. Glenn as he boarded the space shuttle *Discovery* for his return flight to space. The stories about John Glenn represented the ideal elder male, one who was self-sufficient, healthy, and, most important, contributing as a productive self-sustaining citizen. The 77-year-old was also proffered as a scientific object to be probed, studied, and manipulated in order to understand both the limits and abilities of the aging body. Glenn was an example of an ideal aged body, a body that was to be revered, othered, and continually fetishized.

Glenn and Viagra were linked together repeatedly, on talk shows, in cartoons, and in newspaper accounts. The sports page of the *New York Post* began an article about quarterback Steve DeBerg, who made NFL history for being the oldest person, at age 44, to start at any position, by saying, "In this year of Viagra rejuvenating middle-aged men and John Glenn taking his 70-something body back into space, we understand that advancing age doesn't necessarily mean a decline in enthusiasm, performance or production" (Willis 1998: 079). This article transposed the anxiety of the aged body of a 77-year-old to that of the baby boomer at 44, while simultaneously linking sports and sex. This transference is played out in the advertising of Viagra with Bob Dole as the original poster-elder, quickly replaced by younger representatives such as racecar driver Mark Martin, and the then 37-year-old Texas Rangers first baseman Rafael Palmeiro. As Toby Miller (1998) argues, "The male body is standard currency in sporting discourse: on display, at work, measured, and evaluated—in short, objectified for the purposes of pleasure—as nowhere else in contemporary life" (103). Viagra was quickly becoming a drug not just for the elderly, but also for the younger-than-baby-boomer sportsmen.[14]

In 1998, investments also became imperiled as many aging citizens increased their insurance policies with the understanding that upon their retirement at age 65 they would need a significant amount of funds to supplement their Social Security. Joseph B. Treaster (1998) of the *New York Times* reported that millions of Prudential Insurance Company of America policyholders were compensated "to end a class-action suit" because "for more than a decade, company agents repeatedly made false promises" (C 1). Treaster (1998) reported that Prudential often "told customers that they could trade in old policies for more coverage at no extra cost, that premiums would vanish after a few years, and that the policies they were buying were actually retirement plans" (C1, C5). The rampant anxiety over caring for oneself in old age was the impetus for many to increase their insurance policies and to seek supplements to Social Security.

In addition to anxieties over funding Social Security and taking care of the already-aged and those soon to be, the fear of Y2K was also prevalent, especially regarding the timely distribution of Social Security checks. On December 29, 1998, President Clinton announced that the Social Security Administration had corrected any computer problems to ensure that Social Security checks would be paid on schedule in 2000 (Pear 1998: A 14). As Robert Pear reported, Clinton also took the opportunity to note that the system repairs were emblematic of the policy changes that needed to be corrected in order to maintain Social Security's solvency. Clinton was reported as asking Congress to step up to the task at hand. Needless to say, the anxieties over funding old age ran rampant through popular discourse in political, social, and economic spheres.

In 1998, Viagra entered the market of an aging population of baby boomers, one of whom turns 50 every 8 seconds. As Katz (1996) explained, "At one and the same time," the aging "are characterized as a financially secure, healthy, homogenous, powerful interest group, and a massive, dependent burden on welfare, health programs, and the tax base generated by the currently shrinking workforce" (6). With their anxieties over health care, Social Security, and economic stability, baby boomers who valued their prowess in the polis were ready to maintain their standings in a culture that values youth at any price, whether cosmetically or pharmaceutically induced. As Carl Elliot (2003) describes in his book *Better Than Well*, "Consumer capitalism works, at least in part, by presenting consumers with a vision of the good life. This vision of the good life suggests the ways in which a consumer's own life does not measure up, and which could be remedied by the consumer product" (119). At a time when one is filled with anxiety and uncertainty, the desire to maintain and reclaim one's vitality is provided by personal enhancement technologies found in products like Viagra.

The term "erectile dysfunction" emerged out of the U.S. National Institute of Health Consensus Development Conference on Impotence in 1992. Not only did this term replace the common term "impotence," but it also signified a shift in professional attention from the mind to the body of the afflicted subject.[15] The term "impotence" implied that the failure to become erect resulted from the man's personal issues and not from a particular medical state.[16] The change in name signifies a change in the definition of the cause of a lack of sexual function in men. Impotence was a problem caused by external or psychological events, while erectile dysfunction had organic and not psychogenic causes. Scientists began to claim that 80% of all instances of impotence/erectile dysfunction were caused by physical problems in the body (Osterweil 1998: 36). Thus, the term "erectile dysfunction" first redefined impotence as a medical rather than a psychological problem. Second, the term transformed the penis into a mechanical instrument, a commodity, so to speak, an object with a particular purpose that physicians could diagnose, treat, and fix. Third, the turn toward "erectile dysfunction" expanded the notion of impotence to include not just the inability to get an erection, but also the function of "satisfactory sexual performance" (Jarow, Kloner, & Holmes 1998: 7).This revised definition has led to a proliferation of men with ED, "some 30 million according to the NIH, half of whom are thought to be under the age of 65" (Jarrow et al.: 7).

In *Lacan to the Letter,* Bruce Fink (2004) explains that in order for something to be a loss, it has to be symbolized, it has to be named. "Absence cannot even be understood as some *thing* until it is named" (139). The change in terminology from impotence to erectile dysfunction suggests more than a shift in emphasis from the mind to the body. Impotence can be thought of as stasis, a state of being at which one arrives through age or infirmity, and where not having to act, getting to rest, can be perhaps a relief. Erectile dysfunction, on the other hand, is a term that suggests that function is once again possible.

By rendering the term "impotence" impotent and erecting the term "erectile dysfunction," the penis was brought fully into discursive circulation and the medical field started asking questions of it as if it were a manual laborer. Was it strong? Hard working? Functioning properly? Did it have longevity? The discourse circulating around "it" was a discourse concerned with stature, strength, and longevity. As the penis began to take on a life of its own, the man who once *had* a penis was now eclipsed by *its* performance, so much so that its dysfunction was displaced onto the man and away from the penis, which after all could always be made to work again. This process is evident in Viagra's online Sexual Health quiz.

Viagra's online Sexual Health quiz aids in determining whether one might have erectile dysfunction. The preface to the questionnaire states:

> You may wonder if erectile dysfunction (ED) is affecting your sexual performance. If so, take this short quiz. The results will tell you if you have signs of ED. Remember, the right answers are the ones that best describe you.

The visitor is invited to name his dysfunction, and by naming his dysfunction as ED, he is then in a position to overcome his dysfunction, his lack. The Sexual Health quiz consists of the following five questions:

> 1) How do you rate your *confidence* that you could get and keep an erection?
>
> 2) When you had erections with sexual stimulation, *how often* were your erections hard enough for penetration (entering your partner)?
>
> 3) During sexual intercourse, *how often* were you able to maintain your erection after you had penetrated (entered) your partner?
>
> 4) During intercourse, *how difficult* was it to maintain your erection to completion of intercourse?
>
> 5) When you attempted sexual intercourse, *how often* was it satisfactory for you? (emphasis in the original,http://www.viagra.com/about-erectile-dysfunction/ed-test/sexual-health-quiz.aspx)[17]

The scoring consists of five categories: 1) severe ED; 2) moderate ED; 3) mild to moderate ED; 4) mild ED; and 5) no sign of ED. A score of mild ED reports: "Based on group data from several studies, nearly 90% of men with mild ED improved erections with Viagra versus 42% of men taking a sugar pill" (http://www.Viagra.com). For those whose score indicates severe ED, the report suggests:

> You should talk to a doctor about improving your sexual health. Your doctor can suggest effective treatment options like VIAGRA. VIAGRA has been shown to work for men with all degrees of ED. Based on group data from several studies, 68% of men with severe ED improved erections with VIAGRA versus 15% of men taking a sugar pill. (http://www.Viagra.com)

The affirmation of the dysfunction offers its own treatment and after this self-diagnosis, Pfizer provides a link to "ED-friendly" doctors "in your area." The available responses to the questions suggest that sexual health is dependent upon being able to "almost always or always" become erect and maintain an erection hard enough for penetration, always maintain an erection, easily maintain an erection until completion of intercourse, and, of course, almost always be sexually satisfied. The ideal of what sex should or can be is implicit in the online quiz through the available options for response. This ideal will be discussed shortly in terms of a *jouissance* of the Other.

Examining Viagra's advertisements illuminates a biopolitical strategy—the manipulation of the biological body for political and social ends—through which it is revealed that men must govern their material and immaterial bodies for the purpose of sustaining their potency as contemporary capitalist subjects. The concept of potency has long been linked with social and political power. For example, John Milton employed the concept of impotency in 1674 when he wrote, "Any rich man who through age or other impotence is unable to serve the Public" (*Oxford English Dictionary* on-line, 1989). Lexically, impotence entered common parlance as the description for the modern male subject's relationship to his (aged) body, to his ability to "serve the Public," and in relation to his material wealth. Here, three forms of potency are articulated to the male body: virility, agency, and wealth. These three disparate modes of being propel the male body into affective circulation. Pfizer's Viagra commercials successfully link Milton's traditional enlightenment concepts of masculine potency to contemporary symbols of masculinity including youth, wealth, upward mobility, and social power.

Biopolitical Power

The pharmaceutical influence on the body is a form of biopower that exerts political force through the chemical reconstitution of the physical body. As Foucault (1990) explained, "It was the taking charge of life more than the threat of death that gave power its access even to the body" (143). In the first volume of *The History of Sexuality*, Foucault (1990) offers a historical account of how sex became a political issue through the use of biopower: That is to say, sex became a political issue on the axes of disciplining bodies and controlling populations. This intersection revealed "the theme of political operations, economic interventions...and ideological campaigns.... [Sex] was put forward as the index of a society's strength, revealing of both its political energy and its biological vigor" (146). The mechanisms of power addressed the body through the discipline of sex in order to control the population socially, economically, and politically. This implies that to maintain one's viability as a productive citizen, in order to properly serve the state, one has to maintain (and properly govern) one's sexual prowess. "In a society of sex," states Foucault, "the mechanisms of power are addressed to the body, to life, to what causes it to proliferate, to what reinforces the species, its stamina, its ability to dominate, or its capacity for being used" (147). Sex is situated as the mainstay in one's ability to demonstrate potency and productivity. As a Viagra mailer claimed in 2005, "Let's face it, there's nothing like sex."

Biopolitico power illustrates the working of economic power and politics on and through our bodies in contemporary life. Viagra as a cultural and historical phenomenon addresses social and political problems with technological and pharmacological solutions that are played out on the most intimate parts of the body, those that signify one's libidinal energy and potency. Viagra not only allows men to maintain their virility in the bedroom, but its effects are also suggestive of the good life and good citizenship: looking good, economic success, having leisure time and money to vacation—in short, maintaining (and perhaps gaining) one's economic, social, and political power.[18]

In the commercial "Bob" (analyzed below), the protagonist arrives at a cocktail party and proceeds to circulate through the crowd. Each person whom he encounters inquires if he has altered his appearance. In each instance, Bob replies, "No." In another commercial, the protagonist named "Joe" has a similar experience except, unlike Bob, Joe is at work. At the conclusion of both commercials, the viewer is informed that each man has recently spoken to his doctor about Viagra. To be clear, neither Bob nor Joe has used Viagra; they have simply spoken to their doctor about a obtaining a free sample. Taken together, these commercials illuminate that a particular form of affect operates similarly at work and outside of work. This suggests that work and life become almost indistinguishable as the affect necessary for personal fulfillment is conflated with the affect necessary for professional advancement. Masculinity, money, and power are necessary for success in all areas of life. The potential for masculine sexual performance, and its articulation to material wealth and social power, is the affective quality that Pfizer is proffering in pill form.

Pfizer's "Bob" Commercial

> The doorbell rings; Bob, white, handsome, and 40-something, enters a cosmopolitan party and hands the attractive black hostess a gift-wrapped package. She asks, "Hey Bob, did you get a hair cut?" He re-

> plies, "No." The camera follows Bob as he moves through the crowd and is approached by a handsome Asian man: "Hey Bob, did you lose weight?" Bob responds, "No." Finally, Bob reaches his destination, an attractive, white, 40-something woman, who inquires, "Did you just talk to the doctor?" to which Bob responds, "Yup." Then Bob and the woman place their foreheads together in an intimate moment. The male voice-over poses the rhetorical question and its answer: "What's different? He finally asked his doctor about Viagra. Find out if a free sample is right for you." At the conclusion of the commercial the voice-over, once again, states, "Ask your doctor if Viagra is right for you." Text appears on the screen: "Ask your doctor. See the difference," while the voice-over reiterates, "Ask your doctor and see the difference." (Bob, 2002)

This Viagra commercial offers a sophisticated glimpse into adult sexuality—along with its many ironies—at the beginning of the new millennium. On the surface, this commercial sells sex without any explicit reference to sexual intercourse. The upper-middle-class, 40-something adults are attractive and the multicultural aspect of the advertisement implies a sense of cosmopolitanism without crossing cultural boundaries such as interracial or same-sex partnering. At first glance, Bob's marital status is ambivalent, but upon closer inspection Bob is, indeed, wearing a wedding ring, informing the viewer that Bob's companion is his wife and that heteronormative standards of intimacy are intact.

The inquiries into Bob's appearance as he circulates through the room imply that Bob *appears* different, better even—more independent, confident, fit, and better looking—yet, this alteration eludes his peers' ability to pinpoint *what exactly* is different about Bob. They can see the difference, but they are unable to pinpoint what *is* different. Only when Bob arrives at his destination and his wife inquires if he has spoken with his doctor and Bob replies in the affirmative, do we learn what is different: Bob had a conversation with his doctor regarding his erectile dysfunction and, as implied by the voice-over, he obtained a sample of Viagra. This difference lacks any outward material quality. Bob had a conversation and received medication for his dysfunction, but he has not yet taken Viagra. Therefore, he physically remains the same. What has altered is his affect: He enters the party with the confidence of a person who is able to act; he no longer appears impotent even though he has not yet taken his medication, nor has he had sex. This Viagra commercial sells the potential to act, to be confident. Affective change is difficult to pinpoint; it escapes our ability to grasp it *exactly*; the best we can do is to circle around it. How is it then that we are to speak about that which escapes definition: How do we discuss affect?

Spinoza and Affect

Louis Althusser (1971a) argued that the only means by which to understand the unconscious is through its "effects" (204–205). Affect, like the unconscious, cannot be known directly because it does not operate within the linguistic register; therefore, the only means in which to analyze its expression is to point to its effects. The seventeenth-century philosopher Spinoza (1678/2000) described *affect* as "the idea of any mode, by which the human body is affected by external bodies, must involve the nature of the human body and at the same time the nature of the external body" (*Ethics*, part II, proposition 16). As discussed in the Introduction, Spinoza's notion of affect contains a double meaning: *Affectio* refers to the body as affected by an external body, and *affectus* refers to the transition in the body from one state to another (Deleuze 1988: 49). Affect refers to an external cause that combines with another body either to increase or to decrease the body's power of acting. Spinoza referred to an increase in a body's power of acting as joy and, conversely, a decrease in a body's power of acting as sadness.[19] For example, in the case of Viagra, if one were to take Viagra, he would be affected in such a way as to have an erection. His erection will carry within it the external cause, the drug sildenafil citrate, and the man will attribute his erection to the external cause (under the brand name Viagra). His power of acting, to perform sexual intercourse, would then be said to have increased and not diminished, and this would create a sense of joy. Therefore, *affectio* refers to the material effectof one body on another body and *affectus* refers to the immaterial affect (joy/sadness) of one body on another body. While both forms of affect are expressed in the Viagra advertisements, I focus primarily on the immaterial affects (*affectus*) including those of confidence and charisma. Therefore, I argue that our contemporary form of capitalism subsumes and circulates not just material bodies, but bodies' immaterial affects as well. While capitalism has always subsumed immaterial qualities, what is intensified in this particular historical and cultural moment is the prevalence of pharmaceutical corporations that promote the chemical inscription of the body into capitalist circulation from the inside out. While this subsumption may result in pleasure, the experience of pleasure often constitutes a misrecognition of agency and the deployment of actual affective power.

Pleasure and power bring to the forefront the relationship between the penis and the phallus and, subsequently, Jacques Lacan's notion of *jouissance.* For Lacan, the phallus is not the biological penis, but rather the signifier for power in a given economy of desire. Phallic *jouissance* is an experience of pleasure that, in the last instance, does not live up to its anticipated desire for the sole reason that the pleasure has been attained and experienced. Once pleasure is experienced, desire is reignited. Phallic *jouissance* is, therefore, not as pleasurable, in the last instance, as was hoped. Although phallic *jouissance* may eventually end in disappointment, it is important to note that phallic *jouissance* is, nevertheless, the experience of pleasure in real life. Conversely, there is another form of pleasure, "*jouissance* of the Other," which is an idealized form of pleasure expressed often via film, television, and fiction, through representations of sex and desire and the narrativized identification with an other. *Jouissance* of the Other operates through the perpetuation of desire; it is the idealized *jouissance* that can be attained only by the *next* thing, the thing that, by definition, is always just out of reach. "Were there another *jouissance* than phallic *jouissance*," lamented Lacan (1998), "it shouldn't be/could never fail to be that one" (59). All we can actually experience is phallic *jouissance*—the sex we have in real life—and that experience often fails in comparison to the sex desired, to the idealized sexual encounter experienced by the Other.

Phallic *jouissance* cannot help but be fallible as it is structurally dependent on both a rise and a letdown.[20] This is what Spinoza would refer to as an immanent structure because it contains that which causes its rise as well as its decline. Pfizer's Viagra commercials and promotional materials articulate this phallic desire to an Other *jouissance*, to a nostalgic desire (and nostalgia by definition is always a desire for something that never was), or to a future desire of how sex could be. There is a disconnection between what Bob desires and the signification of his desire as it is displaced onto Viagra. Viagra cannot fully satisfy Bob's desire for actual potency as it is structurally limited to a real process that will always let him down and keep the fulfillment of his desire directed toward the future. Lifestyle medicine works in precisely this way: It is not a cure, but must be continually consumed over and over again. "This satisfaction...*fails* to fulfill me—it always leaves something more to be desired," explains Bruce Fink (emphasis in the original, 2004: 160). This is the definition of phallic *jouissance*: "Phallic *jouissance* lets one down, comes up short" (160). Pfizer's advertisement, like most advertisements, refers to phallic *jouissance*, the desire for a pleasure that can be experienced, but links it to *jouissance* of the other, whether in a form of nostalgia or a future desire.

Yet, in Pfizer's Viagra advertisement *jouissance* operates on another level of *jouissance*, a *jouissance* that operates beyond phallic *jouissance*. Lacan describes this as "an existence that stands apart, which insists as it were from the outside, something, not included on the inside" (Fink 2004: 22 n24).[21] The *jouissance* that ex-ists outside—prior to consuming Viagra—is, for our purposes, an affective potency in the form of confidence, joy, pleasure, and charisma. But this affective potency is never felt enough; it is a potency that once obtained by the subject becomes immediately phallic again; that is to say, it is fallible and, like the penis itself, will always eventually fail. Thus, this self-confidence that exists beyond and before Viagra is always precarious and uncertain. The Viagra commercial illuminates a surplus pleasure that exists in the form of an affective potency. This ad presents the viewer with an image of surplus *jouissance*, an affective potency, even prior to the phallic *jouissance*: *It is an anticipation of affective pleasure before the actual pleasure lets you down*. And this anticipation of potency is precisely how Viagra works to induce affective desire. As Fink (2004) explains in regard to the phallus, "It is not what is physically present that is of value, at this level, but, rather, something more abstract, something that is not accessible to sight or touch" (137). This is the definition of affective potency, and affective potency is, therefore, intimately connected to the logics of contemporary capitalism. In the following, I analyze how circulation is essential to the functioning of capitalism in order to argue that affect, like capital, gains its power through circulation, and how a potential gain in power/potency is what is really offered by Pfizer's Viagra advertisements.

Circulation

Viagra works materially in the body through the process of circulation. According to Viagra's website (http://www.Viagra.com), "ED occurs when there is a lack of blood flow to the penis. This means that a man can have trouble getting and keeping an erection long enough to have sex. It may happen only once in a while, or more often."[22] The cause of erectile dysfunction, then, is a lack of blood circulation directed toward the penis. Pfizer does not articulate erectile dysfunction as a lack of sexual desire, but rather as a problem of physical circulation. Under the heading "How Sex Affects the Body" in Pfizer's pamphlet *What Every Man (and Woman) Should Know about Erectile Dysfunction*, which accompanies the company's video of the same name, is the following:

> When a man is sexually excited, the penis rapidly fills with more blood than usual. The penis then expands and hardens. This is called an erection. After the man is done having sex, this extra blood flows out of the penis back into the body. The erection goes away. If an erection lasts for a long time (more than 6 hours), it can permanently damage your penis. You should call a doctor immediately if you ever have a prolonged erection that lasts more than 4 hours. (Pfizer U.S. Pharmaceuticals 1999: 17)

The medicalization of intercourse demands that during an erection the penis is disembodied from its person. Blood fills the penis, causing it to expand. We are not informed of any naturally produced chemicals in the brain that may cause one to become sexually aroused. We are informed only about sexual arousal through the direct flow of blood to the penis, designating the penis as a purely mechanical and a nonsensual entity. We are then informed that "after the man is done having sex, this extra blood flows out of the penis back into the body" (Pfizer U.S. Pharmaceuticals 1999: 17). In this passage, the penis is a separate, mechanical instrument that is alienated from the individual. In this description of ED, the relationship between a man and his penis corresponds to the functional structure of alienated labor. Not only is man alienated from his labor as his object of production is no longer his own, now he is also alienated from his body as the penis is no longer his own.[23]

In Pfizer's explanation of "how sex affects the body," there isn't any discussion of semen. There is no ejaculation and the penis is not referred to as potent in the material emanation of semen.[24] The release of the erection is not explicitly a result of ejaculation of semen, but of the blood in the penis flowing out of the disembodied penis back to the body. "The erection goes away," we are told, "after the man is *done* having sex" (emphasis added, Pfizer 1999: 17). The erection subsides upon completion of sex, but any discourse about natural ejaculation of semen is completely absent. After the third-person discussion about "a man" and "a penis," the penis is personalized: "If an erection lasts for a long time (more than 6 hours), it can permanently damage *your* penis" (Pfizer 1999: 17). This now-damaged penis belongs to someone, *to you*. The passage ends by imploring "you" that if "you" have a "prolonged erection" for more than 6 hours you must immediately seek medical attention.

The functioning of a healthy erection is premised on its capacity as a medium for circulation. In the Pfizer passage above, the only time a person is directly linked to the penis is when it is damaged. A damaged penis is defined by its relationship to the circulation of blood: Either blood doesn't circulate into the penis and an erection does not occur, or blood doesn't circulate out of the penis, in which case permanent impotency may occur. These two forms of dysfunction result in the same condition. Thus, it is the circulation of blood that is of primary importance as it fills the penis, causing it to expand, and then leaves the penis, resulting in its flaccidity.[25] The discourse surrounding potency, health, and sex literally and symbolically *circulates* around the concept of circulation. Both the body and capital can be known only through difference because the only means by which to understand the operation of one sphere (the body) is to compare it to another (capital), as each is part of a larger structure knowable only through relations of difference.[26] Capital is creative and generative, and just as blood flows through the body, continually creating and sustaining life through the mere process of its circulation, capital also requires circulation for its growth and expansion. As Antonio Negri (1991) explains, "*Circulation* is, above all, *the expansion of the potency of capital*" (emphasis in the original, 112).[27]

As postmodern capitalism has shifted emphasis from production to circulation, the desire to throw one's body into circulation seems to follow this logic. Marx recognized the importance of circulation to the success of the capitalist. If we read Marx's passage cheekily with the penis and Viagra in mind, the process of circulation becomes clear:

> His person, or rather his pocket, is the point from which the money [the penis] starts and to which it returns. The expansion of value, which is the objective basis or mainspring of the circulation...becomes his subjective aim, and it is only in so far as the appropriation of ever more and

> more wealth in the abstract becomes the sole motive of his operations, that he functions as a capitalist, that is, as capital personified and endowed with consciousness and a will....The restless never-ending process of profit-making alone is what he aims at. This boundless greed after riches, this dispassionate chase after exchange-value, is common to the capitalist and the miser; but while the miser is merely a capitalist gone mad, the capitalist is a rational miser. The never-ending augmentation of exchange-value, which the miser strives after, by seeking to save his money from circulation, is attained by the more acute capitalist, by constantly throwing it afresh into circulation. (Marx 1954: 150–151, as cited in Gupta 2001: 21–22)

The miser, the one who keeps his money out of circulation and contains his potency in his pocket, is the one who cannot enlarge his wealth. It is the "acute capitalist" that is well endowed, and who understands the never-ending expansion that can be attained by the continual and constant "throwing it afresh into circulation." The capitalist knows that he must continually throw his sex into circulation, and in order to throw his sex into circulation, he must have the proper mechanism: He must have an erect penis. The age-old problem for those without wealth—one must have money to make money—becomes: One must have an erection in order to insert his sex into circulation (at least according to the heterosexual standards of sexual capital) in order to expand its value and to gain surplus sexual capital. To enter into sexual circulation, he must possess "in his pocket" an erection. "Is that capital in your pocket, or are you just happy to see me?" is the unspoken refrain to those who encounter him.[28] To manifest one's material sexual function, he has to implicate himself in the economy of pharmaceutical drugs in order to enlarge his pocket and throw his sex into circulation and produce surplus. As Pfizer's *Patient Summary of Information* notes, "Viagra does not cure erectile dysfunction. It is a treatment for erectile dysfunction" (1999). The continual cycle of treatment is a mandate for men to maintain their capital and their sexual potency.

Affective Potency

Circulation is the "cutting edge of capitalism" because, "historically, surplus-value resulting from production has decreased while surplus value resulting from circulation has increased" (LiPuma & Lee 2004: 9). One means in which derivatives make money is through the process of arbitrage or the buying of currency in one market and the selling of that same currency in another market for a profit. As the shift in capital has produced new forms of business and labor, it has also affected how we live. As LiPuma and Lee note, "These circulation systems are leading to a transformation in the habitus of culture itself" (10). We are directed to circulate our physical bodies and affective selves as a means in which to contend with the economic and social anxieties that pervade daily life. Marx recognized the importance of circulation for economic and capital growth. I focus on the rise of personal strategies of living where one's social, and increasingly economic and political capital is dependent upon the continual circulation of abstract or immaterial qualities like confidence, personality, and charisma. For instance, the affective potency offered by the Viagra advertisement takes the form of confidence and charisma that exists in the *potential* for an erection.[29]

In *$urplus: From Spinoza to Lacan*, A. Kiarina Kordela contends, "The surplus...is conceived as surplus-value in economy, and, as surplus-enjoyment on the level of the signifier and the subject" (2007: 42). She cites Marx's formulation that explains surplus-value and exchange-value:

> Certainly M [money] becomes M + ΔM, £100 becomes £110. But considered qualitatively, £100 is the same as £110, namely money.... The value of the £110 has the same need for valorization [*Verwertung*] as the value of £100, for they are both limited expressions of exchange-value.... At the end of the process, we do not receive on the one hand the original £100, and on the other the surplus-value of £10. What emerges is rather a value of £110, which is in exactly the same form, appropriate for commencing the valorization process, as the original £100. At the end of the movement, money emerges once again as its starting point. (As cited in Kordela: 42–43)

Reading this passage, Kordela explains that surplus-value is, in effect, exchange value. She states, "In the realm of experience, we cannot ever have a surplus-value in our hand; what we hold is exchange-value" (43). She continues: "Surplus-value is a concept, an idea with no empirical referent, which we infer from the purely quantitative difference between the originally advanced and the resulting amounts of exchange value. Nevertheless, it is the cause of both capital and of all things" (43).

Therefore, surplus-value is the excess that is derived from exchange value. Surplus-value is known through the difference between the original value and the value for which it is exchanged. Circulation is necessary for surplus-value, for as Negri (1991) explains, "Even though circulation does not produce surplus value, it nonetheless enables capital to produce surplus-value at every point of the circulation" (112). This is why, as Marx contends, "Capital cannot arise from circulation, and it is equally impossible to arise apart from circulation" (as cited in Kordela 2007: 43). Thus, as Kordela concludes, surplus-value is "the cause and the effect of everything that exists" because surplus-value would not exist unless things were exchanged and things would not be exchanged if it weren't for the potential of producing surplus-value (43).

The affective potency of the male protagonist in the Viagra commercial is produced in each nodal contact that he has with another person. The praise derived from others exceeds the material (exchange) value of Viagra and delivers surplus-value experienced as a bodily or affective sensation that occurs *prior to the consumption* of the pharmaceutical. Affective potency is not produced through sex.[30] Viagra's value, as depicted in this commercial, resides in the surplus-value of an affective potency that is prior to the actual phallic *jouissance*. This affective potency is produced through circulation and by coming into contact with other bodies as "affect does not reside positively in the sign or commodity, but is produced only as an effect of its circulation" (Ahmed 2004: 120). Bob basks in his affective potency. Ownership of the "little blue pill" affectively alters Bob prior to consuming his medication and experiencing its actual chemical alteration. The sample packet of Viagra, like money in the pocket, is enough to alter the affect of those who possess it. Possessing the material object offers symbolic pleasure that is manifested in a representation of the power to act, while Bob's affective potency (surplus-value) is generated through circulation. In the following section, another Viagra ad is analyzed to further illuminate the relations between impotency and circulation.

(Im)potency

The following is a description of Pfizer's 2002 Viagra commercial "Joe," described by Jay Baglia (2005) in his book *The Viagra Ad Venture*:

> A tall, handsome black man is seen emerging from the office of the "Medical Group." He wears a smile.... "Joe" is a white-collar professional and appears to be in his late thirties to early forties. Dressed in an ex-

> pensive suit, we see him enter and cross the vast lobby of a high-rise office building and go into an elevator. In the elevator he encounters a coworker who takes notice of Joe and, presumably, Joe's quiet confidence. This coworker—a white man, wearing spectacles, and much shorter than Joe—asks, "Hey Joe, did you get a haircut?" Joe replies simply, "No." ...Once the elevator arrives on the floor of their workplace and they disembark, Joe encounters more questions—"Did you just get back from vacation?"..."Did you shave your mustache?" "Is that a new suit?" "Are those new shoes?" To all these questions Joe answers, "No." He does not engage any of his inquisitive colleagues any further. But even sequestered in his office, Joe fields more questions: "Did you get a promotion?" his male sidekick asks. "No," Joe replies. "Did I?" the coworker inquires. "No," responds Joe yet again. Still answering questions, Joe leaves the office and walks confidently through the parking lot, presumably on his way to his car. His cellular telephone rings, whereupon, after a laugh, Joe remarks to the mystery caller, "Yes." (80)

Baglia argued that Joe's power resides in his status as the boss, and we "know this because he is not beholden to any of his colleagues, he occupies a large office, and he comes and goes as he pleases" (80). I want to offer an alternative reading to suggest that Joe's position as the boss is not certain and regardless, it is the *affect* of the boss that is of importance in Viagra's advertisement. Joe hosts a multiplicity of inquiries about his altered appearance, but his cohorts are unable to pinpoint what is different about Joe as there appears to be no material change. He didn't get a haircut; he didn't have a vacation; he didn't shave his mustache; he isn't wearing new clothes. His physical presence remains unchanged but his affect has altered. His affective change and newfound confidence are not due to his actually achieving upward mobility within the capitalist marketplace, but rely on an affective alteration that *suggests* that he is upwardly mobile, and that he possesses the *potential* for economic advancement. What has changed is that Joe has the *affect* of the boss, not that he *is* necessarily the boss. With the depiction of Joe's new affective potency, the advertisement suggests that Joe is not only socially but also economically mobile. Thus, there appears to be a correlation between the bedroom and the boardroom, as Joe's not-yet-chemically-induced-erection is circulated as affective potency in his professional life.

Baglia (2005) argued that in this representation of a successful African American man, "Pfizer reveals its expectations: black men can be sexual and successful as long as they are modeling hypersexuality for white men and only if this sexuality and success is not practiced with white women" (81). I want to argue that there is something else going on in this representation. Joe is depicted as successful in business and in life, but the logic of the commercial reveals that this power stems from his admission of his own impotency. His affective potency is not articulated to a masculine dominance of virile stereotypes of African American men. Rather, Joe is potentially potent in the social and economic registers because of the presentation of his upward mobility and not because of physical strength and hypersexuality; his potential potency is premised on his actual impotency. Although the social context for the "Bob" advertisement is a cocktail party and the context for the "Joe" advertisement is the corporate workplace, both commercials cite the same form of affective potency as the mark of social and economic advancement. Here, then, the affect required for success takes the same form in both work and outside of work.

As both commercials demonstrate, Viagra promises the *appearance* of social and economic success, but not its actual attainment. Viagra *simulates* affective potency in order to mask what it cannot deliver: material physical health and the social and economic potency that is related to it. Viagra offers a simulation of potency that, nevertheless, works in the same way as contemporary capitalism. Jean Baudrillard (1994) wrote on the subject of simulation, "To dissimulate is to pretend not to have what one has. To simulate is to feign to have what one doesn't have. One implies a presence, the other an absence" (3). Both Bob and Joe simulate the affect of social potency via the indexing of their own lack of potency. Their simulated social potency does not produce any actual power on its own. Baudrillard further explained that "pretending, or dissimulating, leaves the principle of reality intact: the difference is always clear, it is simply masked, whereas simulation threatens the difference between the 'true' and the 'false,' the 'real' and the 'imaginary'" (3). Affective potency suggests the *appearance* of power—so much so that Joe's and Bob's upward economic and social mobility appears real to those they encounter. Bob and Joe rely on their affective potency, the appearance of power, as if they were participating in arbitrage—in the hope that this appearance of potency can garner actual potency in a different realm.

Viagra offers a semblance of power or, more specifically, a misrecognition of one's affective potency as power. Both Bob and Joe are recognized for appearing different, and they misrecognize the simulation of power or affective potency as real, material power. In actuality, both men remain impotent. Moreover, they have yet to demonstrate that they can overcome their dysfunction even with the aid of Viagra; regardless, their dysfunction will remain even if they momentarily overcome their impotence. As a result, their desire for potency as well as the immaterial power they gain in both work and social settings become structurally *dependent* upon their impotency rather than on an actual potency.

Conversely, they do possess the appearance of power in the form of affective potency. With each nodal contact, both Bob and Joe receive affirmation from others for their affective change. Unfortunately, the potentials inherent in affective potency, including friendship, connection, and collectivity, are not fully actualized. Neither Bob nor Joe capitalizes on these nodal encounters to combine with external bodies to generate and expand their affective power. Thus, while both are affected, neither of them lives up to the potential of his power, and so it remains in the realm of potential. In Lacan's terminology, their affective *jouissance*, in the end, is merely phallic *jouissance*. Although affective *jouissance* operates via circulation just as capital does, there is no material action that occurs. The moments of possibility are foreclosed on as both miss the chance nodal contacts that are necessary for the creation and expansion of new forms of becoming. The acute capitalist seeks the "expansion of value" through the "appropriation of ever more and more wealth" (Marx 1954: 150–151). Bob and Joe fail to produce surplus out of their affective potency because they are unable to combine with those along the way to appropriate and create more power, more capital. Like misers, they harness their affect as they repeatedly say, "No." The form of potential illustrated by Bob and Joe is only virtual and, thus, left unrealized. The potential that *is* actualized here is capital's potential, in that consumers are continually circulated into the grips of the pharmaceutical company. Bob and Joe will remain stuck in a cycle of desire without attaining surplus because even their medically aided sex reverts back to phallic *jouissance*. In every respect they remain, in the last instance, impotent.

This begs the question: Who has the power to act in these texts/contexts? The answer is the sexual partner.[31] Although this text clearly attempts to reestablish patriarchal order, the sexual partner or feminine other is the external body that acts on his body, inducing him to "call the doctor," and likewise this other has the power to accept or reject his (non)erection. His only actual power in this text/context is to please the other, and we never know to what extent he is able to exert this power. The moment when each man says, "Yes" to his partner is the event through which he valorizes himself, and we can only remain hopeful that this valorization and connection will lead to actual affective potency in the form of collectivity and connection. Viagra's ads proffer an affective potency that is circulated in the semblance of actual social and economic power. This desire for affective potency is produced and reproduced via the medium of circulation. Within the nodal moments when Bob and Joe come into contact with other bodies, is the moment that their affect is affirmed. This cycle maintains the subject in a cycle of impotent production. Only through the continual recognition of his impotency is the desire for potency induced. Affective potency is acquired through circulation, and to circulate is to recognize that not to circulate is to remain impotent.

Pillow Talk

> If someone has done something which, he imagines, affects others with pleasure, he will be affected with pleasure accompanied with the idea of himself as cause, or, he will regard himself with pleasure. (Spinoza, *Ethics*, part III, proposition 30)

In the final image of the "Bob" Viagra ad, Bob and his wife press their heads together in a moment of intimacy and affirmation. She affirms Bob's actions and he, in return, is affected by her in the realm of pleasure—the pleasure he experiences is pleasure for being the cause of her pleasure. If there is affective power in this text/ context it takes this form of affirmation. Affective potency carries with it the potential to actualize new ways of being through the power of circulation. These moments of human contact must be captured and expanded upon and once again thrown back into circulation in order to accumulate a collective mode of affective power. To think about Viagra without linking it to the cultural and economic anxieties embedded in potency, as well as the logics of capitalism, fails to *capitalize* on the potentials inherent in affective potency.

The importance of circulation is made all the more apparent in Viagra's (2008) advertising campaign Viva Viagra. Take, for instance, the "Tango" ad, in which a wealthy, white couple dance their way into the bedroom. The commercial begins with the image of the husband channel-surfing on one end of the couch and the wife skimming through women's magazines on the other. We soon begin to hear tango-influenced music. The husband turns off the TV and looks at his wife. He throws the remote control out the window, she throws out her women's magazines, he throws out his golf club, she throws out the telephone, and soon they are dancing through the house until they reach the bedroom. They dance through the door and then close it. The male voice-over states, "Once you've dealt with the things that come between you, don't let erectile dysfunction get in the way. Viva Viagra. Viagra, most prescribed ED treatment, can help you experience a more satisfying sexual experience." The physical coming together of bodies and their circulation together is where affective potency stems from. He leads and she willingly follows, once again maintaining heteronormative stereotypes of masculinity.[32]

In the same ad campaign, the commercial "Viva La Surprise" features a middle-aged man taking dance lessons as a surprise for his wife. This commercial has been rightly critiqued for its racial use of the exotic other as the dance teacher (Ovalle 2008). The non-white ethnic woman as dance teacher adds cultural capital to her student and they circulate around the dance floor. The voice-over states, "Whatever steps you're taking to impress your partner, don't let erectile dysfunction get in your way." Again, we are made aware that sexual intimacy takes work, but that at least erectile dysfunction can be easily remedied. This man is working on his moves to impress his wife and has the added benefit of learning his moves from an "exotic" dance instructor. Although he obviously must pay for the services of his dance instructor, the added value of the "exotic" other is brought into circulation and employed for the pleasure of the white couple. The voice-over continues, "Viagra, America's most prescribed ED treatment, can help you enjoy a more satisfying sexual experience" and then, "To learn more, take a spin around Viagra.com. Now is the time to take the lead. Ask your doctor if Viagra is right for you." Once again, affective potency is premised on the circulation, literal and figurative, of affecting bodies.

More recently, something interesting has happened in Viagra's commercials. There is no longer any dancing or romance. There is no longer even a mention of a partner. Viagra's most recent advertising campaign, "This Is the Age of Taking Action," speaks to a more precarious economy and to a do-it-yourself, neoliberal subjectivity.[33] Viagra's more recent ads focus on individual self-sufficiency and less on the pleasures that partnership brings.

In this current precarious and uncertain economy, Viagra moves its settings outside of the dance halls and into the mythic U.S. West and the rugged outdoors, which are often used in advertisements to represent masculinity in its most hegemonic and traditional forms.[34] Take for instance Viagra's commercial "Stuck" (2011), which speaks to the theme of rugged individualism while referencing traditional masculine traits of self-reliance and physical strength.[35]

This commercial features a white, attractive male in his late 40s who is hauling horses on a dirt road. His truck gets "stuck" in the mud. He relies on his own ingenuity and uses the horses that he is hauling to pull the truck out of the mud. The voice-over states:

> You've reached the age where you don't back down from a challenge. This is the age of knowing how to make things happen. So why would you let something like erectile dysfunction get in your way? Isn't it time to talk to your doctor about Viagra? Twenty million men already have. With every age comes responsibility. Ask your doctor if your heart is healthy enough for sex. (Stuck, 2011: http://www.viagra.com/viagra-tv-commercial.aspx)

Here we have good old-fashioned work, masculine work in which one must rely on his own resourcefulness in order to survive. This neoliberal moment is not about appearing to have the affect that is necessary to survive, but rather by embodying a particular masculine affect that does survive by utilizing his resources. The protagonist is competent and knows how to "make things happen." In this instance, he harnesses the horsepower, literally, from the horses. This Viagra man is less urban and more rugged than the men in the Viagra ads discussed earlier; he must demonstrate to himself his own self-reliance. He becomes his own witness to his potency. If he is "stuck," he must utilize the resources available to him in order to get "unstuck." To remain "stuck" is to be physically, socially, and economically "impotent." He is left to his own resources, his own innate and acquired horsepower, to alter his situation. Our protagonist does not pick up his cell phone and call for help; rather, he goes it alone out in the middle of nowhere, all by himself, except for the horses whose power he must harness for his benefit because, as the Viagra ad informs us, "You don't back down from a challenge." You "know how to make things happen." When it comes to his erectile dysfunction, though, he is implored to take the responsibility to call his doctor.

Even the coloring of this ad campaign is less vibrant and rich than the previous campaigns discussed. These muted colors of blue and gray speak to the seriousness of the economic downturn and to the fact that many don't have anyone or anything to rely on except for themselves. This speaks to the importance of "knowing how to make things happen," and relying on yourself in an enterprising and entrepreneurial manner. Moreover, Viagra's commercials in the This Is the Age of Taking Action ad campaign imply that taking action is taking Viagra and that a man's potency is his ability to go it alone and take care of business. His affect is now one of self-reliance and he doesn't need anyone to witness it; his gaze is turned completely inward. Or in Spinoza's words, "He will regard himself with pleasure" (*Ethics*, part III, proposition 30), as in these ads there is no one to dance with.

In the same campaign, the commercial "Gas Station" plays with the same themes of self-reliance and do-it-yourself know-how. The protagonist's phallic power is represented not by literal horses, but rather by the horsepower in his vintage Camaro, which overheats. He drives to the garage and instead of asking the mechanic for assistance, he walks into the store and purchases a tall bottled water. After drinking out of the bottle, he pours the remainder into the Camaro. Now, they both are hydrated and have reclaimed their potency. He did this without the assistance of the mechanic, signifying that he is responsible for his own potency (and, perhaps, that he is financially broke). In addition, he reclaims his manhood in front of the mechanic; the mechanic bears witness to his reclamation of his potency. He not only individually demonstrates that he is capable of making his own erection, but this demonstration is witnessed by another, a weaker and older man.

In each of these advertisements, a woman or a romantic partner is absent. The divide between the public sphere and the domestic sphere is rigid in these ads. The only nod toward the feminine other is that both the "Stuck" and the "Gas Station" commercials end with a vehicle pulling toward or into a garage. The Viagra symbol then has an orgasmic explosion and bursts in the sky. Once again, he is the cause of his own pleasure and that pleases him. His potency is not a collective effort nor is it for the pleasure of his partner.

In the grand finale of the campaign, the commercial "Anthem" offers a montage comprising former commercials. The voice-over to the montage sums up the campaign:

> You like who you are; the man you've become. You've learned something along the way, about the world and yourself. This is the age of knowing what you are made of. And knowing how to get things done. So why would you let something like erectile dysfunction get in your way? Isn't it time to talk to your doctor about Viagra? Twenty million men already have. You didn't get to this age by having things handed to you. This is the Age of Taking Action. (Anthem, 2011: http://www.viagra.com/viagra-tv-commercial.aspx)

The affect that one must embody in these advertisements is one that is—represented visually—active, strong, traditionally masculine, and completely self-reliant. In these ads there is no group of guys jamming together like in the popular "Viva Viagra" commercial, nor is there a loft party, or a dance lesson. Everyone is out to take care of himself; everyone must be an "entrepreneur of himself" (Foucault 2008: 226) and work independently to keep himself in circulation. In these adds, if one lacks in social and economic potency, he has no one to blame but himself. And, according to these final ads, he has no romantic partner to consider or to rely on. He is alone.

As Viagra is ready to sing its swan song, its "Anthem" reveals that Viagra too has changed with the times. No longer are Viagra commercials suggesting that with a little social potency and boasting the affective attributes of confidence and charisma will one easily appear to have it all and to be upwardly mobile. No longer is there time or money for the leisurely tango through the house or dance lessons. Sadly, Viagra commercials reveal, much like the GM commercial in the Introduction to this book, that you are all by yourself and that you must rely on your own affective potency in order to throw yourself back into circulation to garner capital and perhaps, now more than ever, you need Viagra.

"In an affect economy," Patricia Clough (2007) reminds us, "value is sought in the expansion or contraction of affective capacity. In this sense, affect is a power or potential that cannot be limited. Power or potential face obstacles to expansion rather than limitations" (25). For cultural scholars, explicating affective potency paves the way for critics to illuminate the nodal intersections of bodies and the potentials present in affective relationships. Illuminating the potentials of affective pleasures is a beginning toward a political project that, although bound in capitalist circulation, may expand through collective power and could actualize into potent political activity.

Life in contemporary capitalism is a life in which the subject must continually circulate himself in order to garner more capital. The aim of this circulation is not a destination or endpoint; there is no such stable, safe endgame. We can hope for nodal encounters of bodies coming together and affecting each other in pleasure and joy and granting both the power of action. As Michel Foucault (1990) aptly warned, "We must not think that by saying yes to sex, one says no to power" (157). On the contrary, by saying yes to sex via Viagra, we are saying yes to a stylized and mediated life and hopefully while admitting our own impotency we are beginning to recognize our own power. While this implicates us further into the logics of capitalism, it also reveals the power of affective potency and it especially reveals that potency is most potent when it connects with others. If the Viagra ads teach us one thing, it is that life and potency are more enjoyable and pleasurable when shared with others, and that going it alone, while it may seem necessary is, well, lonely. In the end the potential of affective potency remains to be realized and its realization, as read through these ads, is garnered through combining and collectivity with others.

The previous chapter illustrated how psychotropic medications as a technology function in accordance with capitalism and existing social relations in order to produce effective and affectively appropriate workers throughout various twists and turns in the economy. In addition, it explicated the emergence of affective medication that coincided with women's entry into the workforce and their social and economic relationship to both paid and unpaid labor. In this chapter—and I recognize the ironic twist of moving from women and paid labor to men and sexual or immaterial labor—I contended that affect, like capital, gains both its actual and potential power through circulation.

In the following chapter, we turn our attention to children and ADHD medication. More specifically, we examine how children are constructed as "abilities-machines" (Foucault 2008: 229). To conceptualize children as "abilities-machines" or future workers means that in order to be a "good" caregiver and to properly care for our children, parents and teachers are required to invest in them now, as an investment in their future abilities to earn money. In order to explore this phenomenon, the following chapter reads direct-to-consumer advertisements of ADHD medication alongside of the fictional film *Thumbsucker*, which chronicles a teenager's upward social and academic success, with a little help from Ritalin.

Notes

1 King nailed one of the most obvious contradictions of the Bush administration's position via sex. The administration said it would approve Medicare coverage for Viagra if the prescription were medically necessary while simultaneously funding only those schools that proffer abstinence-only sex education.

2 http://www.huffingtonpost.com/2011/08/01/obama-birth-control-health-insurance_n_914818.html?view=print&comm_ref=false

3 Italian Marxist theorists have explored the relationship between affect, immaterial labor, and contemporary capitalism (see, e.g., Hardt 1999; Hardt & Negri 2000, 2004; Lazzarato 1996; Virno 1996, 2004).

4 For more on the body and its necessity to remain flexible see Martin (1994, 2000).

5 For scholarly work on DTC advertising see the *Journal of Health Communication*'s (2004, vol. 9) special issue.

6 The United States is one of two countries to allow direct-to-consumer advertising for pharmaceuticals. The growth of lifestyle medication coincided with the relaxation of direct-to-consumer broadcast advertising regulations in August 1997. New Zealand is the other country to allow direct-to-consumer advertising, although New Zealand has had a voluntary ban on direct-to-consumer advertising since December 2004 ("New Zealand to Ban DTC" 2005).

7 T. J. Jackson Lears (1983) referred to the selling of self-actualization as a "therapeutic ethos stressing self-realization in this world—an ethos characterized by an almost obsessive concern with psychic and physical health" (4).

8 This formulation is not new. Althusser combined Marx, Spinoza, and Lacan in his writings. For instance, in his essay "Ideology and Ideological State Apparatuses (Notes Towards an Investigation), Althusser (1971b) developed his theory of "ideological state apparatuses" on the theoretical foundation of the "Marxist 'theory' of the State" (138). In his definition of ideology, he employed Lacan's notion of "imaginary" and "real" as he stated, "Ideology represents the imaginary relationship of individuals to their real conditions of existence" (163). Moreover, he employed Marx and Spinoza to describe the immanent formulation of ideology: "As is well known, the accusation of being in ideology only applies to others, never to oneself (unless one is really a Spinozist or a Marxist, which, in this matter, is to be exactly the same thing)" (175).

9 As *Media Week* ("Viagra, Like Its Fans" 2010) acknowledged, "The product created a new category that soon saw competitors—specifically, Eli Lilly's Cialis and Bayer's Levitra. Viagra now makes $1.9 billion a year for Pfizer, the top seller of the three. It's a remarkable achievement no matter how you look at it" (23).

10 Pfizer contacted Dole to be a spokesperson for ED after Dole's appearance on *Larry King Live*, in which "Bob Dole asserted that Viagra is 'a great drug' in response to King's questions abut prostate cancer and impotence" (Baglia 2005: 60). In addition, Meika Loe (2004) explained that "Pfizer's first print and television ads for Viagra did not appear until nine months after the debut, in early 1999, featuring presidential candidate Bob Dole selling ED" (56). Loe described the ad as Dole appearing "formally and patriotically dressed in a blue suit, red tie, and white shirt . . . urging men to speak to their doctors about ED . . . in relationship to prostate cancer" (56). Bob Dole's sexual prowess was again highlighted in 2001 during a Pepsi advertisement campaign that aired during the Academy Awards. The commercial featured Britney Spears in a sexually provocative performance. The commercial pans out from Britney's performance to those watching her on television. The advertisement concluded with a shot of Bob Dole watching the television commercial as he sat in his overstuffed chair with his dog by his side. His dog barked; Dole responded, "Easy, boy."

11 The popular press was fascinated with Viagra's timely emergence on the brink of the new millennium, especially as baby boomers were dominating headlines along with Social Security concerns, the fear of Y2K, and the Clinton-Lewinsky scandal (see, e.g., Horvitz 1997a, 1997b; Leland 1998; Leland & Murr, 1997).

12 Melissa Deem (1999) has argued that Clinton's sex scandal and "the feminist discourses circulating in and through the Clinton sex scandal demonstrate that the primary manner in which feminism gains major media attention is through the anxiety over the bodies of men" (86–87). Viagra also brings to the forefront issues of women's pleasures and desires only as an afterthought to men's desires and abilities to perform sexually. Although this chapter does not grapple with these important issues, it is necessary to note that in February 2004 Pfizer abandoned testing women's responses to Viagra. According to Mitra Boolel of Pfizer's research team: "There's a disconnect in many women between genital changes and mental changes. This disconnect does not exist in men. Men consistently get erections in the presence of naked women and want to have sex. With women, things depend on a myriad of factors." Dr. Boole argued that a woman's sex organ is her brain and, therefore, his team is now examining how drugs affect women's brain chemistry (as cited in Harris 2004).

13 "According to the Census Bureau projections, the number of people younger than 50 will decline between 1990 and 2020, while the 50-plus population will grow by 76 percent" (Horvitz 1997a).

14 A recent study that surveyed male college students' use of Viagra in the Chicago area found that 57% of those who took Viagra did so to treat ED; 29% used Viagra as a performance enhancer; and 64% mixed their erectile dys-

function medication with other legal and illegal drugs (see Newswise press release at http://newswise.com/p/articles/view/519849).

15 As noted in an earlier footnote, Pfizer, ironically, has turned away from studies of female genitalia and toward studies of female brain chemistry.

16 According to Toby Miller (1998) "'impotence' has displaced 'frigidity' in the period since the 1970s" and "since the mid-1980s, self-administered injections of prostaglandin to relax penile tissue and heighten blood flow have been on the market, and in 1966(1996?) the U.S. government for the first time approved one such treatment, Caverject" (124–125).

17 Although the advertisements for Viagra are heteronormative, the questions posed in this online quiz allow for the interpellation of gay men through the ambiguous term "partner." In addition, the Viagra.com website has a section for partners, which also refrains from any discourse that suggests that the partner is a woman. The on-line quiz was last accessed on Aug. 14, 2010. The quiz also appears in the promotional mailer "For every puzzle, there's a solution" (Pfizer, February 2002).

18 As Giorgio Agamben (2000) articulates, "Human beings—as beings of power who can do or not do, succeed or fail, lose themselves or find themselves—are the only beings for whom happiness is always at stake in their living, the only beings whose life is irremediably and painfully assigned to happiness. . . . This immediately constitutes the form-of-life as political life" (4).

19 Spinoza (1678/2000) stated, "By emotion [affect] I understand the affections of the body by which the body's power of acting is increased or diminished, helped or hindered, and at the same time the ideas of these affections" (*Ethics*, part III, def. 3).

20 Fink (2004) placed the phallic back into *jouissance*: "'Phallic' as 'fallible,' we try to hear the 'fallibility' in the 'phallus'. Phallic jouissance is the jouissance that fails us, that disappoints us" (159). This formulation is important. It is an immanent structure in a Spinozist sense in that both its rise and its decline occur without an external cause.

21 Rather than being intimate, it is "'extimate.'" Lacan, discussing the absurdities that are spoken in analysis to enter into "the unconscious" wrote: "From that emerges a speaking [*dire*) that does not always go so far as to be able to "'exist'" with respect to the words spoken *ex-sister au dit*]" (as cited in Fink 2004: 22). In a footnote, Fink noted that "Lacan used [this formulation] to talk about an existence that stands apart, which insists as it were from the outside, something, not included on the inside. Rather than being intimate, it is 'extimate'" (see Fink 2004: 22 n24).

22 Retrieved from http://viagra.com/ed/theRealIssue.asp

23 In a discussion on alienated labor, Marx (1964) explained that "alienated labour takes away the object of production from man, it also takes away his species-life, his real objectivity as a *species-being*, and changes his advantage over animals into a disadvantage in so far as his inorganic body, nature, is taken from him" (emphasis in the original, 128). Marx continued, "Just as alienated labour transforms free and self-directed activity into a means, so it transforms the species-life of man into a physical existence" (128).

24 In order to be clear that the blood in the penis is not ejaculated, as this would feminize the penis, the reader is informed that this "extra blood flows out of the penis back into the body." (For a history of male ejaculation in philosophy, art, and literature see Aydemir 2007.)

25 In reading Viagra's materials, I have yet to come across any discussion of using Viagra as a fertility treatment. In the *Patient Summary of Information*, (Pfizer 1999) there is a disclosure that states, "Viagra does not protect you or your partner from getting sexually transmitted diseases, including HIV—the virus that causes AIDS" (rev. 4).

26 Another way in which to understand this is through the concept of a homology.

As A. Kiarina Kordela (2007) explained,

> The homology between economic and semantic [somatic] value as two of the domains of differential substance precludes the classical Marxist assumption that the "base" (economy) determines the "superstructure" (sign), as well as its idealist bourgeois inverse. Both are directly caused or determined to exist in this way by the differential substance whose modes they are. (40)

Or as Lacan (1977) stated,

> There are thoughts in this field of the beyond consciousness, and it is impossible to represent these thoughts other than in the same homology of determination in which the subject of the *I think* finds himself in relation to the articulation of the *I doubt.* (Emphasis in the original, 44)

Following the Spinozist differential structure employed by both Lacan and herself, Kordela (2007) continued,

> And since knowledge is knowledge of causes, neither capital nor the sign can be known if examined in isolation, as separate fields, since they are both caused by one and the same substance. The analysis of capitalist economy, therefore, must be included among the sciences whose object is a mode of the differential substance, such as the analysis of all fields that involve the examination of language. (41)

27 The complete sentence reads: "Therefore *circulation* is, above all, *the expansion of the potency of capital*; and for the same reason it entails the *appropriation* of all the social conditions and their placement in *valorization*" (emphasis in the original, Negri 1991: 112).

28 I thank Brynnar Swenson for this insightful wordplay.

29 In *Écrits,* Lacan (2006) explained, "It is thus that the erectile organ—not as itself, or even as an image, but as a part that is missing in the desired image—comes to symbolize the place of jouissance" (passage 822).

30 This is not to say that there isn't a surplus *jouissance* derived from sex, only that in the Viagra commercial we have no indication of this.

31 In the commercial "Joe," we do not know whether the person that he is speaking to is male or female. This ambiguity has been pointed out by others

including Baglia (2005) and Mamo and Fishman (2001). I thank Jay Baglia for pointing this out to me.

32 Interestingly, this commercial at least acknowledges that there may be other issues that come between couples besides erectile dysfunction. This commercial obviously does not advocate therapy, but it at least recognizes external barriers (besides an inability to get an erection) to sexual intimacy.

33 Pfizer, in a move uncommon for drug companies whose medications are soon to become generic, doubled its price of Viagra from its original costs in 1998 and also increased its advertising expenditures, spending $101 million, up 5%, on television adds in 2009 ("Viagra, Like Its Fans" 2010).

34 Images of the Marlboro man readily come to mind.

35 http://www.viagra.com/viagra-tv-commercial.aspx

FOUR

Children as Abilities-Machines

ADHD and Future Workers of America

> There are signs that mental conditions involving constant shifting in time and space, emotionally or cognitively—namely manic depression and Attention Deficit Hyperactivity Disorder (ADHD)—have been undergoing a dramatic revision in American middle-class culture, from being simply dreaded liabilities, to being especially valuable assets that can potentially enhance one's life in the particular social and cultural world now inhabited by many middle-class Americans. —Emily Martin (2000: 512)

> The contemporary trend away from long term labor contracts, towards temporary and part-time labor, is not only an effective economic strategy, freeing corporations from contracts and the expensive commitments of health care and other benefits, it is an effective strategy of subjectification as well. It encourages workers to see themselves not as "workers" in a political sense, who have something to gain through solidarity and collective organization, but as "companies of one." They become individuals for whom every action, from taking a course on a new computer software application to having their teeth whitened can be considered an investment in human capital.—Jason Read (2009: 7)

Attention deficit with hyperactivity disorder (ADHD) is the disorder of our time. Nearly 10% of children in the United States are diagnosed with ADHD despite critics who argue that ADHD is not a "real" disorder and others who argue that ADHD is overdiagnosed (Akinbami et al. 2011: 1).[1] This chapter explores popular discourses of ADHD, specifically direct-to-consumer advertisements of prescription medication, and the manner in which we are directed to manage our children through psychopharmacology. I argue that this form of management helps produce productive and well-behaved children both at school, at home, during extracurricular activities, and even during summer vacation, the most sacred leisure time.

Popular discourses of ADHD and its often-prescribed treatment of stimulant medication reveal a form of subjectivity that coincides with the ideal worker in the knowledge and service industries. The attributes of this subjectivity include the performance of sociability, keen focus, and task completion, while sustaining and building relationships. Many of these attributes are encompassed under the umbrella term of "good communication" skills. As will be explored below, these attributes are now required of even our youngest citizens. Prescription medication for disorders like ADHD is one means in which we can invest in our children to hone and discipline their communication skills and affective abilities so that they will be productive laboring citizens.

Known as a disorder of communication, ADHD is often described as the inability to pay attention and get along well with others (Baird, Stevenson, & Williams 2000). According to the ADHD gurus Hallowell and Ratey (1995) in their popular press book *Driven to Distraction*, "Receptive language problems can affect both what you take in and what you are able to put out" and output, or "expressive language problems, can affect what you are able to write or speak as well as what you are able to conceptualize within your brain" (33). ADHD is often explained in reference to communication such as an inability to remember things that aid in future actions, talking out of turn, being slow at acquiring internal speech and therefore an inability to self-regulate external speech (Baird et al. 2000). Baird et al. (2000) argue that there is a link between attention and language acquisition: "Language skills compete with other cognitive activities for the attention system, and thus the evolution of language could not in fact be independent of the evolution of attention" (17). Communication as a symptom of ADHD is common in popular narratives of ADHD, and with the consumption of stimulant medication, these discourses inform us that communication skills can be improved.

Cultural Representations of ADHD

The benefits of stimulant medication for ADHD are made clear in Mike Mills's film adaptation of Walter Kirn's novel *Thumbsucker* (Stephenson 2005). *Thumbsucker* is the quintessential, albeit fictional, narrative of a teenage boy's academic and social success after his diagnosis of ADHD and the consumption of Ritalin-like medication. The film presents itself as a critique of the use of stimulant medication and likens the consumption of Ritalin to masking one's "real" or "authentic self." Although the film is a critique of ADHD and stimulant medication, *Thumbsucker* ultimately reveals that the protagonist's success is premised on the use of stimulant medication. In this coming-of-age story, the 17-

year-old protagonist, Justin (Lou Taylor Pucci), experiences behavioral and interpersonal difficulty at school and at home. He secretly sucks his thumb for solace and comfort. A diagnosis of ADHD and a Ritalin-like prescription are soon to be the anodyne for all of Justin's difficulties. This is foreshadowed in the following scene.

Justin sits in debate class admiring Rebecca (Kelli Garner), an attractive young animal lover who sports her liberal views on her chest with a T-shirt that reads "Club Sandwiches, Not Seals." During class, Rebecca makes an eloquent environmental argument about the ever-increasing pollution of oceans. Justin stares in awe of Rebecca until he is jolted out of his trance when the debate coach, Mr. Geary (Vince Vaughn), asks Justin to refute Rebecca's argument. Justin responds, "Actually, I agree with Rebecca. I saw a show on Animal Planet how they were giving depressed male baboons Prozac...." Justin's reference to Animal Planet, depressed male baboons, and Prozac sets the scene for the pharmaceutical treatment of affective disorders in teenagers. The analogy is as follows: Justin, the male, is in his own Animal Planet of high school, and the use of Prozac to cure the male baboon's depression foreshadows the use of pharmaceuticals for the treatment of Justin's own affective disorder.

Justin is soon interrupted by Mr. Geary and chastised for his ineptitude in formulating an appropriate response to Rebecca's performance.

> This isn't glee club; it's debate club. If you researched, you'd have the confidence to have an opinion, and if you had an opinion that's based on facts gathered from your research, then you are confident to speak. And speaking confidently does what class? That's right, speaking confidently wins minds. (Mills 2005)

The foregoing scene illuminates Justin's inadequacies in performing the appropriate communication skills and the necessary affective behavior that must be enacted in order to present oneself as academically successful and socially viable. According to Mr. Geary, Justin fails at conducting the research that is required for his academic success and he is unable to speak with "confidence," and therefore to "win minds." He is humiliated in front of his love interest, his incompetence is revealed to the class, and he flees the scene to the boys' bathroom where he proceeds to unabashedly suck his thumb.[2]

Eventually, Justin and his parents are called to a meeting with the principal and debate coach, Mr. Geary. The school principal (Kit Koenig) informs Justin's parents that Justin "has always shown a lot of promise." She continues, "But I feel that something comes between him and his potential and with college just ahead, Justin needs to maximize, right now." The principal continues, "I feel that in light of recent behavior that Justin needs an adjustment."

> Principal: Justin, have your ever suspected that you were different than other teenagers? Not as patient. Can't finish what you started? Terrified of being left alone but angry when you feel crowded?
>
> Justin: A little.
>
> Principal: It's classic hyperactive teen. Um, attention deficient hyperactivity disorder, ADHD. We'd like you to think about a stimulant drug treatment for Justin.
>
> Audrey (Tilda Swinton) [Justin's mother]: You mean like Ritalin?
>
> Principal: That's one of many of the drugs that a doctor could prescribe. There's Adderall, Clonidine...
>
> Mike (Vincent D'Onofrio)[Justin's father]: If this is all just coming down to medication....Look I think my son could handle this if he puts his mind to it.
>
> Principal: Mr. Geary, don't you feel that Justin could do much better?
>
> Mr. Geary: Justin has exhibited, you know, some of the behaviors that fit this particular profile.
>
> Audrey [reading a brochure on ADHD]: Excuse me, these symptoms they have listed here, they are pretty vague: "Ignores information," "makes mistakes." "Seems restless," "avoids, dislikes or reluctance to engage in work that requires sustained mental effort." What do you think, Justin?
>
> Justin: So my problems are just because I'm hyper? (Mills 2005)

In this brief encounter, Justin is interpellated into an ADHD diagnosis by the school's administrative apparatus. Justin's parents remain skeptical and demonstrate concern about medicating Justin. On the one hand, his father dismisses the idea of medication and translates Justin's problems to his lack of discipline. "Look I think my son could handle this if he puts his mind to it."[3] Justin, on the other hand, expresses relief that there is a reason for his social ineptitude and misbehaviors. A diagnosis of ADHD articulates his problems directly to his body, ignoring any age-appropriate factors such as his sexual awakening, tensions with his family, and his unexplained attachment to his thumb. Justin's feelings of alienation are not due to external circumstance, basic teenage angst, or even any Oedipal issue that may cause his Freudian attachment to his thumb, but rather Justin's issues are described as an affective disorder. A diagnosis of ADHD offers Justin relief that his problems are "just because I'm hyper" (Mills 2005).

The good news for Justin is that the stimulant medication works. Justin becomes the top debater, excels at school, and has success with girls. His academic performance is enviable. After taking his stimulant medication, Justin feels immediately transformed. He reads *Moby Dick* in its entirety and answers questions regarding the novel in class poetically and insightfully. When the class is asked to speak on "whiteness" in *Moby Dick*, Justin speaks up: "Whiteness speaks to eternity; the blankness of uninterrupted time; it represents both innocence and extinction, the beginning and the end." After consuming the medication Justin speaks eloquently, articulately, and confidently. Ecstatic about his transformation and his accomplishment of reading *Moby Dick*, he awakens his brother (Chase Offerle), exclaiming, "I've changed. It works. I never thought I would feel so clear." Justin immediately transforms from an apathetic and unmotivated student into a successful student who articulately and insightfully communicates his knowledge. This movement represents the narrative trajectory of ADHD. The immature, unmotivated, and socially awkward youth transforms from underachieving, disruptive, deviant adolescent into a successful and motivated model young citizen through the consumption of stimulant medication.

ADHD

ADHD is continually ranked as the most prevalent mental diagnosis of children and teens, affecting 10% of school-age children in the United States (Baird et al. 2000; U.S. Drug Enforcement Administration). According to the Centers for Disease Control and Prevention (CDC), ADHD has increased 3% each year from 1997–

2006, and as of 2007, 5.4 million children between the ages of 4 and 17 have been diagnosed with ADHD.[4] In 2007, 2.7 million children were on prescription medication for their ADHD (CDC). Although this is a spreading global phenomenon (see Lloyd, Stead, & Cohen, 2006), "90% of the world's consumption of Ritalin is in the United States" (Stephen 2000: 20) and the "U.S. manufactures and consumes five times more MPH [Ritalin] than the rest of the world combined (DEA).[5] The CDC reports that there is a substantial increase in the percentage of children diagnosed with ADHD, "with nearly one in 10 children aged 4–17 years diagnosed with ADHD by 2007" (CDC "Increasing Prevalence 2010). This is a greater annual increase of 5.5% from 2003–2007 (CDC "Increasing Prevalence" 2010). According to the CDC, an epidemic of young people, most often boys, are prescribed stimulant medications to control their symptoms.[6] While the diagnosis of ADHD has been on the rise in recent years, the symptoms of ADHD are anything but new.

The symptoms of ADHD have long been associated with children. For instance, in 1848 a German physician, Heinrich Hoffmann, wrote a book for his children in which one character was "Fidgety Phil" and another "Harry Look in the Air." Fidgety Phil was described as the hyperactive child, while Harry was the inattentive one (Wolraich & Baumgaertel 1996: 168). In 1902, George Still, who would become England's first professor of pediatrics, presented a series of three lectures in which he described his observations of 43 children using adjectives such as "aggressive, defiant, excessively emotional, and lacking inhibitory volition who were also noted to have impaired attention and over-activity" (Wolraich & Baumgaertel 1996: 168). Just as the symptoms of hyperactivity and inattention date back as early as the emergence of pediatrics as a discipline, these symptoms also have a terminological history as evidenced by the American Psychiatric Association's *Diagnostic Statistical Manual* (*DSM*).

Symptoms that describe ADHD today, such as restlessness, inability to focus, and hyperactivity, were once referred to as a host of diagnoses including "organic driveness," "minimal brain damage," "hyperkinetic impulse disorder," "minimal brain dysfunction," "hyperkinesis," "hyperactive child syndrome," and, more recently, "attention deficit disorder" (Mayes & Erkulwater 2008: 309–310). In the first *DSM*, no distinction was made between disorders in children and those in adults (Mayes & Erkulwater

2008: 311). In the second incarnation of the *Diagnostic Statistical Manual* (*DSM-II* 1968) the childhood disorder of "hyperkinetic reaction of childhood (or adolescence)" is described as a "disorder characterized by over activity, restlessness, distractibility, and short attention span, especially in young children." The description continues to state, "The behavior usually diminishes in adolescence" (50). The *DSM-III* expanded the descriptions of child and adolescent disorders. Descriptions of child and adolescent disorders were "listed with significantly more elaborate description and diagnostic criteria than the one paragraph provided by *DSM-II*" (Mayes & Erkulwater 2008: 311). For instance, in the *DSM-II*, only one paragraph was written to describe the symptoms of "Hyperkinetic Reaction of Childhood." By the publication in 1980 of the *DSM-III*, we see for the first time the terms "Attention Deficit Disorder" (ADD) and "Attention Deficit Hyperactivity Disorder" (ADHD) with a description that spanned multiple pages (from pages 41–45).

Russell Barkley (2006) described ADD as a "radical reconceptualization [from that in *DSM-II*] of the Hyperkinetic Reaction of Childhood diagnosis to that of ADD (with or without Hyperactivity)" (19). Children with hyperactivity are described in the *DSM-III* as "being on the go, 'running like a motor,' and having difficulty sitting still. Older children and adolescents may be extremely restless and fidgety." The current symptoms of ADHD as described in the most recent *DSM-IV-TR* (2000) include:

> Often fails to give close attention to details or makes careless mistakes in schoolwork, work, or other activities;
>
> Often has difficulty sustaining attention in tasks or play activities;
>
> Often does not seem to listen when spoken to directly;
>
> Often does not follow through on instructions and fails to finish school work, chores, or duties in the workplace (not due to oppositional behavior or failure to understand instructions);
>
> Often has difficulty organizing tasks and activities
>
> Often avoids, dislikes, or is reluctant to engage in tasks that require sustained mental effort (such as schoolwork or homework);

Often loses things necessary for tasks or activities (e.g., toys, school assignments, pencils, books or tools);

Is often easily distracted by extraneous stimuli;

Often fidgets with hands or feet or squirms in seat;

Often leaves seat in classroom or in other situations in which remaining seated is expected;

Often interrupts or intrudes on others (e.g., butts into conversations or games).

Is often 'on the go' or often acts as if 'driven by a motor.' (92)

The subjective criteria of the current descriptions of ADHD are recognizable to most parents in describing the behavior of their children. The age for the onset of ADHD continues to increase with each subsequent edition, prompting a potential increase of young people diagnosed with ADHD.

With each edition, the *DSM* increases the age of onset for ADHD, allowing for more and more people to find a diagnosis under its continually expanding umbrella. Unlike the *DSM-II*, which describes that a child will grow out of his or her disorder, the *DSM-III* (1980) explains, "Though excess motor activity frequently diminishes in adolescence, in children who have the disorder, difficulties in attention often persist" (41). The *DSM-III* describes the onset of symptoms of ADD/ADHD as typically occurring by the age of 3 (42). The *DSM-IV* increases the age of ADD/ADHD onset and states "some hyperactive-impulsive or inattentive symptoms that caused impairment must have been present before age 7 years" (78). While the current *DSM* states that onset is usually "before age 7" the proposed *DSM-V* will increase the age of onset to age 12. This increase in the age in which symptoms present themselves will increase the prevalence of the disorder in young people, and, therefore, will increase the prevalence of ADHD prescription medication.[7]

Although there is no known cause of ADHD, historically ADHD and its former incarnations have traversed the spectrum of causes including bad parenting, poor diet, allergies, brain injury, deviance, and moral defect (see, e.g., Mayes & Erkulwater 2008; Nadesan 2010: 131–137). The popular press simply refers to ADHD as a "disorder of its time" (Herr 2010). Stephen Herr (2010) for the *Christian Science Monitor* states, "ADHD appeared to be a reasonable theory that might help people address genuine concerns. Raising children can be hard, especially when adults are tired, frustrated, overwhelmed, and riddled with self-doubt" (para 6). "This is, beyond question, an American phenomenon," states a *Newsweek* article titled "Mother's Little Helper" (Hancock 1996: 50). Neuropsychiatrist Sydney Walker refers to ADHD as "symptoms of modern life, rather than symptoms of modern disease" (as cited in Gladwell 1999: 80). And Sam Anderson (2009) explains, "Obviously,...a culture of BlackBerrys and news crawls and Firefox tabs-tools...focuses us all into a kind of elective ADHD." The argument that the popular press presents is that we are all challenged in the area of attention due to the multiple demands on our time and energy, the continual flow of information and stimulation, and the requirements of multitasking just to keep pace with the world around us. No wonder we are distracted and fidgety.

Whether ADHD is a symptom of contemporary culture, or whether it is a long-standing disorder that affects a growing number of children, the discourse of ADHD functions to produce effective and efficient young people and better capitalist workers of us all. As will be discussed below, the discourse of ADHD both informs consumers of the proper affective qualities that we are all to embody as well as directs us toward a diagnosis of ADHD as a means of investing in our children as "abilities-machines."

Investing in Children as "Abilities-Machines"

By definition, to be a "good parent" or a "good teacher" and even a "good doctor," is to invest in your children, students, and patients in such a manner as to help them "maximize" their potential. In *Thumbsucker*, Justin's parents and his debate coach do just that. They intervene to help Justin "maximize his potential" so that he is better prepared to gain admittance into a good college by being a better student with appropriate academic skills and affective behavior. Justin, his parents, and the school invest in Justin's human capital, in his potential for academic and social success, which is an investment in his foundation for future economic success in contemporary capitalism.

In his discussion regarding the rise of neoliberalism, Foucault (2008) refers to the investment in human capital as an investment in one's "abilities-machines" (229). This term is particularly useful as it links human capital, defined as that which connects the "abilities," know-how, knowledges, and immaterial skills, "the set of all those physical and psychological factors which make someone able to earn this or that wages" (224), to the "machine," which processes the apparatuses, codes, and techniques that are required for these abilities to be transformed into productive value within capitalism.

Whereas liberalism was premised on a model of exchange, neoliberalism is premised on model of competition (Foucault 2008: 12; Read 2009: 4). As Jason Read (2009) explains, classical liberalism "establishes a homology: just as relations in the marketplace can be understood as an exchange of one good for another, the state or social contract can be understood as an exchange of certain freedoms for a set of rights and liberties" (Read 2009: 4). This neoliberal turn means that the state operates according to the logics of the market; the state intervenes and regulates the market on behalf of the market. Wendy Brown (2003) explains that this "neoliberal rationality" is one that "while foregrounding the market, is not only or even primarily focused on the economy; rather it involves *extending and disseminating market values to all institutions and social action*, even as the market itself remains a distinctive player" (emphasis in the original, para 7). This extension of market values extends over all spheres of life including the constitution of subjectivity and the governmentality of (future) workers.

The sphere of market rationality—one that is premised not on exchange but on competition—extends into the sphere of our most intimate and personal lives. Classical liberalism focused on "exchange," the exchange of one good for another, the exchange of freedoms for rights. Neoliberalism focuses on competition, entrepreneurship, and the maximizing of profit (Brown 2003; Read 2009). A neoliberal logic suggests that decisions are made based on the rationality that we live in a society based on fierce competition and spreading scarcity. This "financialization of daily life," to borrow a phrase from Randy Martin (2002), constructs a logic in which everyday life decisions are made via a cost-benefit analysis. These life decisions run the gamut from education decisions such as if and where to attend college, to which self-help program to follow to lose weight, to where and when to purchase a house, to health-care decisions, to decisions on whom to marry.

The most vital and important investment that we can make is in our own human capital, and that of our children, a capital investment that will allow us to work for as much capital as possible for as long as possible. Human capital, Foucault (2008) explains, "is made up of innate elements and other, acquired elements" (226). This neoliberal form of governing one's self and children is premised on the freedom to invest in one's self and therefore one's own capital. An investment in human capital takes the form of a market rationality, a cost-benefit-risk analysis. Is the investment worth the costs of the investment; do the benefits outweigh the costs; and is the risk worth it? In others words, is there a potential financial gain on the investment? A college education is a case in point. A college education is a financial investment in one's human capital. This financial investment is made on the premise that there is a future financial return on the investment that is greater than the original investment.

ADHD as a medical diagnosis and stimulant medication as a treatment for the disorder provide a means to govern and manage human capital. The discourses of ADHD suggest that it is a genetic disorder located in the brain and that it is "hereditary." In all human capital there are innate elements and acquired elements (Foucault 2008). "There are those we call hereditary," explains Foucault, "and others which are just innate; differences which are, of course, self-evident for anyone with the vaguest acquaintance with biology" (227). Heredity difference opens up a new system of management in which the risk for contracting "this or that type of disease at a given age, during a given period of life, or in any way at any moment of life" is measured and monitored (227). As Foucault explains, "In other words, one of the current interests in the application of genetics to human populations is to make it possible to recognize individuals at risk and the type of risk individuals incur throughout their life" (227). Genetic makeup, a person's innate human capital, is open to potential risk that we can now begin to prepare for, manage, correct, or overcome with a goal of maximizing value.

Acquired human capital is of special interest to the neoliberal subject. As Foucault (2008) explains, "Obviously, the neo-liberals pose their problems and set out their new type of analysis much more from the angle of acquired human capital, that is to say, of the more or less voluntary formation of human capital in the course of individuals' lives" (229). An investment in human capital is an investment in the production of "abilities-machines, which will produce income" (229). In answer to the question: "What constitutes this investment that forms an abilities-machine?" (229), Foucault turns to parenting as a model of producing "abilities-machines." He states,

> Experimentally, on the basis of observations, we know it is constituted by, for example, the time parents devote to their children outside of simple educational activities strictly speaking. We know that the number of hours a mother spends with her child, even when it is still in the cradle, will be very important for the formation of an abilities-machine, for the formation of a human capital, and that the child will be much more adaptive if in fact its parents or its mother spend more rather than less time with him or her. (229)

Foucault's turn toward parenting as a primary example of investing in human capital, in a child's "abilities-machine," is significant as it illustrates the primary relationship—the relationship between parent, especially mother, and child—a relationship in which the investment in a child's human capital must begin as soon as possible, often even prior to birth from the coupling process to genetic testing and other technologies of birthing. It is not enough for a mother to spend a significant amount of quality time with her child; she must attend to her child's (potential) human capital in all arenas. The investment in human capital, in producing "abilities-machines," also takes into its analysis "medical care and, generally speaking, all activities concerning the health of individuals, which will thus appear as so many elements which enable us, first, to improve human capital, and second to preserve and employ it for as long as possible" (Foucault 2008: 230). Therefore, to invest in our child's human capital is, by definition, to be a good parent, to help our child's "abilities-machine" so that he or she will be productive and receive a financial benefit from our investment in his or her (mental) health.

In the film *Thumbsucker*, Justin's parents followed the logic of neoliberalism by investing in their son's mental health and human capital. They did what any good parent would do and assisted Justin in "maximizing his potential," so that he could get into a good college, solidify his economic foundation, and increase the investment in his human capital. This investment in one's human capital, this entrepreneurial spirit within neoliberalism, intensifies the relationship with the self. It "carries responsibility for the self to new heights," as Wendy Brown (2003: para 15) notes. The individual is governed in such a way as to learn to become "an entrepreneur of himself" (Foucault 2008: 226). He or she is given the responsibility to improve and invest in innate attributes, to invest in one's human capital through new technologies and medical interventions. The advertising of ADHD drugs is a clear example of the manner in which parents are directed toward a diagnosis of ADHD for their children and prescription medication as a means in which to improve upon their child's "human capital" and their own.

Advertising the Ideal Child/Worker: Advertising ADHD

This cultural narrative suggests that life and school are better for all involved with stimulant medication. For instance, Justin's newfound "health" is articulated in the language of many lifestyle medication advertisements. In a meeting with Mr. Geary, the debate coach, Justin shares that the medication is working, and when asked how he feels he replies: "I feel like me; I never really did before" (Mills 2005). This discourse mirrors advertisements for ADHD medication as well as it suggests that there is an authentic subject in each of us just ready to emerge. Articulated in a manner that suggests that there is an authentic subject, many lifestyle medications promise to "let the real you come through" (Glaxo-SmithKline 2004). The authentic self, the "real you," is one that corresponds to our historically and culturally situated ideal subject. For example, an Adderall XR print advertisement (2004) states:

> Schoolwork that matches his intelligence
>
> Friends that ask him to join the group
>
> Family hours that last for hours
>
> A real solution for ADHD

This idea that there is an authentic self, a self that is not culturally and historically situated, pervades lifestyle advertisements. The "real you" embodies the subjectivity that is a better version of your already existing self, a you that is "better than well" (Elliott 2003). Justin continues: "It used to be kind of a hassle to put on underwear in the morning, but now it's kind of easy, you know. I actually listened to the words to the Pledge of Allegiance today, and it gave me chills" (Mills 2005). Mr. Geary affirms this alteration in Justin by explaining that he always had a sense that Justin had a "real sensitivity to language" and that he knows Justin is smart and "[sees] a lot more than [he] takes responsibility for and that kind of perception...can't be taught by anyone" (Mills 2005). These affective attributes that Mr. Geary describes have an uncanny resemblance to the narratives of ADHD found in popular press, self-help books. For instance, as described in the bestseller *Driven to Distraction*,"[Those with ADHD] can also be unusually empathetic, intuitive, and compassionate, as if in that tangled brain circuitry there is a special capacity to see into people and situations" (Hallowell & Ratey 1995: 10). Justin has always been smart and it's not suggested that the medication magically instills intelligence, but the medication does heighten Justin's ability to focus, communicate his knowledge, and act confidently, all of which aid in his communicative labor. An inability to perform these proper affective attributes is articulated to ADHD, and its "cure" in pill form is advertised directly to parents.

For those of us who live in the United States, it may be hard to remember a time in which the airwaves did not bombard us with advertisements for prescription medication. Like other forms of deregulation, the lobbying efforts of pharmaceutical companies and the developments in the Food and Drug Administration (FDA) resulted in the relaxation of the once strict guidelines that prevented advertising prescription medication directly to consumers. The FDA's Modernization Act of 1997 opened the door for pharmaceutical companies to directly sell their pharmaceuticals and the disorders that attend them. By the latter part of the 1980s, pharmaceutical advertisements were found in newspapers and magazines. While the FDA permitted broadcast of pharmaceutical advertisements directly to consumers in 1997, advertising stimulant medications did not appear until 1999 due to a 1971 United Nations prohibition on psychotropic drug advertising that was signed by the United States, although never implemented by law (Singh 2007: 149). In 1999, drugmakers pushed the edge of the deregulation envelope and ran advertisements for ADHD medication in women's magazines and on cable television, opening the floodgates for ADHD medication to be advertised directly to consumers. *Time* (Novak 2001) magazine reported the following:

> In one ad, drug maker Celltech shows a smiling boy and his mom with the message: "One dose covers his ADHD for the whole school day," plus the drug's name, Metadate CD. The ad is running in a dozen magazines, including *Ladies' Home Journal*, which has two more ADHD drug ads in the same issue—from Shire Pharmaceuticals (maker of Adderall) and McNeil Consumer Health Care (Concerta). These ads don't name any medications, but they do give toll-free numbers for more information. McNeil also has a similar ad on cable TV. (para 4)

This commercialization presented directly to consumers helped to make ADHD and its stimulant medications (Adderall, Concerta, Vyvanse, etc.) common household names. Beginning with the earliest DTC advertisements, children treated for ADHD were represented as happily excelling at school and making mom proud. Today, as discussed later in this chapter, advertisements for ADHD promote symptom control at school, at home, and even during the summertime.

ADHD advertisements offer happiness and success through a diagnosis of ADHD and stimulant medication. Many ads present us with a young person, often a boy, who isn't reaching his potential; who is failing at school; has few friends; and often disappoints himself, his teachers, and his parents. For example, the following Concerta advertisement promises academic achievement and better interpersonal relationships. A young boy sits at a desk with a pen in hand. The text reads, "Alex has ADHD" and then follows the progression of a school assignment for a "Book Report on U.S. Presidents." One option: "Starts Concerta→goes to the library with Matt→gets to know George Washington→makes teacher proud." The other option follows a different logic: "Leaves backpack on bus→argues with sister→George who?→teacher calls mom." Below the images of Alex the text states, "If your child struggles with attention deficit hyperactivity disorder (ADHD), Concerta can help them [*sic*] get on the path to success" (Janssen Pharmaceuticals 2008). Just as with Justin, the narrative logic argues that those who are treated with prescription stimulant medication for ADHD excel at school and earn the praise and kudos of parents and teachers alike. Conversely, those who suffer from ADHD and are not receiving stimulant treatment will forget important things such as a backpack, will obviously fail at completing homework assignments, will inevitably argue with siblings, and will garner teacher complaints. There is only one option for happiness and success and that is a diagnosis of ADHD and treatment by its stimulant medication.

The advertisements of ADHD promise parents a return on their investment in the form of a child who is productive and socialized, and has potential for success in neoliberal capitalism. Another Concerta (Janssen Pharmaceuticals 2009b) advertisement, similar to the previous ad, features a redheaded boy sitting in a classroom, smiling. The text offers two different scenarios of "a typical school day." One scenario: "Forgets homework—> keeps interrupting teacher—> eats lunch alone —> time to ask your child's doctor about Concerta?" Or, the advertisement's overtly better alternative: "Starts Concerta—> pays attention during class—> interacts better with classmates—> focuses on homework." The ideal child, therefore, is one who is happy and productive at school. He is able to focus on his homework and even remembers to bring it to class with him the following day, he does not talk out of turn during class and does not interrupt his teacher, he gets along well with his classmates and eats lunch with others, and this child is "content," as illuminated by his small smile. Importantly, the "better" option relies upon consumption of his prescription medication for the treatment of ADHD.

A child's misbehavior at home combined with misbehavior at school often leads to a diagnosis of ADHD (Rafalovich, 2004; *DSM-IV* criteria C). According to Rafalovich (2004), "The troubles that most commonly spark the process of diagnosing a child with ADHD originate in the child's school" (131). These troubles are articulated in two ways: as academic difficulties, "denoting an inability to competently engage in the achievement of classroom assignments," and as social difficulties, "denoting interpersonal conflicts with other students and/or teachers" (131). As Rafalovich explains, "If their case is presented effectively, parents may act in ways that fit with the school's interests: recommendations for clinical referrals are accepted, children become clinically evaluated, and medication is often administered" (147).

Schools may no longer offer a skill-set or trade to guarantee a career for life, but schools still maintain an important relationship to the production of future workers.[8] As labor forms change, so have the practices of discipline within the schools. While physical punishment is no longer the norm, the rise of medical technologies and personality disorders provide a new means of managing the affective and behavior attributes of young people. As the school is and has always been a central site for the production of a future productive laboring citizenry, the techniques employed to manage children shift and change over time in order to meet the conditions of the workforce. This emphasis on affective skills and "prosocial behavior" renders the education system not just "an instrument for the production of employable citizens, [but] the school is now also widely regarded as one of the central sites for some of the most important aspects of ongoing social management" (Tait 2001: 95). As Gordon Tait (2001) argues, "Schools have always sought to govern the behaviour of pupils, and the pathologisation of specific forms of conduct is simply a new tactic within a very old and familiar strategy" (95). The school as a central site in social management and personality training finds significant benefits in the labeling of young people.

> Identifying, organizing and treating non-conforming children as ADHD and ODD sufferers serve a dual purpose: first, there are significant administrative benefits from ongoing intervention, in the form of better and easier management, both in the home and the classroom. Second, there is a greater social acceptability for a child to be suffering from a medical condition than there is for one whom might otherwise be regarded as willfully naughty. (Tait 2001: 97–98)

Therefore, through a diagnosis of an ADHD disorder, children are easier to manage at school and home than they would be for a mere disobedient personality. Moreover, just as we saw with Justin, a diagnosis of ADHD allows a child to be positioned as suffering a medical condition that is articulated to brain chemistry and not to external causes. A medical disorder demands that proper care includes medical treatment and in the case of many affective disorders in the age of "evidence-based medicine," the proper medical treatment is articulated as stimulant medication.

Recently, medical doctors have readily confessed that they diagnosis economically disadvantaged youth with ADHD in order to prescribe them stimulant medication to help them succeed at school. The rationale is that if society is unwilling to invest in external and environmental remedies then the child him or herself has to be altered. In a *New York Times* (2012, October 9) interview, Dr. Anderson explains, "We've decided as a society that it's too expensive to modify the kid's environment. So we have to modify the kid" (Schwarz 2012).[9] As many middle- and upper-middle-class students readily take stimulant medication to bolster their high achievement, students in the lower economic realm seek stimulant medication in order to gain some academic achievement in schools that are often failing. One eleven-year-old described why he uses the medication: "To help me focus on my school work, my homework, listening to Mom and Dad, and not doing what I used to do to my teachers, to make them mad" (Schwarz 2012). While many young people may not necessarily have ADHD, for students in the lower economic bracket, the stimulant drug treatments function in the place of other resources like tutoring, counseling, and well-funded public schools.

The "freedom" to "choose" a diagnosis of ADHD, and to consume stimulant medication as its treatment, speaks to a neoliberal subjectivity that works to improve an individual's innate abilities. In our current historical and cultural moment, an improvement in innate abilities is an improvement in affect and communication. Each advertisement reveals a child who will be productive in contemporary capitalism. The child gets along well with others and behaves in such a manner so as not to cause trouble at either home or school (work), and is content with his position in life. According to ADHD advertisements, the use of pharmaceuticals as a form of social management is an appropriate investment in a child's abilities-machine. This chemical restructuring of a child's brain renders difference invisible and functions to reconstruct young people so that they can meet the current demands of labor—that is to say, they are able to focus, complete tasks, and get along well with others. As Toby Miller (2008) contends, "ADHD and Ritalin offer a means of identifying, naming, curtailing, and channeling unproductive, uncontrolled, disruptive exuberance, such that 'troubled' young people lead disciplined lives, making them over without allocating vast human resources to monitor and direct them" (75). Following the neoliberal logic of investing in our children's human capital, a child's innate rambunctiousness is redirected through pharmaceutical consumption to academic success and social well-being. This investment is an investment in the child as a future worker.

This medical diagnosis is an efficient means of managing young people to meet the contemporary requirements of social behavior and workplace productivity. Miller (2008) argues that because of the medical management of young people, "classroom conduct and scholastic results are made over by an invisible and inexpensive device; Ritalin is, as per the wider designer-drug phenomenon, central to US upward mobility fantasies of transcendence through purchase" (76). Miller suggests that in our consumer-oriented and "makeover culture," children can be reconstructed through pharmaceutical medicine that clearly coincides with the cultural desires for upward advancement. This desire is increasingly heightened in times of economic precarity and uncertainty. What a relief it would be if we could provide our children economic security, social happiness, and a better life through a pill.

Advertisements for ADHD medications locate the child at school or in reference to school (such as doing homework) because a diagnosis of a child's mental health disorder often originates at the school. Rafalovich (2004) explains, "Schools are the most common institutional context for the discovery of children's troubles that are believed to be indicative of ADHD, and schools are the most involved institutions in moving a case of suspected ADHD toward a formal medical diagnosis" (129). As represented in *Thumbsucker*, schools may be the first contact for parents regarding their child and a mental health or behavioral disorder. Although current laws and fears of liability circumvent what many teachers are allowed to say to parents, schools still remain the central site in which a child's social behavior and academic performance are assessed, graded, and discussed with parents. The school as an institution requires a particular model of behavior of young people and this model coincides with the simultaneous competition and cooperation that is required of workers today.

College Students and ADHD

Young people are quite aware of the precariousness of the economy and the difficulty of finding and keeping a job. When asked, young people report high levels of stress and anxiety due to external circumstances and the fear of what has been referred to as the "falling middle class" (Ehrenreich 1990). For instance, *The American Freshman: National Norms Fall 2010* survey found that "the emotional health of college freshmen [...] has declined to the lowest level since an annual survey of incoming students started collecting data 25 years ago" (Lewin 2011). Students today "feel buffeted by the recession and stressed by the pressures of high school," and "worried about their own college debt and job prospects when they graduate" (Lewin 2011). The article continues,

"Campus counselors say that survey results are the latest evidence of what they see every day in their offices—students who are depressed, under stress and using psychiatric medication, prescribed even before they came to college." According to the study itself, "More students self-identified as having ADHD (5%) or a psychological disorder (3.8%) than any other disability/condition" (Higher Education Research Institute at UCLA 2011). Students also report that the current economy influenced their college choice. According to the survey results, "Coupled with the decrease in perceived emotional health and increased pressures and the financial concerns students have, the expectation to seek personal counseling in college is also at an all time high" (Higher Education Research Institute at UCLA 2011), signifying that young people are not immune to the pressures to succeed in a precarious and uncertain economic environment and that many will seek to invest in their abilities-machines via an investment in their mental health and well-being, even if that means seeking out a mental disorder diagnosis or at least the stimulant drugs that are prescribed to treat it.

As students face increasing pressures to succeed in an economy that is precarious and unstable, it seems reasonable that the rise of prescription drug use on college campuses has increased in recent years. As *The American Freshman* (Higher Education Research Institute at UCLA 2011) reports, "Student responses show that at the same time that emotional health has been trending downward and feeling overwhelmed has been trending upward, self-ratings on academic ability and drive to achieve have been moving up." To meet the drive to achieve and to overcome the sense of being overwhelmed, many students admit to buying, selling, and using stimulant medication without a doctor's prescription. Matt Lamkin (2011) reports for the *Chronicle of Higher Education* that while the rate of alcohol consumption in college students has remained stable, the use of illicit prescription drugs has risen and now their use is second only to that of marijuana. In research conducted by Alan D. DeSantis, at least 34% of university students have used ADHD drugs such as Ritalin and Adderall as a study enhancer, and approximately 60% of the University of Kentucky's juniors and seniors have used stimulant medication (as cited in Lamkin 2011).

The growing rate of stimulant medication use for the enhancement of academic performance has led to an increasing number of students feigning ADHD in order to secure a prescription of their own (Sollman, Ranseen, & Berry 2010). Kendra Nichols (2004), in an article for the *Chronicle of Higher Education*, "The Other Performance-Enhancing Drugs," explains that "a growing number of college students [...] are using Adderall and similar drugs to help them prepare for tests and term papers" (41). As more college students are diagnosed with ADHD, the availability of stimulant medication to treat ADHD has increased on college campuses, "and the use of prescription stimulants as study aids has become prevalent among peak performers and procrastinators alike" (43). Many students find that they are able to stay focused longer, which allows them to study longer. As one college student noted, he felt "zoned in." This same student "read 100 pages of his textbook in three hours, a task that normally would have taken him much longer," and "the information stuck in his head," earning him an A– on the exam (as cited in Nichols 2004).[10]

The increase on college campuses of stimulant medication as an academic enhancer and study aid signifies the neoliberal, competitive environment in which young people find themselves. Students learn to understand achievement from the cultural cues around them. Our cultural achievement is premised on competition and monetary reward. As Lamkin (2011) explains, "High school students compete for college admissions"; "college students compete for grades, then jobs"; "employees compete for promotions"; and the competition continues on. When competition reigns, one can hardly blame young people for investing in their abilities-machines and seeking out academic performance enhancers in the form of an ADHD diagnosis and its stimulant medication. The social management of young people is not strictly a top-down approach. Young people do have agency, and in this case many young people use their agency to their academic advantage in seeking out a diagnosis for ADHD or at least its stimulant treatment, much like Justin did.

There Is No Holiday

While ADHD advertisements traditionally focus on improved abilities at school, the newer medications that last longer are advertised as controlling symptoms of ADHD well into the after-school hours. The advertisements for ADHD argue that there is no holiday or time off from ADHD for you or your child. The appeal is that your child will be focused, productive, and well behaved both at school and at home. For instance, a print advertisement for Vyvanse suggests that ADHD should be medically treated from morning until night. In "Fairytale" (Shire 2010g) the viewer is presented with an image of a mother and daughter in their pajamas, reading before bed. The text reads: "Vyvanse: Shown to provide consistent ADHD symptoms control even at 13 hours after taking.

> 7:00 am Ate breakfast and took Vyvanse
>
> 12:00 pm Paid attention in my English class
>
> 5:00 pm Focused on my science homework
>
> 8:00 pm Read a fairy tale with mom before bed

The advertisement argues that after consuming the medication, the child is able to focus on schoolwork during the day, focus in English class during the lunch hour, focus on science homework at dinner time, and at eight o'clock at night, enjoy reading a book with mom. The only meal the child seems to eat during the appropriate time is breakfast, and that is when she takes her stimulant medication. During the noon hour and the five o'clock hour, the child is focused on her schoolwork and we are not sure when she eats, but we learn that she only needs to consume her stimulant medication with breakfast. According to this advertisement, the child's symptoms are supposed to be controlled for 13 hours a day, and the child is working on schoolwork for most of that time. Even the leisure activity of reading a fairytale before bed becomes about focus and control, instead of relaxation and pleasure. Both mother and daughter smile at you from the advertisement as yet another productive day has been achieved.

Whereas at one time physicians suggested that people taking stimulant medication should take a "medication holiday," ADHD advertisements argue that an ADHD child should be medicated all the time. A medication holiday is advised for medications, like stimulants, in which patients are likely to build a tolerance. A medication holiday or a weekend off medication allows for the medication to remain effective, without having to increase dosage. ADHD advertisements inform the reader that there is no holiday from ADHD; advertisements suggests that children with ADHD should take their medication throughout the year. The discourse of ADHD does not offer a "cure"; instead, like other lifestyle drugs, ADHD medication offers only the management of symptoms, and advertisements for ADHD medication argue that symptoms should be managed all the time so that the child can always be focused and productive. Vyvanse capitalizes on the importance of the continual management of ADHD symptoms all day, every day. Vyvanse advertises, "Consistent symptom control for ADHD." "Consistent Kevin throughout the day, even during homework," states the ad. The text continues:

> Kevin's ADHD symptoms weren't controlled throughout his busy day. His teachers, coaches and even his friends didn't know the Kevin I know.
>
> Vyvanse has been shown to provide consistent ADHD symptom control from morning, through homework and family time, for up to 12 hours.
>
> In a Vyvanse clinical study, parents reported ADHD symptom control at approximately 10:00 am, 2:00 pm and 6:00 pm, demonstrating consistent symptom control.
>
> I wish others could see the child I see. (Shire 2010h)

According to the advertisement, Kevin's symptoms weren't under control. And because Kevin's symptoms weren't under control, his ability to be productive and focused was unknown to his teachers, coaches, and even his friends. With the consumption of the medication, Kevin's symptoms are consistently controlled throughout the day. Again, a smiling Kevin reveals that he is happy with his medically controlled and productive self.

This advertising campaign for "consistency" illustrates that children need to perform the same affective behavior both inside and outside of school. "Consistent Carl" (Shire 2009b) is consistent "throughout the day even after school." The image of a young boy, constructing a model race-car with a friend, looks up with a smile. "When Carl's ADHD symptoms are controlled, even at 6:00 pm, he's able to focus and pay attention so friends can see the child I see." We are presented with a well-behaved and socially engaging child who meets the expectations of the parent. The text proclaims, "Vyvanse has been shown to provide significant symptom control for up to 12 hours from morning through homework and family time."[11] The ability to complete homework and maintain relationships after school is just as important as good behavior and academic achievement while at school. A child's ADHD symptoms must always be controlled. These ads indicate that the same type of affective behavior is required in both school and home time; that there is never a day off or an evening free of attention deficit hyperactivity disorder; there is no time in which a child should not be focused, or productive, or well behaved.

An advertisement featuring a young girl and boy sitting side-by-side boasts, "Vyvanse: Shown to provide consistent ADHD symptom control even at 13 hours after taking" (Shire 2010b). The timeline duplicates "Consistent Kevin's," with the exception that at eight o'clock at night, this child helps his "sister with homework." Again, we learn that the social skills and affective attributes that are required for success at school are required for success and stability at home too, and not only is a child supposed to be productive and focused on his own work, but he should be able to cheerfully help his sister too.

Each moment of a child's day is increasingly taken over by the management of their ADHD symptoms. A Concerta (Janssen Pharmaceuticals 2009a) advertisement published at the beginning of summer states, "ADHD does not take a summer break." The ad features a light-skinned African American boy at a Little League game.[12] The scenario: "Little League→stays on Concerta→listens to coach→focuses during batting practice→ice cream party with team." Or, the other option, "Little League→can't find glove again→picks dandelions in outfield→annoys teammates→time to ask the doctor about staying on Concerta through the summer?" The tag line reads, "During the summer, Concerta can help keep your child on the path to success in managing ADHD." The benefits include the following: "Concerta can help improve your child's focus," "Concerta improves social interactions as reported by teachers and parents," "90% of parents surveyed said their child is more likely to have positive interactions with friends and family when taking Concerta on weekends and over the summer." These advertisements inform the viewer that ADHD encompasses the entire temporal structural of a child's life. There is no "free time." Even summertime, the time that is devoted to leisure and childhood dreaming and vacations and summer camps, is now colonized by the consumption of ADHD and its stimulant medication.

There is no holiday. Just as there is no differentiation between work and leisure time for adults as discussed in the previous two chapters, the discourse of ADHD argues that there is no differentiation between academic and nonacademic time for children with ADHD. They are required to perform the same affective behavior, communication skills, and to focus and exude social likability all of the time.

What's Up with Boys and Their Moms?

Overwhelmingly, ADHD is touted as a "boy's disorder." According to Concerta's brochure (ALZA Corporation 2010), the signs and symptoms of ADHD in children include "having trouble paying attention in class or completing homework," a child who is "constantly out of his or her seat," a child who has difficulty waiting for "his or her turn when playing games," a child who has "trouble paying attention," is easily "excited" or "hyperactive, and acts impulsively." "ADHD can affect a child's ability to sit still, focus and follow directions." In addition, "symptoms of ADHD can impact a child's social interactions." Furthermore, "ADHD symptoms can affect children all day, every day" (4–5). Psychologist Peter Briggin, known critic of ADHD, refers to this list as "a list of behaviors that annoy adults" (as cited in Stolberg 2002: 59). These behaviors are repeatedly linked to "boy behaviors," and boys are more likely to be diagnosed with ADHD than girls.[13] According to Concerta's informational webpage, "In the United States, approximately 9% of the school-age population is diagnosed with ADHD. It's the most commonly diagnosed behavioral condition in children today. Twice as many boys are diagnosed with ADHD as girls" (http://www.concerta.net).[14]

Many antifeminist and conservative commentators (see Kleinfeld 1998; Leo 1999; Sommers 2000) have argued that the problem with boys is inherently the fault of educators (especially women educators) and progressive school reforms that have opted for cooperative learning to the detriment of the competitive and rote learning of traditional, masculinist education paradigms (Titus 2004).[15] They have argued that education has become too female-centered and has disadvantaged and discriminated against boys and traditional boy behavior. What the critics of cooperative learning overlook is the function of the school as a training ground for work-life, and as a site that reproduces social relations. Through the pathologizing of the behavior of inattention and hyperactivity, and the prescription of medication for this "neurological and genetic" (Barkley 2006) disorder, boys are more likely to be treated for ADHD than girls. As Barkley explains, "Males are more likely than females to exhibit aggressive and antisocial behavior, and such behavior is more likely to get a child referred to a psychiatric center for treatment" (108).

The *DSM-III* and *DSM-IV* diagnostic criteria mirror the behaviors that interfere with the new labor trends and that prevent affective and communicative labor. Self-described conservative Michael Fumento (2003) wrote an essay for the *New Republic* to demystify the use of Ritalin. He characterized the idea that "ADHD is part of a feminist conspiracy to make little boys more like little girls" as a myth. The following is Fumento's summary of conservative thought on the matter of medicating boys:

> Many conservatives observe that boys receive ADHD diagnoses in much higher numbers than girls and find in this evidence of a feminist conspiracy. (This, despite the fact that genetic diseases are often heavily weighted more toward one gender or the other.) Sowell refers to "a growing tendency to treat boyhood as a pathological condition that requires a new three R's—repression, re-education and Ritalin." Fukuyama claims Prozac is being used to give women "more of the alpha-male feeling," while Ritalin is making boys act more like girls. "Together the two sexes are gently nudged toward that androgynous median personality...that is the current politically correct outcome in American society." George Will, while acknowledging that Ritalin can be helpful, nonetheless writes of the "androgyny agenda" of "drugging children because they are behaving like children, especially boy children." (19)

What we see in much professed conservative literature as described by Fumento is the anxiety over medications like Ritalin that affect affective behavior in ways that are perceived as erasing gendered attributes. The fear of androgyny speaks to an anxiety over traditional gender roles and, I would suggest, the prevalent role of affective labor in contemporary society. However, more conservatives are recognizing the benefits of treatments for ADD and ADHD. According to Fumento,

> Kerri Houston, national field director for the American Conservative Union and the mother of two ADHD children on medication, agrees with much of the criticism of public schools. "But don't blame ADHD on crummy curricula and lazy teachers," she says. "If you've worked with these children, you know that they have a serious neurological problem." (19)

Although many conservatives still contend that the wrongdoings of public education and cooperative learning are an impediment to boys, they are able to agree that there is a neurological disease taking hold of children today.

The treatment of ADHD works through medications like those described above in order to prepare the youthful body for affective labor. The fact that more males than females are diagnosed with ADHD on the one hand may appear as a reconditioning of traditional masculine behavior, yet, on the other hand, through the use of Ritalin like drugs, these boys are being prepared for professional affective labor. The affective state apparatus of the school reproduces white, male, patriarchal dominance through the use of medication[16] in order to maintain masculine dominance in the workforce.[17] As the population changes, an increase in the percentage of female workers suggests an inherent threat to male dominance in the workforce.[18]

Boys are not alone in the commercial representation of ADHD. In many advertisements, boys and their mothers are "squarely in the visual and metaphoric center" (Singh 2007: 150). In a Concerta advertisement (Janssen Pharmaceuticals, 2010b), the text states:

> His math homework is two days late.
>
> It's in his backpack, which he left on the bus.
>
> Again.
>
> It feels like everyone is giving up on him.
>
> I need a way to help him, but all I have is tears.
>
> —Laura, Kyle's mom.

An image of a deserted school dominates the ad. The text continues, "ADHD can be a lonely experience for both the child and the parent. But Laura is not alone. And neither are you. Learn why moms just like you have made the decision to talk to their child's doctor about Concerta, a treatment with 9 years of proven safety and results in treating ADHD symptoms." This ad highlights this relationship between mother and son, and the desire for mothers to have successful and well-behaved sons. Combined with statements like "I wish others could see the child I see," this discourse indicates that mothers see their child's potential, and their own potential as a parent of a well-behaved child.

In her historical analysis, Ilina Singh (2007) analyzes early Ritalin advertisements directed to physicians to underscore that these advertisements position "problem boys with their problematic mothers" (138). As she explains, early ads "make a direct link between the behavior and appearance of children to the behavior and appearance of the mother and suggest that the clinician's tool, Ritalin, can help manage all these appearances" (145). In contemporary direct-to-consumer advertisements, women who come across ADHD ads "learn that successful mothers have successful sons, and that drug intervention is a sign of maternal love and care" (Singh 2007: 150). Singh provides the example of an Adderall advertisement ("Finally a Hug" 2004, reprinted in Singh 2007) in which a mother embraces her son who earned a B+ on his schoolwork. The advertisement reads:

> Schoolwork that matches his intelligence.
>
> Friends that ask him to join the group.
>
> Family hours that last for hours.
>
> A real solution for ADHD.

Singh argues that "the point of drug treatment, as depicted in this ad, is not simply good behavior; the real promise is an enhanced relationship between mother and son" (150) and this relationship is secured through the treatment of ADHD.

In the advertisement featuring Laura, Kyle's mom, discussed above, Laura feels despair indicated by her tears. The tears are significant. Just as Laura does not want others to give up on her son, she does not want others to give up on her skills as a mother. Treating Kyle for ADHD symptoms with stimulant medication redeems Laura's parenting abilities as she makes the investment in Kyle's abilities-machines and allows others to see both herself and Kyle as embodying the "appropriate" attributes for each of their subjectivities. Soon, mom herself will be interpellated into more than the discourse of ADHD; she will also be interpellated into the diagnosis of ADHD.

Singh (2007) raised the question, "Why boys?" and proposed the answer "Because mothers" (151). This troubled relationship becomes more interesting as adults, and specifically mothers, are now the fastest growing population of ADHD sufferers. In the United States, ADHD is the most common mental disorder after depression in adults (National Institute of Mental Health 2009). Adults on ADHD medication between the ages of 20 and 44 doubled between 2000 and 2004, surpassing the pediatric population by 44% (Medco Press Release 2005). The spending on ADHD drugs for this age group grew by more than 325% during the same time period (Medco Press Release 2005). Adult ADHD is described as a "chronic neurobehavioral disorder." Just as with ADHD in younger people, there is no real certainty as to what causes ADHD, and "the lack of a precise physiological marker for ADHD further increases the difficulty of making an accurate diagnosis" (Goodman 2007: 319). According to Goodman, "Adults with ADHD often function below their ability for much of their lives" (320). Schulte (2011) reports that "adults with ADHD have been found to be more likely to lose a job, change a job or not show up for work, costing an estimated $77 billion a year in workplace failure." (Just as with depression discussed in Chapter 1, mental health is calculated in economic terms of lost work time.) Moreover, "they are more likely to get divorced, go broke or be arrested." They tend to have more difficulties with relationships and substance abuse. In addition, they have "lower educational attainment and earning potential" (Schulte 2011).[19] In this discourse, untreated ADHD in young people results in the economic and personal failure in untreated ADHD in adults, just as described in *Achieving the Promise* (discussed in Chapter 1).

This "medicalization of underperformance" (Conrad & Potter 2000) shifts with the ADHD sufferer from the school to the workplace. Whereas an untreated ADHD child lacks focus, forgets things, talks out of turn, and is unable to complete tasks such as homework in a timely manner, work-specific descriptors of ADHD include "inefficiencies at work," "difficulty sitting through meetings," working multiple jobs, working long hours, and feeling "overwhelmed" (Goodman 2007: 319). In each case, ADHD results in the loss or potential loss of an economically productive subjectivity.

Brigid Schulte, writing for the *Washington Post* (2011), provides a cultural narrative of adult ADHD in an article titled "More Women Have ADHD…or Is It the Stress of Modern Life?" The question is never answered, but the rhetoric of ADHD abounds. A busy mother of two learns about ADHD after a teacher recommends that her 6-year-old son see a behavior specialist. While completing the paperwork she begins to see herself in the questionnaire. Anthony is described in the common narrative form, "though he's smart, he has a tough time of sitting still, getting going on things that bore him, such as homework, and [...] he is easily distracted or frustrated at school." Mom had to quit the job she loved because of her inability to work and take care of the children and house with her undiagnosed ADHD. The article claims, "What has traditionally been expected of women—keeping house, doing laundry, grocery shopping, organizing children's activities, paying bills—are exactly the mundane and organized tasks most difficult, if not impossible, for a wandering and impatient ADHD brain" (Schulte 2011). Once the mom is diagnosed with ADHD, her comments echo that of Justin in the movie *Thumbsucker*, "It's kind of a relief, knowing I have ADHD...rather than just thinking I am nuts" (Schulte 2011). Medco Health Solutions (Sept. 28, 2006), found that "parents of children on an ADHD medication are nearly 10 times more likely to take an ADHD drug themselves than those without a child using those drugs." Moreover, "in households where both a parent and child began treatment for the first time in 2005, nearly 60 percent of those parents were moms" (Medco Health Solutions, Sept. 28, 2006). This increase in women as ADHD sufferers suggests that Singh is correct. The problem with boys *is* their mothers and the treatment for this problem is to medically treat them both for ADHD disorders.

Mothers are interpellated into the discourses of ADHD via their child's diagnosis of ADHD. Singh's argument concerning the ADHD phenomenon in regard to "problem boys and problematic mothers" finds its conclusion in the treatment of both mother and son for their ADHD. To solidify that mothers are ultimately held accountable for their child's behavior via their child's ADHD, the discourse of ADHD links the cause of ADHD directly to genetics. For example, according to a Concerta brochure (ALZA Corporation 2009) on adult ADHD, "76% of ADHD is due to our genes" (5). Unlike most other genetic diseases in which the parent worries about passing on a genetic disease to his or her child, the discourse of ADHD works the other way around. "If you think your child has ADHD, you may too." The brochure inquires: "Are you more like your child than you think? Your child has trouble paying attention at school—you get distracted at work" (4). The text continues, "Any parent of a child with ADHD knows it's hard work helping your child manage his or her condition. Now, ask yourself this question: Is it more difficult for us to stay focused and organized because I have ADHD too?" (5). The brochure informs the reader that

> the truth is ADHD can occur in anyone, from professional athletes to CEOs. ADHD can occur in both men and women, and in people of all ages—children, teens and adults. Approximately 60% of people who had ADHD symptoms as a child continue to have difficulties as adults. Even if you weren't diagnosed as a child, you may have had ADHD. (5)

The rhetorical construction of ADHD begins with the child's behavior and attitude and then is articulated as a problem and disorder with the parent. The parent is directed to manage her symptoms or else she is failing her child. As the brochure contends (ALZA Corporation 2009), "Think about it. If you have trouble focusing and staying organized, it may affect how well you can help your child stay focused and organized" (13). The text uses the care of the child as a reason to get treated for ADHD. "That's why it's important to find out whether or not you have ADHD—and get treatment if you do" (13). As ADHD can happen to anyone at anytime in his or her life cycle, we are trapped in the consumption of pharmaceuticals as there is no "cure" offered in the discourse of ADHD, only self-management of the disorder through medication. And if you don't happen to have ADHD, according to the brochure, "your child's *other parent* might" (emphasis added, 10).

What we see in the rhetorical construction of ADHD is a whole heteronormative family of underperforming and underachieving individuals that suffers from ADHD. A case in point is a *Newsweek* (Hancock 1996) article aptly titled "Mother's Little Helper," which describes a family of ADHD sufferers.

> That's no surprise to the Schmidt family of Rochester, Minn. Over the past three years, all five have been diagnosed with attention deficit. The first case was Stephen, 8, who appeared to be hypersensitive and hard of hearing. "You would look straight at him, and say something, and he'd always say "What?" says Joan, 40, his mom. The psychiatrist determined that Stephen, Dennis, 37, and Daniel, 10, all had ADHD. Joan and her daughter, Maggie, 5, were found to have ADD, without the hyperactivity. One child takes Ritalin, another the antidepressant Wellbutrin. The rest take daily combinations of Ritalin for ADHD, plus antidepressants (Prozac, Wellbutrin or Paxil) for accompanying depression. (53)

Following the cultural script, the young boy, Stephen, at age 8, is diagnosed with ADHD. Subsequent to Stephen's diagnosis the rest of the family follows suit including his 5-year-old sister. The problem child indicates problems in the rest of the family. If children can be helped by a diagnosis of ADHD and its stimulant medication, it seems reasonable that their parents can too. The treatment of affective disorders is an investment in the abilities-machines of the entire family unit, each individually and in the family as a whole.

The discourse of ADHD advertisements sells us a contemporary form of neoliberal subjectivity for the whole family. We learn that we are to be productive and focused in our work, leisure, and home life throughout all our phases of life from early childhood until late adulthood. Success means that we are able to complete tasks in a timely fashion and get along well with others. If we are unable to adequately perform these affective behaviors, we will fail in the knowledge economy and, the narrative goes, in life in general. We, like Justin in *Thumbsucker*, just might find hope in a diagnosis of ADHD. For as Justin says excitedly to his parents, "It says I will have more confidence and self-control; I will have better relationships." And who among us does not desire to reach our potential, have more confidence, and have better relationships?

Conclusion: Abilities-Machines and Their Monsters: Back to Justin

Investing in a diagnosis of ADHD medication is one means in which to invest in a child's abilities-machine and success as a contemporary capitalist worker. The advertisements of ADHD medication demonstrate that this investment is well worth the risks of a medical disorder and its prescription medication. *Thumbsucker* suggests just as much as well. The limits of medication and the risk of medication are in the fine print in advertising discourse. To close this chapter, I return to the film *Thumbsucker* and Justin, its protagonist, to argue that even though this film presents itself as a critique of ADHD, what it reveals is that stimulant medication does work and in the end, this film reifies that medicating youth is a worthwhile investment in their abilities-machines.

Returning to Justin and the critique of ADHD as presented by *Thumbsucker*, this section explores the negative side effects of stimulant medication and their consequences. These side effects are illustrative of the limits of the affective attributes induced through the consumption of ADHD medication. The limit of the appropriate affective attributes for productive capitalist workers is met when Justin's affect is too competitive and strategic and when he overmedicates, crossing the threshold into what his debate coach refers to as monstrous behavior.

Justin's pharmaceutically treated "neurochemical self" is soon put into contrast with Rebecca's new pot-smoking—another stimulant drug with different outcomes—boyfriend. Rebecca quits the debate team in order to spend more time with her boyfriend, while Justin takes her spot on the team and enjoys the success of his newly medicated-induced, productive self. Justin, poised and competent, wears a tie to his debate competition and does exceedingly well. In his first sparring on the topic of TV and violence, Justin respectfully intervenes in the debate to argue that "images aren't reality," and that we must "distinguish between images and life." Justin appears cognizant of his opponent and rhetorically diffuses potential intensity. "Mark, I understand the spirit of your refutation but society and its conception of reality are inextricable," argues Justin. However, images do affect others, and Justin reaps the benefits of his new self-presentation. The subtext of the exchange is that Justin is a mere image created by his medication. But this new image does matter, as Justin's immaterial attributes have very material consequences.

Justin appears calm and collected and demonstrates his communicative abilities and listening skills to his debate opponents when he employs his rhetorical sensitivity to state things such as "Mark, I understand the spirit of your refutation," before destroying his opponent's argument. Justin soothes his opponent: "You're angry and that's human, but that's not a solution." He continues, "We have to overcome the idea that everyone is the same" (Mills 2005). The notion that "everyone is not the same" suggests that with prescription drugs some semblance of normalizing appropriate affective behavior is possible. Justin is correct, "everyone is not the same," and some may have the advantage of altering their affective potential through medication, while others may not. Regardless, Justin's new "image" makes life look better, and for Justin in many ways it is better. Performing the appropriate affect has served Justin well. These debate scenes function as an underlying commentary on kids and the use of Ritalin and, while the most damning comments come from Justin, ironically, he also experiences the most success he has ever had.

Employing the power of his rhetorical skills, Justin finds a means in which to cooperate with others—by "speaking confidently" and "winning minds." His interpersonal and sexual awakening also benefits as he effortlessly persuades his debate coach to allow him to room with his young female teammates rather than with his male coach. Then, Justin manages, with prompting from his all-female teammates, to request that Mr. Geary purchase them alcohol. The coach acquiesces and delivers a six-pack to the team, the contents of which are then mixed with schnapps. Fueled by the alcohol, Justin manages to initiate a playful half-naked romp with his teammates. Employing his new sense of interpersonal communication, when the coach knocks on their door in response to a noise complaint, Justin, buttoning up his shirt, replies to the coach's question: "Do you think I'm stupid?" with contrived empathy and sincerity. "You're not stupid. You just feel left out" (Mills 2005). The next morning Justin wins the regional debate tournament and the first-place trophy. In all respects, Justin is affectively adjusted, and this improvement has led to competent communication skills, interpersonal success, and academic achievement, all as promised by ADHD's promotional material.

Justin's newly affected personality causes his own demise. His rhetorical sensitivity and confidence morph into pedantic and competitive arrogance. At the (regional) tournament, Justin tells his opponent, "Look, Kevin, your pro-disarmament views do not reflect the current international climate. They just reflect your need for everything to be nice, to be friendly, but humans are inherently hostile" (Mills 2005). Justin's argument affronts the very idea of affective labor as a collective and cooperative mode of action. When Kevin attempts to intervene, Justin continues unequivocally, "I don't think you know what your point really is. Now if we are to take disarmament seriously, I propose that we look at the real weapons, our minds" (Mills 2005). The reference to "our minds" as the "real weapons" is a tongue-in-cheek reference to ADHD as a chemical imbalance of the mind and, therefore, its treatment is one centered on the mind. If people are "inherently hostile," then medication that transforms hostility into cooperation offers an alternative model of productive force. Too much of a good thing is never a good thing. As Justin becomes addicted to his medication, his debate strategies begin to lack substance and rely more and more on his affective performance. Justin becomes edgy, competitive, self-righteous, and downright hostile.

After the tournament, when his debate coach inquires how Justin feels, Justin replies, "Tired, but good." When Mr. Geary asks, "Why do you feel good?" Justin aggressively retorts, "Because I am winning." When asked about learning, Justin offers the abrupt comment, "I am learning how to win." To this, his coach responds, "You are so hungry, Justin. I never really took that into account" (Mills 2005). Justin's affective state has exceeded the boundaries of teamwork. He is angry, competitive, commanding, irritable, and out of control. He no longer expresses the rhetorical sensitivity, collective and interpersonal attributes, and the ability to adequately read various social contexts. Instead, Justin comes home from winning the regional tournament to fight with his family. Soon he takes another pill (he is now overmedicating) and joins his mother outside while she smokes a cigarette and proceeds to argue with her. His antagonistic behavior is heightened into a manic state as he takes yet another pill and manically pens a fabricated story to submit with his NYU college admission application. He claims that both of his parents are mentally ill and that is the reason that his grades are not of the caliber of other applicants. He composes a heart-wrenching story of triumph over circumstance and articulates his dream of working in broadcast media to help others.

Justin's behavior mirrors the side affects of stimulant medication. Concerta warns that your child should stop taking the medication if "aggressive behavior or hostility develops or worsens while taking CONCERTA" (http://www.concerta.net/children/adhd-medication-safety-index.html). And an advertisement for ADHD medication Vyvanse exhorts, "Tell your doctor immediately" if your child "exhibits aggressive behavior or hostility" (Shire 2010f). These warning signs of aggressive behavior and inappropriate communication signify out-of-control affective behavior. Justin's aggressive behavior continues until it reaches its limit point, illuminating which type of affective responses are inappropriate for proper subjectivity in the knowledge economy.

At the championships, Justin has his final breakdown: Justin's opponent witnesses him taking his medication in the men's room and informs Justin that his medication "is just three molecules away from cocaine." Justin states that it calms him down and his debate opponent retorts that Justin's medication actually just speeds him up so much that it gives him focus. He then calls Justin a "speed freak." Justin's subsequent tournament is a disaster and his arguments are senseless:

> I think you are confusing tone and content. I mean tone has tone, but content is silent.... It's not quite silent, it's just that the tone is muted; tone should inhere in the content....If silence is neutral then the tone will be quieter and the content would be neutral but heard. (Mills 2005)

At this point, Justin has lost his communicative advantage and now is just a nonsensical junkie. Justin's demise is likened to that of an addict, a cocaine addict. Justin gets called out for taking his prescribed stimulant medication as a performance enhancer and the reference to cocaine turns Justin into an addict. Prescription medication is fine; but illegal medication is deviant. The reference to stimulant medication like Ritalin being ascribed attributes of cocaine is not novel, and the recreational abuse of Ritalin is high, most likely because of its cocaine-like effects. According to the DEA (U.S. Department of Justice, Drug Enforcement Administration 2011), stimulants are abused because they "produce a sense of exhilaration, enhance self-esteem, improve mental and physical performance, increase activity, reduce appetite, [and] extend wakefulness for prolonged periods" (43). It is not shocking then that "the increased use of this substance for the treatment of ADHD has paralleled an increase in its abuse among adolescents and young adults who crush these tablets and snort the powder to get high" (para 2).[20] Young people can readily obtain methylphenidate from classmates and friends who are prescribed the stimulant medication.[21] As discussed earlier in this chapter, many young people illegally secure a quick study fix via ADHD medication.

The following day, Justin's debate coach tells him directly, "Justin, it's my professional opinion that you have become a monster."

> Justin: What? You used to love me.
>
> Mr. Geary: Don't get grandiose with this.
>
> Justin: What was that all about my gift and you told me, you built it up, you told me I have a talent?

Mr. Geary: You do. You have a real intensity. You have a great understanding of group dynamics, but there are also a lot of things you need to work on, Justin, like glibness, arrogance, self-control, should I go on?

Justin: At least I still have a dream. (Mills 2005)

These qualities of "glibness, arrogance, self-control" can be viewed as traditionally masculine characteristics, and it could be argued that, as labor has become more affective, concerned with cooperation, small group communication, and the like, the newly acquired arrogant and overly confident characteristics that Justin displays have made him into a "monster." In any event, he is certainly no longer sucking his thumb.

There are side effects to stimulant medications. These side effects occur for Justin when he is abusing his drugs by overmedicating. The affect of aggressiveness and arrogance are viewed by his coach as inappropriate and "monstrous."

Justin and his debate coach represent the divide between liberalism and neoliberalism. The debate coach, Mr. Geary, premises his relationship on one of exchange. He will exchange his teaching and belief in Justin if Justin does his best for the team. Justin has embraced the neoliberal moment in which competition and winning is what, ultimately, matters. Justin breaks with the former liberalism as he gets a taste of winning and success.

Even though Justin is "winning," the film suggests that there is a limited threshold to performance in a competitive situation. This reveals that in this neoliberal competitive moment, workers need to present the affect of cooperation, collaboration, and likeability, while still being competitive and self-focused. It is not enough just to be smart, skilled, or even competent; the performance of affect requires the proverbial "smile" to accompany all phases of work, as each ADHD advertisement presents. As the nature of work itself relies on the ability to communicate information, the attitude in which this is done has taken on more importance.

The investment in our youths' abilities-machines as an investment in their affect coincides with the immaterial labor demands of contemporary capitalism. An investment in affect is required for any hope of success in the knowledge economies and service industries. Acquired investments are all the more vital in a precarious economy with a precarious labor force. The investment in affect is made all the more salient via an affective state apparatus—the contingent coming together of pharmaceutical corporations, medical diagnosis, the school, the family, and the individual—as we are all encouraged and we all desire to invest in ourselves and our children, and by focusing on the performance of our child's affect we are increasingly directed to examine our own.

Thumbsucker fails in its final moment as it reveals itself as a liberal text premised on a liberal subjectivity of authenticity. As soon as Justin goes off his medication, he goes back to sucking his thumb. Let's pause momentarily. Justin, after being called a "speed freak" by his debate opponent and "a monster" by his debate coach, ends up throwing away his medication. The next day he is withdrawn and sickly. Following the discourse on ADHD, children who come off these drugs will often seek alternative forms of medication and, in this case, Justin returns to his love interest, Rebecca, and starts smoking marijuana. This drug also creates an affective response in Justin, although not quite the academically productive one caused by Ritalin. Justin and Rebecca constantly get high and finally have an intimate physical relationship. When Justin finally shares that he loves Rebecca, she rebukes him and refers to their burgeoning sexual intimacy as "just a teenage experiment" (Mills 2005).

At the conclusion of the film, Justin, on a flight to New York for a summer program at NYU, falls asleep and dreams of his future employment as a news anchor and awakes to find his original comfort, his thumb, happily in his mouth. The "thumb" never really went away, the effects of the stimulant medication only veiled it. Upon awakening, he sees the attractive woman sitting next to him and says, "Hi, I'm Justin," and she responds, "Hi," and they both look away and then at each other (Mills 2005). The film concludes with the idyllic image of Justin running gleefully through the streets of New York City. And this is where the film fails. If Justin is going to succeed in the future that he desires, a life in which his work—and it is work that he dreams about—is delivering the evening news as all the people in his life watch him from their respective homes, then Justin is going to have to do more than suck his thumb. The only success that Justin has had in the film—at school, at home, and in his social life—is when he was taking his medication for his diagnosis of ADHD. Even when overmedicating, Justin was succeeding. He won the debate championship and he fabricated his application to NYU. Justin's success throughout the film was based on his diagnosis of ADHD and its pharmaceutical treatment.

This chapter reveals that in direct-to-consumer advertising and in many popular discourses of ADHD, to be a good parent is to invest in your child's potential. This investment is one that is not made carelessly; rather, it is based on a benefits-risks analysis and if the benefits include academic success, extracurricular excellence, and a well-behaved and well-liked child, then the risks of prescription medication may be overlooked.

Through the use of prescription medication and a diagnosis of ADHD parents can invest in their child's future by investing in pharmaceutically induced affective behavior now. Moreover, parents, especially moms, can invest in their own "abilities-machines" by investing in their own affective performance as parents. The discourses of ADHD suggest that we all should perform the appropriate affective skills for success in neoliberal capitalism as it is currently practiced. An affective disorder and its pharmaceutical treatment is just another investment in one's abilities-machine.

In this chapter, Justin provides a narrative foil for the promises found in ADHD and reveals that success is measured by the yardstick of contemporary capitalism, which is often defined as individual achievement. As Justin and the promotional materials for ADHD reveal, the affective disorder of one family member affects the entire family. The concluding chapter provides a brief glimpse into the mood disorders of the family's favorite member, the dog.

Notes

1 According to a *Newsweek* article (Hancock 1996), "Critics dismiss the drug [Ritalin] as just a behavioral 'quick fix' for children forced to live in an impatient culture that feeds on deadlines, due dates, sound bites and megabytes" (para 5).

2 The high school setting is much like the professional office in that it requires a particular type of affective performance. Melissa Gregg (2010), in her analysis of workplace affects and demands of "friendliness," explains, "Much like high school, the office is shown to have strict rules of behavior that can result in punishment, discipline, and ostracism" (263). And just as in the workplace, in high school "the toilet becomes a key dramatic location [...] because it is the one site free from surveillance—it provides a temporary reprieve from the exhaustive performance of [...] cool" (261).

3 According to Ilina Singh (2003), "Fathers' perspectives on ADHD behaviours, diagnosis, and drug treatment can be categorized along two dimensions: 're-luctant believers' and 'tolerant non-believers'" (308).

4 http://www.cdc.gov/ncbddd/adhd/data.html

5 http://www.justice.gov/dea/pubs/pressrel/pr951020.htm

6 According to the CDC, "Boys (13.2%) were more likely than girls (5.6%) to have ever been diagnosed with ADHD" (http://www.cdc.gov/ncbddd/adhd/data.html).

7 http://www.dsm5.org/ProposedRevisions/Pages/proposedrevision.aspx?rid=383#

8 Cultural theorists such as Foucault and Althusser have long recognized the importance of the school as a site of discipline and ideological training, respectively.

9 Article retrieved from http://www.nytimes.com/2012/10/09/health/attention-disorder-or-not-children-prescribed-pills-to-help-in-school.html?pagewanted=all&_r=0.

10 Even professional athletes, after the much-publicized scandals of the illegal use of steroids and other performance enhancers, are seeking a diagnosis of ADHD in order to secure a prescription for stimulant medication to enhance their work performance.

11 Vyvanse also has an advertisement featuring a girl, "Consistent Casey" (2009), with her father looking on approvingly. The text is the same as that for "Consistent Kevin."

12 Many of the ads that I found featured white children. The fact that this ad features an African American boy in the context of playing sport and not in the context of the classroom opens itself up for critique.

13 This by no means suggests that girls aren't implicated in affective disorders. In fact, ADD has been described as the feminine version of ADHD: "But there is another kind of ADD that shows no hyperactivity whatsoever. Indeed, these people can be underactive. This is the child, often a girl, who sits at the back of the classroom daydreaming, or the adult who moves serenely within a cloud, never quite present anywhere" (Hallowell & Ratey 1995: 9).

14 http://www.concerta.net/children/about-adhd-what-is-adhd.html

15 Titus (2004) noted that Kleinfeld and Sommers had been sponsored by the Women's Freedom Network (WFN) and the Independent Women's Forum (IWF), which are conservative antifeminist groups (158).

16 Diller (2002) reported at the President's Council on Bioethics "that in Canada and in the United States, while there are pockets of under-use, ADHD diagnosis and stimulant use is primarily a white middle and upper-middle class phenomenon" (http://biotech.law.lsu.edu/research/pbc/transcripts/dec02/session3. html).

17 According to the U.S. Census Bureau 2004 American Community Survey, men with graduate or professional degrees make, on average, $68,239, while females with professional or graduate degrees make, on average, $46,004 (a difference of $22,235). Even as immaterial labor has become the dominant form of labor, gender discrepancies abound.

18 According to the *Occupational Outlook Handbook*:

> The numbers of men and women in the labor force will grow, but the number of women will grow at a faster rate than the number of men. The male labor force is projected to grow by 9.1 percent from 2004 to 2014, compared with 10.9 percent for women. As a result, men's share of the labor force is expected to decrease from 53.6 to 53.2 percent, while women's share is expected to increase from 46.4 to 46.8 percent. (http://www.bls.gov/oco/print/oco2003.htm)

19 http://www.washingtonpost.com/lifestyle/magazine/more-women-have-adhd--or-is-it-the-stress-of-modern-life/2011/04/08/AFx1Vo8E_story_2.html

20 http://www.justice.gov/dea/druginfo/concern_meth.shtml

21 http://www.justice.gov/dea/druginfo/concern_meth.shtml

CONCLUSION

By Way of the Family Dog

> Pets are family too! [...] Take good care of them. They'll love you forever.
> —Happy Paws ad (*O, The Oprah Magazine* 2007(October))

> [We] live in and through the use of one another's bodies.
> —Donna Haraway (2008: 79)

> At Pfizer we understand that dogs aren't just pets, they're members of the family.
> —animalhealth.pfizer.com

A discussion of the neoliberal American family and lifestyle drugs is incomplete without at least a bone thrown to the beloved family dog. As the Happy Paws ad above clearly indicates, "Pets are family too," and if the family takes "good care of them," the family pet will "love you forever." Rhetorically constructed as both a dog and a member of the family, our canine companions are increasingly diagnosed with the same mood and affective disorders and prescribed the same prescription pills as their human companions.

As with other lifestyle drugs discussed in this book, the promotional materials for doggie drugs reveal the proper affective behavior required of both canine and human. Similar to the discourse of lifestyle drugs for humans, the discourse of lifestyle drugs for canines also ignores altering the real and material conditions that cause the disorder. In the following, I offer a brief discussion of canine lifestyle drugs to illustrate that even the family dog is affected by life in neoliberal capitalism. Next, I discuss lifestyle drugs and their embedded relationship to work, and finally I answer the question that has been avoided throughout this book: Should drugs be viewed as good or as bad?

Dogs, Drugs, and Desires

There is something quite interesting going on when the family pet shares the same affective disorder and the same prescription medication as its human companions. How are we to understand our family pet and its affective disorder in relation to our own? Let's begin with Eli Lilly's (2005) question posed in the "Depression Hurts" commercial: "Who does depression hurt?" The answer:

"Everyone." An image of the family dog, with a tennis ball in its mouth, looking longingly at the camera, illuminates that the family dog is affected by its human companion's depression. This reveals that a person is responsible both for her depression and its affect on others, even the family dog. Significantly, this also reveals that dogs are depressed when their human companions are unable to play and engage with them. These issues, combined, inform us of the interrelationship between humans, companion dogs, and affective behaviors.

The rise in mood-altering medications for companion species for disorders such as depression, separation anxiety, compulsive disorder, and even obesity reveals that even the family dog is held to a particular affective standard (Vlahos 2008). This is not surprising as the companionship between humans and animals is co-constructed. Donna Haraway (2008) explains, "Relations are constitutive; dogs and people are emergent as historical beings, as subjects and objects to each other, precisely through the verbs of their relating" (62). A dog's subjectivity is constituted through its social relations to its human counterparts and its historical and cultural moment just as humans are. Family pet companions offer a view of the human family, including a glimpse of the affective attachments they desire.

Similar to the parents discussed in the previous chapter, a "pet-parent" (as the pet industry refers to them), is a good parent that desires his or her canine to be healthy, happy, well behaved, and socially accepted. And just as lifestyle drug advertisements for ADHD render visible the qualities that parents and children should embody, the discourses regarding canine health illuminate the proper and improper behavior of pet-parent and canine companion.

Take, for instance, the story of Max, a 3-year-old German shepherd. In a featured article in the *New York Times Magazine* aptly titled "Pill-Popping Pets," James Vlahos (2008) shares the story of Max and his pet-parents:

> Max fields tennis balls with his dexterous forelegs and can stand on his hindquarters to open the front door. He loves car rides and will leap inside any available auto, even one belonging to strangers. [...] "He's agile," Allan says. "He's healthy. He's a good-looking animal." Michelle adds, "We love him to death." That is why they had no choice, she says. The dog simply had to go on psychoactive drugs. (para 1)[1]

Max has a problem with his tail, sometimes chasing it and chewing on it "often for hours on end." Max's pet-parent describes Max as "a junkie needing a fix" (Vlahos 2008). Max's compulsive obsession with his tail landed Max a prescription of clomipramine, an antidepressant often prescribed to humans under the brand name Anafranil. Max's drug was renamed Clomicalm and meat flavoring was added to make it tastier for him and his canine peers. Clomicalm is approved for the treatment of separation anxiety, but in the case of Max, it was prescribed for its off-label use for the treatment of compulsive disorder (Vlahos 2008).

Max is not alone in receiving pharmaceutical care from his human family. An increasing number of pet owners feed their pets medicinal "treats." According to the American Pet Products Association (APPA), "77 percent of dog owners and 52 percent of cat owners" provided medication to their pets in 2006, which is an increase of 25 percent from 2004 (as cited in Vlahos 2008). The pet industry continues to grow despite a faltering economy. *Pet Product News* (March 17, 2011) reports, "The pet industry continues to perform as recession resistant." Figures from the APPA show that "overall spending in the pet industry grew by 6.2 percent from $45.53 billion in 2009 to $48.35 billion in 2010." Pet owners, like Max's owners, are willing to spend more on higher-end care for their family pet. With 46.3 million households caring for a canine pet, animal and companion care is a booming business (APPA Industry Statistics and Trends).[2]

According to the APPA, pet-parents "are willing to pay almost any price when it comes to caring for their pets" (APPA 2011). APPA president Bob Vetere explains that pet services are "growing at a fast rate because pet owners are treating their pets as they would their children. Highest quality nutrition, health care, and preventative maintenance for pets means they are living longer and happier lives" (*APPA* 2011). People are willing to spend more and more money on their family pet including spending on "products and services similar to those that humans enjoy" (Vetere, as cited in APPA 2011). Pet-parents are expected to spend over $50 billion for the care of their animal companions in 2011, which is a 5.1% increase from the previous year (APPA 2011). Vetere explains that the growth of the pet care industry is likened to that of the baby industry. "It seems many pets owners have accepted that their pets are like children," states Vetere (APPA 2011).

A Pfizer (2010) advertisement for vaccinations makes explicit the pet's relationship to the family. The ad features an image of an African American toddler in full color at the top right hand of the page. The text to the left of her reads:

> Working on vaccines for children. Pfizer is committed to improving health and well-being at every state of life. Today, there are many vaccine preventable causes of death worldwide in young children. That's why we're working tirelessly to bring vaccines to every child, giving them a shot at preventing life threatening infectious diseases. (Pfizer 2010)[3]

At the bottom of the left-hand corner is a black and white picture of a pug puppy. And the text to the right of this image reads:

> And those who act like them. Pfizer is working to keep every member of your family healthy. We discover and develop some of the leading vaccines and prescription medicines that help pets live longer and healthier lives. See how we're putting our commitments to work at Pfizer.com/vaccines. (Pfizer 2010)

And there it is. The pharmaceutical industry encourages consumers to think of their pets as another child in the family. And as many parents think of their pets as children, then the affect of their pets takes on a particular significance.

Doggie Prozac

"Has Your Dog's Behavior Changed Recently?" inquires the Elanco's website for its doggie Prozac, Reconcile. The text continues:

> It could be separation anxiety.
>
> You're getting complaints from the neighbors about his barking. He jumps on you when you walk through the door. You're cleaning up messes after a long day of work. Your new couch is in shreds. Your front door has been clawed to splinters.
>
> If this sounds like your dog, he or she might be suffering from a clinical condition called canine separation anxiety. When dogs become upset by their owners' absence, the stress can lead to abnormal behaviors. In fact, up to 17% of dogs in the U.S. may be affected by separation anxiety—and many of them go undiagnosed. But there's hope. (http://www.reconcile.com)[4]

From this brief blurb, the symptoms of separation anxiety become clearer: barking loud enough to for the neighbors to complain; jumping on you the moment you walk in the door; going to the bathroom indoors; tearing up the furniture and clawing at the door. These misbehaviors are clearly triggered by being left alone all day in the house. The Reconcile website does not suggest finding a companion for your dog while you are away or providing some outdoor space for your dog to romp in. Instead, it offers prescription medication as the answer to the pet's misbehaviors.

Similar to ADHD advertisements of mom and child discussed in the last chapter, the discourse of Reconcile's website couches the dog's behavior in a "relationship problem" between the pet-parent and the dog. Reconcile offers a way to "restore" the relationship between the pet-parent and the companion pet. According to the website, "With help from your veterinarian, you can restore your relationship with your dog" (www.reconcile.com). Just as with ADHD, once a child is treated, he or she will have better relationships with parents, peers, and siblings. Drugs are the means to restoring these relationships.

Unlike ADHD advertisements involving mom and child, Reconcile promises not only to restore this relationship, but also to relieve the pet-parent of any guilt for the dog's behavior. Reconcile's website addresses the concern of a pet-parent—"I wonder if he tears things up to get even with me. Maybe it's my fault"—with the following explanation:

> Dogs are social animals, and they naturally bond with family members in their household. When separated from their family, certain dogs can become extremely stressed. These dogs act out as a result of the fear and anxiety triggered by their separation from you. Many dog owners mistakenly assume these behaviors are a result of spite, disobedience or poor training. The important thing to remember is that your dog is suffering from a treatable medical condition.[5]

In this discourse, the pet-parent is relieved of any blame, but as with parents of children with ADHD, a pet-parent is a better parent if his or her pet-companion is being treated for its disorder. Once again, we see that the cause of separation anxiety—being alone for long stretches of time and reacting negatively to this solitude—is ignored while the negative behavior is rearticulated into a "treatable medical condition." The pet-parent is not viewed as the cause of the pet's affective disorder even if it is the pet-parent that leaves the dog alone for most of the day. No, the cause is rhetorically constructed as a medical condition that is readily treatable with a prescription antidepressant. Like the depressed women in Chapter 2, the dog's material conditions will not change. It will still be left alone for most of the day, locked up in a crate in the house. Although, once treated with prescription medication, the dog will not seem to mind as much.

Elanco the maker of Reconcile offers an online questionnaire to complete and share with your veterinarian. The questions include the following: "Does your dog…greet you excessively when you return home, even after a short separation? Become agitated or distressed when you prepare to leave? Display destructive behavior only when left alone? Exhibit any other behavior you find unacceptable or would like to change?" (http://www.reconcile.com/about-separation-anxiety/separation-anxiety-questionnaire.aspx). After completing the questionnaire the pet-parent can then print it out and take it to the veterinarian. Just as with other online questionnaires that help determine if you have a particular disorder, this questionnaire is provided so that you can present the behaviors that make your family pet a candidate for pharmaceutical intervention.

The questionnaire informs the reader how the pet should behave. The canine's responsibilities include the protection of the family, even if the canine is alone all day. The dog must be "happy" to see the family, without being riddled with anxiety when the family is away. The family dog must not do its business in the house, but should be housetrained. In short, the job of the family dog is to love the family unconditionally, while causing as little trouble as possible. Or else.

Advertisements for lifestyle drugs, even those for the family dog, once again suggest that by governing our affect appropriately, via lifestyle pharmaceuticals if need be, we are contributing to the "health" of the family. But the family dog reveals something else, too: the effect that life in contemporary capitalism has on all of us. Ironically, the family dog reminds us of our humanness, and like our favorite companion species, we desire sustained connection with and love from others. Negative and disruptive behaviors are a reasonable response to long hours of isolation and confinement. The family dog reveals to the family their affective failings and, therefore, their affective desires for love, safety, and connection with others.

The job of the family dog is to help reproduce the production of labor for the entire family. That is to say, the family dog's unyielding love and affection offer the family the affective relations that they need and desire in order to make life and work worthwhile. A happy pet means a well-adjusted family. The family dog is to be well behaved and loving. The family dog is directed to circulate its affect, not in order to garner more capital or potency for itself; rather, the family dog is to make the rest of the family happy through its performance of unconditional love and proper doggie behavior, regardless of the dog's own material conditions. The family dog should not display distress, anxiety, or depression nor remind family members of their own depression, anxiety, and feelings of precariousness.

The investment in the family dog is an investment in receiving the companionship that is desired from the family dog. Unfortunately, as with the other promotional materials of lifestyle drugs discussed in this book, the pet's material circumstances will not change even as its affective reaction to its material situation does. The pet-parent is not providing the pet more social interaction. In fact, the pet-parent may now be able to provide the pet even less social interaction with less guilt. The only change is that the pet is medicated and the medication works to effectively reduce the natural response that the dog feels in relation to its home life in neoliberal capitalism. Therefore, the family canine companion has its own affective labor to perform and it is required to perform it adequately.

The simple argument that I have been making throughout this book is that lifestyle drugs assist each member of the family in their "work" within neoliberal capitalism. Using drugs to work or to be better workers or to have social capital in order to circulate more affectively is certainly not a new practice.

Affecting Work

Stimulants have long been used in assisting workers to produce the required affect for work. The use of stimulants to assist one through the workday conjures images of Herman Melville's (1853) novella *Bartleby the Scrivener: A Story of Wall Street. Bartleby* is the story of a law firm on Wall Street where Bartleby and his colleagues spend their days reproducing multiple copies of legal documents by hand in ink. Each character has his particular stimulant to propel him through the tedious and laborious task of producing copies by hand. Turkey relies on the noonday dinner and brandy to get through the afternoon, while Ginger Nut litters his desks with snacks and ginger cakes. Bartleby is the character who forgoes any stimulants to get him through the day; he is the character who eventually "prefers not to" do anything that is asked of him, who, in the end, dies. The moral of the tale suggests that, even today, each of us must work and do whatever it takes to keep working in order to survive, literally and figuratively. We each must embrace our "flexible survivor" instincts and the stimulants that accompany them.

More recently, corporations like Microsoft have recognized the benefits to employee productivity of offering free Starbucks coffee drinks to their employees. This not only raises morale and improves relations between management and employees, but also provides workers with the caffeine fix they need to make it through a long and potentially boring workday. As the Introduction pointed out, as uncertainty and precarity become increasingly prevalent, use of prescription drugs and other stimulants for depression and anxiety continue to rise.

The body always resurfaces to make its desires known, and drugs are one way in which we attempt to control our bodies, to modulate them to certain particular ends, and to increase their speeds or slow their intensities and to connect with others. The question that I have not yet truly answered is the question of value: Are drugs good or bad? I answer this question in two ways, first by quoting Foucault (1997) and then by quoting Deleuze and Guattari.

> We have to experience drugs. We have to do good drugs that can produce very intense pleasure. I think this Puritanism about drugs, which implies that you can either be for drugs or against drugs is mistaken. Drugs have now become a part of culture. Just as there is bad music and good music, there are bad drugs and good drugs. So we can't say we are "against" drugs any more than we can say we are "against" music. (Foucault 165–166)

The question of whether drugs are "good" or "bad" is the incorrect question to ask. Foucault was adept in noting that drugs are a part of culture and they have been for a long time; therefore, the question of whether they are good or bad is irrelevant as, of course, they are both. Some drugs keep us alive and other drugs get us through the day, which may in fact amount to the same thing as keeping us alive.

Deleuze and Guattari (1987) were adamantly against the addiction to drugs as productive of freedom. They noted that drugs may be used in the search for freedom and to perceive the imperceptible.

> It is our belief that the issue of drugs can be understood only at the level where desire directly invests perception, and perception becomes molecular at the same time as the imperceptible is perceived. Drugs then appear as the agent of this becoming. (283)

While drugs may be an agent to this becoming, Deleuze and Guattari were quick to argue that the addict is not liberated from himself:

> Drug addicts continually fall back into what they wanted to escape: a segmentarity all the more rigid for being marginal, a territorialization all the more artificial for being based on chemical substances, hallucinatory forms, and phantasy subjectifications. Drug addicts may be considered as precursors or experimenters who tirelessly blaze new paths of life, but their cautiousness lacks the foundation for caution. So they either join the legion of false heroes or follow the conformist path of a little death and a long fatigue. (285)

Deleuze and Guattari are skeptical of drugs and their ability to transform material conditions, while Foucault kept open the potential for drugs to offer new forms of pleasure. Drugs are a part of culture—from caffeine to Viagra—and I most certainly agree that they can bring pleasures, but their pleasure must be combined with others' pleasures in order to become engaged with the realm of political action. What matters is not so much being for or against drugs, but to examine how drugs are linked to other practices and processes, how, in other words, they find themselves attached to old and new ways of being and becoming. Drugs can make communication possible. The depressed person may find comfort if she has medication that helps her to go to work and to build social and communicative relationships. Through our relationships with others we can alter our material conditions to make life and work better in neoliberal capitalism. This is why the study of affect is vital: Collectivity, the combining with others and affecting each other to greater joy leads to greater power both individually and collectively.

What I have termed the affective state apparatus (ASA) and explained as the interconnections between already existing apparatuses merging in order to manage the population's affect. For instance, the United States has employed the use of stimulants in order to manage, modulate, and control populations as far back as the colonial practice of providing native populations with alcohol to induce cooperation (Mancall 1995). In *Lifestyle Drugs and the Neoliberal Family*, I argued that there is an emergent state apparatus that works through the capture and constitution of our affect. Unlike in the past, the ASA normalizes the use of drugs across a large section of the population, as was demonstrated by the familial structure of this project. The ASA deploys drugs less as an incentive for work or as a cultural reward to reproduce the conditions of work; rather, drugs are used to make working possible. The drugs that traverse the ASA are given authoritative sanction by medical experts, social workers, the state, the school, and even the family. Drugs are no longer contingent options; they are increasingly regarded as necessary ingredients of everyday life.

In the first chapter, I argued that the government is indeed concerned with capturing and modulating our affect through existing state apparatuses. I extended Louis Althusser's conception of the ideological state apparatus to offer the concept of an affective state apparatus. An ASA differs from an ideological state apparatus by working less on the representational terrain of subjectivity and more on the biopolitical of the body. The ASA is concerned with regulating and modulating the mood and affect of a population. By explicating *Achieving the Promise: Transforming Mental Health Care in America,* I illustrated how a complex network of family, friends, coworkers, and service providers are pulled together to care for the mental health of all. A key component of this new initiative for mental health is the increasingly important role that drugs will play in the care of the self.

In the second chapter, I explored how psychotropic medications that alter one's affect, labor, and social relations function and cooperate to produce more effective, productive subjects. The movement of white married women after World War II from nonpaid work in the home to wage labor illuminated not only the change in labor from production to service-based industries, but also the ways in which women affected labor. The new workforce was a feminized labor force in which the skills necessary for work predominantly included affective and immaterial labor skills.

Alongside the shifting and unstable economy, contingent and temporary work, along with contractual work and telecommuting, workers increasingly began to feel displaced, alienated, and depressed. In order to alleviate these anxieties, each epoch produced its own psychotropic medication to transform the unproductive affect into an affectively productive worker.

In the third chapter, I argued that affect gains its power through circulation, following the logic of capital and the capitalist that must continually throw himself into circulation. Through a critical reading of Pfizer's commercials and promotional materials for Viagra, the importance of circulation was made apparent. Affective and bodily circulation is necessary for the ASA to function, and in order to gain and maintain affective potency and social and economic power.

In the last chapter, I offered a critical reading of the film *Thumbsucker*, along with advertisements for ADHD, to make explicit the link between communication, affect, and labor. Moreover, the construction of investing in children's affective disorders as an investment in their "abilities-machines" was made apparent. And finally, the subject position that mothers encounter in ADHD discourse suggests that the best way to be a good parent is to medicate both the child and oneself.

In this Conclusion, mood disorders and their medication for the family dog illuminate the extensive arm of the affective state apparatus. The family dog is rhetorically constructed as a member of the family and, as such, is diagnosed with similar disorders as the family and prescribed the same pharmaceuticals. Most important, lifestyle drugs targeting the family dog reveal that dogs too are required to perform a particular affect that coincides with neoliberal capitalism. The dog's affective labor includes offering love, companionship, safety, and joy to the family. The family invests in the dog's affective health as an investment in their own.

We "live in and through the use of one another's bodies" (79) as Haraway (2008) states. It is most pertinent to remember this as we continue to negotiate life and work and family in neoliberal capitalism. If we need to use drugs to get through the day, to become better workers, to invest in ourselves and our children's abilities for a more economically secure future, may we also use them to garner collective joy and power, to come together to make life and work less precarious and more pleasurable.

Notes

1 http://www.nytimes.com/2008/07/13/magazine/13pets-t.html?pagewanted=all
2 http://www.americanpetproducts.org/press_industrytrends.asp
3 Pfizer was accused of harming and killing Nigerian children in a 1996 drug trial for an experimental meningitis drug. In 2009 Pfizer settled for $35 million. Four families each received $175,000 for the lost of their child (see McNeil 2011, August 11) (http://www.nytimes.com/2011/08/12/world/africa/12nigeria. html).
4 http://www.reconcile.com/
5 http://www.reconcile.com/about-separation-anxiety/default.aspx

WORKS CITED

Adkins, L., & Jokinen, E. (2008, September). Introduction: Gender, living and labour in the fourth shift. *NORA—Nordic Journal of Feminist and Gender Research*, 16(3), 138–149.

Adult ADHD prescription volume doubles. (2006, Spring). Adult ADHD: Issues and Answers. Retrieved from http://www.med.nyu.edu/psych/psychiatrist/adult adhdnewsletter.html.

Advertising Age (2011, September 5). Late news. Retrieved from http://adage.com/article/late-news/late-news/104442/.

"affective, adj.". OED Online. (September 2012). Oxford University Press. http://www.oed.com/view/Entry/3357?isAdvanced=false&result=1&rskey=Rmy2o X&.

Agamben, G. (2000). *Means without end: Notes on politics* (V. Binetti & C. Casarino, Trans.). Minneapolis: University of Minnesota Press.

Ahmed, S. (2004, Summer). Affective economies. *Social Text*, 22(279), 117–139.

Akinbami, L. J., et al. (2011). Attention deficit hyperactivity disorder among children aged 5–17 years in the United States, 1998–2009. NCHS data brief. 70.

Albin, P., & Applebaum, E. (1988). The computer-rationalization of work implications for women workers. In J. Jenson et al. (Eds.), *Feminization of the labor force: Paradoxes and promises*. New York: Oxford University Press, 137–152.

Aleccia, J. (2011, April 14). Shortage of ADHD drugs sends parents scrambling: Manufacturing delays, heavy demand for Adderall, Ritalin could have serious consequences. nbcnews.com. Retrieved from http://www.today.com/id/42577775/ns/health-kids_and_parenting/#.USTnCugyFCU.

Althusser, L. (1969). *For Marx* (B. Brewster, Trans.). New York: Pantheon Books.

Althusser, L. (1971a). Freud and Lacan. In L. Althusser, *Lenin and philosophy, and other essays* (B. Brewster, Trans.). New York: Monthly Review Press, 195–219.

Althusser, L. (1971b). Ideology and ideological state apparatuses (notes towards an investigation). In L. Althusser, *Lenin and philosophy, and other essays* (B. Brewster, Trans.). New York: Monthly Review Press, 127–186.

ALZA Corporation. (2009, May). ADHD runs in families. Attention deficit hyperactivity disorder: Concerta. Titusville, NJ: Ortho-McNeil-Janssen Pharmaceuticals, Inc.

ALZA Corporation. (2010, June). Does your child frequently have trouble focusing or getting organized? It could be ADHD: Concerta. Titusville, NJ: Ortho-McNeil-Janssen Pharmaceuticals, Inc.

American Pet Products Association (APPA). (n.d.). Industry statistics and trends: Pet ownership. American Pet Products Association. Retrieved from http://www.americanpetproducts.org/press_industrytrends.asp.

American Pet Products Association (APPA). (2011, March 17). Pet industry spending expected to exceed $50 billion in 2011. American Pet Products Association. Retrieved from http://media.americanpetproducts.org/press.php?include=142817.

American Psychiatric Association. (2010a, February 2). DSM-5: Options being considered for ADHD, 1–9. Retrieved from http://www.dsm5.org.

American Psychiatric Association. (2010b). Major depressive episode. Retrieved from http://www.psych.org.

American Psychiatric Association. (2010c). Mood disorders. Retrieved from http://www.dsm5.org.

American Psychiatric Association. (1994). *Diagnostic and statistical manual of mental disorders: DSM-IV*. Washington, DC: American Psychiatric Association.

American Psychiatric Association and American Psychiatric Association Task Force on DSM-IV. (2000). *Diagnostic and statistical manual of mental disorders: DSM-IV-TR*. Washington, DC: American Psychiatric Association.

American Psychiatric Association. (1980). *Diagnostic and statistical manual of mental disorders III (DSM III)*. Washington, DC: American Psychiatric Association.

American Psychiatric Association, Committee on Nomenclature and Statistics. (1968). *Diagnostic and statistical manual of mental disorders (DSM II)*. Washington, DC: American Psychiatric Association.

American Psychiatric Association, Committee on Nomenclature and Statistics, and National Conference on Medical Nomenclature (U.S.). (1952). *Diagnostic and statistical manual [for] mental disorders*. Washington, DC: American Psychiatric Association Mental Hospital Service.

American Psychiatric Association, Task Force on Nomenclature and Statistics, and Committee on Nomenclature and Statistics. (1980). *Diagnostic and statistical manual of mental disorders (DSM III)*. Washington, DC, American Psychiatric Association.

American Psychological Association. (2002, July 23). American Psychological Association applauds final report of President's New Freedom Commission on Mental Health. Retrieved from http://www.apa.org/release/mentalhealth_rpt.html.

Anderson, S. (2009, May 17). In defense of distraction; Twitter, Adderall, lifehacking, mindful jogging, power browsing, Obama's BlackBerry, and the benefits of overstimulation. *New York Magazine*. Retrieved from http://nymag.com/news/features/56793/.

Angell, M. (2004). *The truth about the drug companies: How they deceive us and what to do about it*. New York: Random House.

Aydemir, M. (2007). *Images of bliss: Ejaculation, masculinity, meaning*. Minneapolis: University of Minnesota Press.

Berrios, G.E. (1985). The psychopathology of affectivity: Conceptual and historical aspects. *Psychological Medicine*, 15(4), 745–758.

Baglia, J. (2005). *The Viagra ad venture: Masculinity, marketing, and the performance of sexual health.* New York: Peter Lang.

Baird, J., Stevenson, J.C., & Williams, D.C. (2000). The evolution of ADHD: A disorder of communication? *The Quarterly Review of Biology*, 75(1), 17–35.

Barkley, R.A. (2006). Fact sheet: Attention deficit hyperactivity disorder (ADHD) topics. In *Attention deficit hyperactivity disorder: A clinical workbook* (3rd ed.). Retrieved from http://www.russellbarkley.org/adhd-facts.htm.

Bartlett, T. (2010, June 11). How to fake ADHD [Web log post]. *The Chronicle of Higher Education.* Retrieved from http://chronicle.com/blogs.

Baudrillard, J. (1994). *Simulacra and simulation* (S. F. Glaser, Trans.). Ann Arbor: The University of Michigan Press.

Beckett, S. (1958). *Three novels: "Molloy," "Malone Dies," "The Unnamable"* (P. Bowles, Trans.). New York: Grove Press, 24–25.

Blackwelder, J.K. (1997). *Now hiring: The feminization of work in the United States, 1900–1995.* College Station: Texas A&M University Press.

Blum, L.M., & Stracuzzi, N.F. (2004). Gender in the Prozac nation: Popular discourse and productive femininity. *Gender & Society*, 18, 269–286.

Boodman, S.G. (2006, July 18). *Daily life: Finally getting some attention.* St. Paul, MN: St. Paul Pioneer Press, pp. 1E, 3E.

Bordo, S. (2000). *The male body: A new look at men in public and in private.* New York: Farrar, Straus & Giroux.

Bousquet, M. (2008, September 14). Ritalin generation 1 [Web log post]. *The Chronicle of Higher Education.* Retrieved from http://chronicle.com/blogs.

Bristol-Myers Squibb. (2009a, June). *Getting started with Abilify as an add-on therapy for depression: A patient guide.* Rockville, MD: Otsuka America Pharmaceutical, Inc.

Bristol-Myers Squibb. (2009b, June). *Talking to your healthcare professional.* Rockville, MD: Otsuka America Pharmaceutical, Inc. (SEE UNDER OTSUKA, BELOW, FOR MAGAZINE ADS).

Brown, W. (2003). Neo-liberalism and the end of liberal democracy. *Theory & Event*, 7(1).

Burnett, M., & Trump, D. (Producers). (2004). *The Apprentice* [Television series]. New York: NBC.

Butler, J. (1997a). *Excitable speech: A politics of the performative.* London, England: Routledge.

Butler, J. (1997b). *The psychic life of power: Theories in subjection.* Stanford, CA: Stanford University Press.

Centers for Disease Control and Prevention. (2010). Increasing prevalence of parent-reported attention-deficit/hyperactivity disorder among children—United States, 2003 and 2007. *Morbidity and Mortality Weekly Report*, 59(44), 1439–1443. Retrieved from http://www.cdc.gov/mmwr.

Cevallos, M. (2011, April 20). Most popular drugs in America and how much we spend on medication. *Los Angeles Times*. Retrieved from http://latimes.com.

Charland, M. (1987). Constitutive rhetoric: The case of the "peuple Québécois." *Quarterly Journal of Speech*, 73, 133–150.

Choi, S.M., & Lee,W. (2007). Understanding the impact of direct-to-consumer (DTC) pharmaceutical advertising on patient-physician interactions: Adding the web to the mix. *Journal of Advertising,* 36(3), 137–149.

Clarke, A.E., et al. (2003, April). Biomedicalization: Technoscientific transformations of health, illness, and U.S. biomedicine. *American Sociological Review*, 68(2), 161–194.

Cline, R.J.W., & Young, H.N. (2005). Direct-to-consumer print ads for drugs: Do they undermine the physician-patient relationship? *The Journal of Family Practice*, 54(12), 1049–1057.

Clough, P.T. (2007). Introduction. In P. T. Clough with Halley, J. (Eds.),*The affective turn: Theorizing the social*. Durham, NC: Duke University Press, 1–33.

Conrad, P. (2005, March). The shifting engines of medicalization. *Journal of Health and Social Behavior*, 46(1), 3–14.

Conrad, P., & Potter, D. (2000). From hyperactive children to ADHD adults: Observations of the expansion of medical categories. *Social Problems*, 47(4), 559–582.

Copjec, J. (2006). May '68, the emotional month. In S. Žižek (Ed.), *Lacan: The silent partners*. New York: Verso, 90–114.

Coy, P., Conlin, M., & Herbst, M. (2010, January 18). The disposable worker. *Bloomberg Businessweek*, 33–39.

Daly, R. (2005, December 16). APA says bill biased against MH treatment. *Psychiatry News,* 40(10).

Deem, M. (1999). Scandal, heteronomative culture, and the disciplining of feminism. *Critical Studies in Mass Communication*, 16(1), 86–93.

Deleuze, G. (1988). *Spinoza: Practical philosophy* (R. Hurley, Trans.). San Francisco: City Lights Books.

Deleuze, G. (1990). *Expressionism in philosophy: Spinoza* (M. Joughin, Trans.). Brooklyn, NY: Zone Books.

Deleuze, G. (1995). Postscript on control societies. In *Negotiations, 1972–1990,* (M. Joughin, Trans). New York: Columbia University Press, 177–182.

Deleuze, G., & Guattari, F. (1987). *A thousand plateaus: Capitalism and schizophrenia* (B. Massumi, Trans.). Minneapolis: University of Minnesota Press.

Depression, stress account for most psychiatric claims. (2003, December 8). *Mental Health Weekly*, 13, 6.

Diller, L. H. (2002, transcript) President's council on bioethics: President's council on bioethics: Session 3: Prescription stimulant use in American children: ethical issues. Retrieved from http://biotech.law.lsu.edu/research/pbc/transcripts/dec02/session3.html.

Donohue, J. (2006). A history of drug advertising: The evolving roles of consumers and consumer protection. *The Milibank Quarterly*, 84(4), 659–699.

Donohue, J., Cevasco, J.M., & Rosenthal, M.B. (2007). A decade of direct-to-consumer advertising of prescription drugs. *New England Journal of Medicine*, 357(7), 35–43.

DTC reminder ads axed under PhRMA code; Lawmakers may still seek legislative vix (2005, August 8). *Washington Drug Letter*, 37(31).

Edwards, J. (2010). Viagra, like its fans, faces old age. *Brandweek*, 51(23), 23–24.

Ehrenreich, B. (1990). *Fear of falling: The inner life of the middle class.* New York: Harper Collins.

Eli Lilly. (2003). Prozac. Retrieved from http://www.prozac.com.

Eli Lilly (2005, December). "Depression hurts" [Broadcast Commercial]. Retrieved from http://www.adforum.com/creative-work/ad/player/57679/sxi:2766192.

Eli Lilly. (2008, August). [Advertisement for Cymbalta]. *Real Simple.*

Eli Lilly. (2010, December). [Advertisement for Cymbalta]. *Good Housekeeping.*

Eli Lilly. (2011, August). [Advertisement for Cymbalta]. *Psychology Today.*

Elliott, C. (2003). *Better than well: American medicine meets the American dream.* New York: Norton.

Emanuel, E. J. (2011, August 6). Shortchanging cancer patients [Opinion]. *New York Times.* Retrieved from http://www.nytimes.com/2011/08/07/opinion/sunday/ezekiel-emanuel-cancer-patients.html/.

Feeley, J., & Kresge, N. (2012, July 31). Bayer's Yazmin lawsuit settlements rise to $402.6 million. *Bloomberg Businessweek.* Retrieved from http://www.businessweek.com/news/2012-07-31/bayer-s-yasmin-lawsuit-settlements-rise-to-402-dot-6-million.

Fink, B. (2004). *Lacan to the letter: Reading "Écrits"* closely. Minneapolis: University of Minnesota Press.

Fishman, J.R., & Mamo, L. (2001). What's in a disorder: A cultural analysis of medical and pharmaceutical constructions of male and female sexual dysfunction. In E. Kaschak & L. Tiefer (Eds.), *A new view of women's sexual problems.* Philadelphia: Haworth Press, 179–193.

Foreclosures (2012 Robosigning and mortgage servicing settlement). *New York Times*. Retrieved from http://topics.nytimes.com/top/reference/timestopics/subjects/f/foreclosures/index.html.

Foucault, M. (1990). *The history of sexuality: An introduction.* New York: Vintage Books.

Foucault, M. (1991). Governmentality. In G. Burchell, C. Gordon, & P. Miller (Eds.), *The Foucault effect: Studies in governmentality*. Chicago: University of Chicago Press, 87–104, 93.

Foucault, M. (1997). Sex, power, and the politics of identity. In *Ethics: subjectivity and truth* (P. Rabinow, Ed.). New York: The New Press, 164–173.

Foucault, M. (1995). *Discipline and punish: The birth of the prison* (A. Sheridan, Trans.). New York: Vintage Books, 178.

Foucault, M. (2008). *The birth of biopolitics: Lectures at the Collège de France, 1978–79* (G. Burchell, Trans.). New York: Palgrave Macmillan.

Foucault, M., et al. (1988). *Technologies of the self: A seminar with Michel Foucault*. Amherst: University of Massachusetts Press.

Fraser, M. (2001). The nature of Prozac. *History of the Human Sciences*, 14(3), 56–84.

Freking, K. (2005, May 28). Medicare test gauges prescription subsidy: In 14 states, impotence drug prescriptions given to sex offenders. *Associated Press Online.* http://jacksonville.com/tu-online/apnews/stories/052805/D8AC9SOG0.shtml.

Freking, K. (2005, May 29). Sex offenders get Medicaid-paid Viagra. *Associated Press Online*. Retrieved from: http://www.apnewsarchive.com/2005/Sex-Offenders-Get-Medicaid-Paid-Viagra/id-f1cb40a055d30464af7d9219cef871fd?SearchText=sex%20offenders%20viagra;Display.

Freud, S. (1963). *General psychological theory: Papers on metapsychology* (P. Reiff, Ed.). New York: Collier Books.

Front matter. (1995, Autumn–Winter). *Social Text*, 44.

Fudge, J., & R. Owens (2006). Precarious work, women, and the new economy: The challenge to legal norms. In J. Fudge & R. Owens (Eds.), *Precarious work, women, and the new economy: The challenge to legal norms*. Portland, OR: Hart, 1–27.

Fullagar, S. (2009). Negotiating the neurochemical self: Anti-depressant consumption in women's recovery from depression. *Health*, 13(4), 389–406.

Fumento, M. (2003, February 3). Trick question: A liberal hoax turns out to be true. *New Republic*, 228(4). Retrieved from www.lexisnexis.com/hottopics/lnacademic.

Gagnon, M.-A., & Lexchin, J. (2008). The cost of pushing pills: A new estimate of pharmaceutical promotion expenditures in the United States. *PLoS Med*, 5(1), e1.

Galatzer-Levy, I.R., & Galatzer-Levy, R.M. (2007). The revolution in psychiatric diagnosis: Problems at the foundations. *Perspectives in Biology and Medicine*, 50(2), 161–180.

Gardner, P. (2000). Necessary contradictory discourses: Psychology as expert and cultural negotiator in 2000. *International Journal of Critical Psychology*, 1(1), 130–134.

Gardner, P. (2003). Distorted packaging: Marking depression as illness, drugs as cure. *Journal of Medical Humanities*, 24(1), 105–130.

Gardner, P. (2007). Re-gendering depression: Risk, web health campaigns, and the feminized pharmaco-subject. *Canadian Journal of Communication*, 32, 537–555.

Gardner, P., Metzl, J.M., & Lewis, B.E. (2003). Introduction. *Journal of Medical Humanities*, 24(1), 3–7.

General Motors (2007, February 4) Robot [Commercial] Aired during the 2007 Super Bowl on CBS.

Gibson-Graham, J. K., Resnick, S. A., & Wolff, R. D. (2000). Introduction: Class in a poststructuralist frame. In J. K. Gibson-Graham et al. (Eds.) *Class and its others*. Minneapolis: University of Minnesota, 1–22.

Gill, R. (2010, March 4). Employment, but without benefits [Review of the book *Nice work if you can get it: Life and labor in precarious times*, by A. Ross]. *Times Higher Education* (London, England).

Gill, R., & Pratt, A. (2008). In the social factory?: Immaterial labour, precariousness and cultural work. *Theory, Culture & Society*, 25(7–8), 1–30.

Gladwell, M. (1999, February 15). A critic at large: Running from Ritalin. *The New Yorker*, 80–84.

Glass, L. (2001). After the phallus. *American Imago*, 58(2), 545–566.

GlaxoSmithKline. (2004). [Advertisement for Paxil CR]. *U.S. News and World Report*.

Goldman, R., & Montagne, M. (1986). Marketing 'mind mechanics': Decoding drug advertisements in medical journals. *Social Science and Medicine*, 22(10), 1047–1058.

Goldman, H.H., Buck, J., & Thompson, K. (2009). *Transforming mental health services: Implementing the federal agenda for change*. Arlington, VA: American Psychiatric Publishing.

Goldstein, S. (2006). Is ADHD a growth industry? *Journal of Attention Disorders*, 9(3), 461–464.

Goleman, D. (1992, December 8). A rising cost of modernity: Depression. *New York Times*, p. C1.

Goodman, D.W. (2007, September). The consequences of attention-deficit/hyperactivity disorder in adults. *Journal of Psychiatric Practice*, 13(5), 318–327.

Gould, S.R., Roberts, M.C., & Beals, S.E. (2009). Do state mental health plans address the New Freedom Commission's goals for children's mental health? *Clinical Child Psychology Review*, 12, 295–309, 296.

Greene, R.W. (2004). Rhetoric and capitalism: Rhetorical agency as communicative labor. *Philosophy and Rhetoric*, 37(3), 188–206.

Gregg, M. (2008). The normalization of flexible female labour in the information economy. *Feminist Media Studies*, 8(3), 285–299.

Gregg, M. (2009). Learning to (love) labour: Production cultures and affective turn. *Communication and Critical/Cultural Studies*, 6, 209–214.

Gregg, M. (2010). On Friday night drinks. In M. Gregg & G. J. Seigworth (Eds.), *The affect theory reader*. Durham, NC: Duke University Press, 250–268.

Grossberg, L. (2003). Cultural studies, the war against kids, and the re-becoming of US modernity. *Postcolonial Studies*, 6(3), 327–349.

Grossberg, L. (2005). *Caught in the crossfire: Kids, politics, and America's future.* Boulder, CO: Paradigm.

Gu, Q., Dillon, C. F., & Burt, V. L. (2010). Prescription drug use continues to increase: U.S. prescription drug data for 2007–2008. NCHS data brief, no 42. Hyattsville, MD: National Center for Health Statistics.

Gupta, S. (2001). *Corporate capitalism and political philosophy*. London: Pluto.

Hallowell, E. M., & Ratey, J.J. (1995). *Driven to distraction*. New York: Touchstone.

Hancock, L. (1996, March 18). Mother's little helper. *Newsweek*, 127(12), 50. Retrieved from http://www.thedailybeast.com/newsweek/1996/03/17/mother-s-little-helper.html.

Hansen, R.S., & Hansen, K. (n.d.). What do employers really want? Top skills and values employers seek from job-seekers. Retrieved from http://quintcareers.com/job_skills_values.html.

Haraway, D.J. (1991). *Simians, cyborgs, and women: The reinvention of nature.* New York: Routledge.

Haraway, D. J. (2003). *The companion species manifesto: Dogs, people, and significant otherness.* Chicago: Prickly Paradigm Press.

Haraway, D.J. (2008). *When species meet*. Minneapolis: University of Minnesota Press.

Hardt, M. (1999, Summer). Affective labor. *Boundary* 2, 26(2), 89–100.

Hardt, M., & Negri, A. (2000). *Empire*. Cambridge, MA: Harvard University Press.

Hardt, M., & Negri, A. (2004). *Multitude: War and democracy in the age of empire.* New York: Penguin Press.

Harris, G. (2004, February 28). Pfizer gives up testing Viagra on women. *New York Times*, C 1.

Harris, G. (2011, December 31). F.D.A. finds short supply of attention deficit drugs. *New York Times.* Retrieved from http://www.nytimes.com/2012/01/01/health/policy/fda-is-finding-attention-drugs-in-short-supply.html?pagewanted=all&_r=0.

Harris, G. (2012, February 21). Shipments from abroad to help ease shortage of two cancer drugs. *New York Times.* Retrieved from http://www.nytimes.com/2012/02/22/health/policy/fda-approves-imports-amid-shortage-of-2-cancer-drugs.html?_r=0.

Hartley, H., & Tiefer, L. (2003). Taking a biological turn: The push for a "female Viagra" and the medicalization of women's sexual problems. *Women's Studies Quarterly*, 31(1/2), 42–54.

Harvey, D. (2005). *A brief history of neoliberalism.* New York: Oxford University Press.

Hatch, J., & Clinton, A. (2000, December). Job growth in the 1990s: A retrospect. *Monthly Labor Review*, 3–18.

Henry J. Kaiser, Foundation (2003, June). Impact of direct-to-consumer advertising on prescription drug spending (#6084). Retrieved from http://www.kff.org.

Herr, S. (2010, August 19). ADHD: Has this diagnostic fad run its course? *Christian Science Monitor.* Retrieved from www.lexisnexis.com/hottopics/lnacademic.

Herzberg, D. (2009). *Happy pills in America: From Miltown to Prozac.* Baltimore: Johns Hopkins University Press.

Hesse-Biber, S., & Carter, G.L. (2000). *Working women in America: Split dreams.* New York: Oxford University Press.

Higher Education Research Institute. (2011, January 26). Incoming college students rate emotional health at record low, annual survey finds [Press release]. Retrieved from http://newsroom.ucla.edu/portal/ucla/incoming-college-students-self-191135.aspx.

Higher Education Research Institute at UCLA. (2011, January). The American freshman: National norms Fall 2010 [Research brief]. Los Angeles, CA. Retrieved from http://heri.ucla.edu/pr-display.php?prQry=55.

Hogan, M.F., et al. (2003, July). Achieving the promise: Transforming mental health care in America (final report). Retrieved from http://govinfo.library.unt.edu/mentalhealthcommission/reports/FinalReport/downloads/downloads.html.

Holden, A., & Elden, S. (2005). "'It cannot be a real person, a concrete individual": Althusser and Foucault on Machiavelli's political technique. *Borderlands*, 4(2), e-journal. Retrieved from http://www.borderlands.net.au/vol4no2_2005/eldenhold_foucault.htm

Horvitz, L.A. (1997a). Aging America is big business. *Insight on the News*, 13(45), 38.

Horvitz, L.A. (1997b). Can better sex come in a pill? The nineties' impotence cure. *Insight on the News*, 13(46), 38.

Huang, L., et al. (2005, September). Transforming mental health care for children and their families. *American Psychologist*, 60(6), 615–627.

IMS HEALTH. (2011, April 7). Top therapeutic classes by prescriptions. In IMS National Prescription Audit PLUS. Retrieved from http://www.imshealth.com/portal/site/ims/template.MAXIMIZE/menuitem.6bf189b8c787e60c57b429973208c22a?javax.portlet.prp_8786a91d2ae4940c57b429973208c22a_viewID=merged_results&beanID=1821718402&search=search&additionalParam=&qt=Top+therapeutic+classes+by+Rx&UserSearchRequired=Top+therapeutic+classes+by+Rx#.

IMS Institute for Healthcare Informatics. (2011, April). The use of medicines in the United States: Review of 2010. Retrieved from www.imshealth.com/deployedfiles/.../IHII_UseOfMed_report.pdf.

Jameson, F. (2004). Symptoms of theory or symptoms for theory? *Critical Inquiry*, 30, 403–409.

Janssen Pharmaceuticals. (2008, September). Book report [Advertisement for Concerta]. *Better Homes and Gardens*.

Janssen Pharmaceuticals. (2009a, May). Summer [Advertisement for Concerta]. *Parents*.

Janssen Pharmaceuticals. (2009b, December). For the treatment of ADHD [Advertisement for Concerta]. *Better Homes and Gardens*.

Janssen Pharmaceuticals. (2010a, February). [Advertisement for Concerta]. *Better Homes and Gardens*.

Janssen Pharmaceuticals. (2010b, May). Kyle's mom [Advertisement for Concerta. *Parents*.

Janssen Pharmaceuticals. (2011a). ADHD medication safety. Retrieved from http://www.concerta.net/children/adhd-medication-safety-index.html.

Janssen Pharmaceuticals. (2011b). Concerta website. Retrieved from http://www.concerta.net.

Jarow, J., Kloner, R. A., & Holmes, A. M. (1998). *Viagra: How the miracle drug happened and what it can do for you!* New York: M. Evans.

Jenson, J., Hagen, E., & Reddy, C. (1988). *Feminization of the labor force: Paradoxes and promises*. New York: Oxford University Press.

Jenson, J., Laufer, J., & Maruani, M. (2000). *The gendering of inequalities: Women, men and work*. Aldershot, England: Ashgate.

Jhally, S. (2003). Image-based culture: Advertising and popular culture. In G. Dines & J. M. Humez (Eds.), *Gender, race, and class in media: A text-reader* (2nd ed.). Thousand Oaks, CA: Sage, 249–257.

Johnson, D. (2008). Psychiatric power: The post-museum as a site of rhetorical alignment. *Communication and Critical/Cultural Studies*, 5, 344–362.

Kass, L.R., et al. (2003, October 15). Beyond therapy: Biotechnology and the pursuit of happiness (A report to the President's Council on Bioethics). Retrieved from http://www.bioethics.gov/reports/beyondtherapy/.

Katz, S. (1996). *Disciplining old age: The formation of gerontological knowledge.* Charlottesville: University of Virginia Press.

Kirschner, S.R. (1999). From flexible bodies to fluid minds: An interview with Emily Martin. *Ethos*, 27(3), 247–282.

Kivimäki, R. (2004). In search of boundaries: Changing boundaries in and through teleworking. In Tuula Heiskanen & Jeff Hearn (Eds.), *Information society and the workplace: Spaces, boundaries and agency*. London: Routledge, 178–192.

Kleinfeld, J. (1998). *The myth that schools shortchange girls: Social science in the service of deception.* Washington, DC: Women's Freedom Network.

Kordela, A.K. (2007). *$urplus: From Spinoza to Lacan*. Albany: SUNY Press.

Kramer, P.D. (1993). *Listening to Prozac*. New York: Viking.

Kristeva, J. (1989). *Black sun: Depression and melancholia* (L. S. Roudiez, Trans.). New York: Columbia University Press.

Lacan, J. (1998). *On feminine sexuality: The limits of love and knowledge* (B. Fink, Trans.). New York: Norton.

Lacan, J., & Fink, B. (2006). *Écrits: The first complete edition in English* (B. Fink, Trans.). New York: Norton.

Lamkin, M. (2011, February 27). A ban on brain-boosting drugs is not the answer. *The Chronicle of Higher Education.*

Laparra, M., Barbier, J., Darmon, Il, Dull, N., Frade, C., Frey, L., Lindley, R. & Volger-Ludwig, K. (2004). Managing labour market related risk in Europe: Policy implications. Report of the ESOPE Project.

Lazzarato, M. (1996). Immaterial labor (P. Colilli & E. Emory, Trans.). In P. Virno & M. Hardt (Eds.), *Radical thought in Italy: A potential politics.* Minneapolis: University of Minnesota Press, 133–150.

Lears, T. J. J. (1983). From salvation to self-realization: Advertising and the therapeutic roots of the consumer culture, 1880–1930. In R. W. Fox & T. J. J. Lears (Eds.), *The culture of consumption: Critical essays in American history.* New York: Pantheon, 1–38.

Leis, W., Kline, S., & Jhally, S. (1986). *Social communication in advertising: Persons, products and images of well-being.* Toronto, ON: Methuen.

Leland, J. (1998). Let's talk about sex. *Newsweek,* 132/133(26/1), 62.

Leland, J., & Murr, A. (1997). A pill for impotence? [Cover story]. *Newsweek,* 130(20), 62.

Lenzer, J. (2004a). Bush launches controversial mental health plan. *BMJ: British Medical Journal,* 329(7462), 367.

Lenzer, J. (2004b). Bush plans to screen whole US population for mental illness. *BMJ: British Medical Journal,* 328(7454), 1458.

Leo, J. (1999, February 22). Gender wars redux. *U.S. News and World Report,* p. 24.

Lewin, T. (2011, January 26). Record level of stress found in college freshmen. *New York Times.* Retrieved from http://www.nytimes.com/2011/01/27/education /27colleges.html.

Libbon, S.E. (2007). Pathologizing the female body: Phallocentrism in Western science. *Journal of International Women's Studies,* 8(4), 79–92.

Lipka, S. (2011, January 27). Economy changed freshmen's plans but didn't shake their confidence. *The Chronicle of Higher Education.* Retrieved from http://chronicle.com.

LiPuma, E., & Lee, B. (2004). *Financial derivatives and the globalization of risk.* Durham, NC: Duke University Press.

Loe, M. (2004). *The rise of Viagra: How the little blue pill changed sex in America.* New York: New York University Press.

Lloyd, G., Stead, J., & D. Cohen (2006). *Critical new perspectives on ADHD.* New York: Routledge.

Lloyd, J. (2011, October 19). Antidepressant use skyrockets 400% in two decades. *USA Today.* Retrieved from http://usatoday30.usatoday.com/NEWS/usaedition/ 2011-10-20-Anitdepressant-meds-_ST_U.htm.

Mamo, L., & Fishman, J.R. (2001). Potency in all the right places: Viagra as a technology of the gendered body. *Body & Society,* 7(4), 13–36.

Mancall, P.C. (1995). *Deadly medicine: Indians and alcohol in early America.* Ithaca, NY: Cornell University Press.

Martin, E. (1992). The end of the body? *American Ethnologist,* 19(1), 121–140.

Martin, E. (1994). *Flexible bodies: Tracking immunity in American culture from the days of polio to the age of AIDS.* Boston: Beacon Press.

Martin, E. (1995). Flexible bodies: Health and work in an age of systems. *The Ecologist,* 25, 221–226.

Martin, E. (2000). Flexible survivors. *Cultural Values,* 4, 512–517.

Martin, R. (2002). *Financialization of daily life.* Philadelphia: Temple University Press.

Marx, K. (1954). *Capital: A critique of political economy* (Vol. 1, F. Engels, Ed., S. Moore & E. Aveling, Trans.). New York: International.

Marx, K. (1964). *Early writings* (T.B. Bottomore, Trans.). New York: McGraw-Hill.

Marx, K. (1993). *Grundrisse: Foundations of the critique of a political economy* (M. Nicolaus, Trans.). New York: Penguin Classics.

Massumi, B. (1996). The autonomy of affect. In P. Patton (Ed.), *Deleuze: A critical reader*. Oxford: Blackwell, 217–239.

Massumi, B. (2002). *Parables for the virtual.* Durham, NC: Duke University Press.

Mayes, R., & Erkulwater, J. (2008). Medicating kids: Pediatric mental health policy and the tipping point for ADHD and stimulants. *Journal of Policy History,* 20(3), 309–343.

McDevitt, C. (2009, August 30). Depression and the recession: Cymbalta sales are on the rise. *Washington Post,* p. G2.

McDowell, L. (2008, September). The new economy, class condescension and caring labour: Changing formations of class and gender. *NORA—Nordic Journal of Feminist and Gender Research,* 16(3), 150–165.

McInnis, S.C. (2000, April). The political is personal or why have a revolution when you could be medicated. *Off Our Backs,* 30(4), 10–12.

McNeil Jr., Donald. (2011, August 11). Nigerians receive first payments for children who died in 1996 meningitis drug trial. *New York Times.* Retrieved from http://www.nytimes.com/2011/08/12/world/africa/12nigeria.html.

Mead, S. (2006, June). The evidence suggests otherwise: The truth about boys and girls. Retrieved from http://www.educationsector.org.

Medco Health Solutions. (2006, September 28). Family ties: Major research findings show strong familial link to attention deficit hyperactivity disorder (ADHD) [Press release]. Retrieved from http://medco.mediaroom.com.

Medco Health Solutions. (2006, March 21). New data shows adults continue to outpace children in growth of ADHD medication use [Press release]. Retrieved from http://medco.mediaroom.com.

Medco Health Solutions. (2005, September 15). New research: ADHD medication use growing faster among adults than children [Press release]. Retrieved from http://medco.mediaroom.com.

Melillo, W. (2005). Big pharma's Sisyphean task: drug co.'s work to fend off gov't regulation of DTC ads amid mounting criticism. *Adweek,* 46(44), 18–19.

Metzl, J.M. (2003). *Prozac on the couch: Prescribing gender in the era of wonder drugs.* Durham, NC: Duke University Press.

Miller, T. (1998). *Technologies of truth: Cultural citizenship and the popular media.* Minneapolis: University of Minnesota Press.

Miller, T. (2008). *Makeover nation: The United States of reinvention.* Columbus: The Ohio State University Press.

Montag, W. (2003). *Louis Althusser.* New York: Palgrave Macmillan, 66.

Morrow, D. J. (1998, June 7). Spending it: From lab to patient, by way of your den. *New York Times.* Retrieved from http://www.nytimes.com/1998/06/07/business/spending-it-from-lab-to-patient-by-way-of-your-den.html?pagewanted=all&src=pm.

Moynihan, R., & Cassels, A. (2005). *Selling sickness: How the world's biggest pharmaceutical companies are turning us all into patients.* Vancouver, BC: Greystone Books.

Nadesan, M.H. (2010). *Governing childhood into the 21st century: Biopolitical technologies of childhood management and education.* New York: Palgrave Macmillan.

National Association of Colleges and Employers (NACE). (2010, December 2). Top skills for job candidates. Retrieved from http://www.naceweb.org/Press/Releases.

National Association of Colleges and Employers (NACE). (2011, April). Job outlook 2011: Spring update. Retrieved from www.naceweb.org.

National Institute of Mental Health. (2006, April 1). ADHD medication use held steady in recent years. Retrieved from http://www.nimh.nih.gov.

National Institute of Mental Health. (2009, April 27). ADHD medication treatment associated with higher academic performance in elementary school. Retrieved from http://www.nimh.nih.gov.

National Manpower Council (1957). *Womanpower; a statement, with chapters by the council staff.* New York: Columbia University Press.

National Manpower Council. (1958). *Work in the lives of married women: Proceedings of a conference on womanpower.* New York: Columbia University Press.

Negri, A. (1991). Marx beyond Marx: Lessons on the *Grundrisse* (J. Fleming, Ed.). (H. Cleaver, M. Ryan, & M. Viano, Trans.). Brooklyn, NY: Autonomia.

Negri, A. (1992). Twenty theses on Marx: Interpretation of the class situation today (M. Hardt, Trans.). *Polygraph,* 5, 136–170.

Newman, R. (2006, Spring). "Let's just say it works for me": Rafael Palmeiro, major league baseball, and the marketing of Viagra. *NINE: A Journal of Baseball History and Culture,* 14(2), 1–14.

New Zealand to ban DTC advertising by '06 [Electronic version]. (2005, September 5). Advertising Age, 1. Retrieved from LexisNexis database.

Nichols, K. (2004, December 17). The other performance-enhancing drugs. *The Chronicle of Higher Education,* p. 41.

Nietzsche, F.W. (1996). *On the genealogy of morals: A polemic: by way of clarification and supplement to my last book, Beyond good and evil* (D. Smith, Ed.). New York: Oxford University Press. (Original work published 1887).

Novak, V. (2001, September 10). New Ritalin ad blitz makes parents jumpy. *Time Magazine*. Retrieved from: http://www.time.com/time/magazine/article/0,9171,10 00718-1,00.html.

OECD. (2001). Knowledge, work organisation, and economic growth. Paris: DEELSA/ELSA, 2.

OECD Centre for Educational Research and Innovation. (2001). "Competencies for the knowledge economy." In Science, technology and industry outlook. In *Education Policy Analysis 2001*, Retrieved from www.oecd.org/dataoecd/42/25/ 1842070.pdf.

Osterweil, N. (1998). *Beyond Viagra: Drugs, devices and markets*. London: FT Healthcare.

Otsuka/Bristol-Myers Squibb. (2010, February). [Advertisement for Abilify]. *Better Homes and Gardens.*

Otsuka/Bristol-Myers Squibb. (2010, August). [Advertisement for Abilify]. *Parents.*

Otsuka/Bristol-Myers Squibb. (2010, October). [Advertisement for Abilify]. *Better Homes and Gardens.*

Otsuka/Bristol-Myers Squibb. (2011, July/August). [Advertisement for Abilify]. *Health.*

Ovalle, P. P. (2008, October 30). Viva viagra! Or, how race dances around erectile dysfunction. *Flow TV*, Retrieved from http://flowtv.org/2008/10/viva-viagra-or-how-race-dances-around-erectile-dysfunction-priscilla-pena-ovalle-university-of-oregon/#.

Oxford English dictionary. (1989, 2nd ed.). Oxford: Oxford University Press.

Parker-Pope, T. (2009, April 27). A.D.H.D. drugs linked to higher test scores. *New York Times*. Retrieved from http://well.blogs.nytimes.com/2009/04/27/adhd-drugs-linked-with-higher-test-scores/.

Pear, R. (1998, December 29). Clinton says benefits are safe in 2000. *New York Times*, p. 14.

Pear, R. (2005, February 2). Dispute over Medicare plan to cover erectile treatments. *New York Times*, p. 13.

Pet Product News. (2011 March 17). Pet industry spending tops $48 billion in 2010. Pet Product News. Retrieved from http://www.petproductnews.com/ headlines/2011/03/17/pet-industry-spending-tops-48-billion-in-2010.aspx.

Petersen, M. (2002, August 11). Heartfelt advice, hefty fees. *New York Times*. Retrieved from http://www.nytimes.com/2002/08/11/business/heartfelt-advice-hefty-fees.html?pagewanted=all&src=pm.

Pfizer. (1999, June). *Patient summary of information about Viagra (sildenafil citrate) tablets.* New York: Pfizer.

Pfizer. (2010, July). [Advertisement for Pristiq]. *Real Simple.*

Pfizer (2010, July). [Advertisement for Vaccines]. *Black Enterprise.*

Pfizer. (2011, August). [Advertisement for Pristiq]. *Psychology Today.*

Pfizer. (2012, December). ["Anthem," Commercial for Viagra]. Retrieved from http://www.viagra.com/viagra-tv-commercial.aspx.

Pfizer. (2012, December). ["Anthem," Commercial for Viagra]. Retrieved from http://www.viagra.com/viagra-tv-commercial.aspx.

Pfizer. (2012, December). ["Gas Station," Commercial for Viagra]. Retrieved from http://www.viagra.com/viagra-tv-commercial.aspx.

Pfizer. (2012, December). ["Sail," Commercial for Viagra]. Retrieved from http://www.viagra.com/viagra-tv-commercial.aspx.

Pfizer. (2012, December). ["Stuck," Commercial for Viagra]. Retrieved from http://www.viagra.com/viagra-tv-commercial.aspx.

Pfizer Inc. & Subsidiary Companies. (2010). *2010 financial report: Appendix A.* New York: Pfizer.

Pfizer U.S. Pharmacetuicals. (2002, February). *For every puzzle, there's a solution.* [promotional mailer]. New York: Pfizer.

Pfizer U.S. Pharmaceuticals. (1999, July). *What every man (and woman) should know about erectile dysfunction.* New York: Pfizer.

Pinkus, R.L. (2002). From Lydia Pinkham to Bob Dole: What the changing face of direct-to-consumer drug advertising reveals about the professionalism of medicine. *Kennedy Institute of Ethics Journal,* 12(2), 141–158.

Rabin, K. (Ed.). (2004). Commentary: DTC advertising for prescription medicines: Research and reflections as the second decade ends [Special issue]. *Journal of Health Communication,* 9.

Rafalovich, A. (2007). *Framing ADHD children: A critical examination of the history, discourse, and everyday experience of attention deficit/hyperactivity disorder.* Lanham, MD: Lexington Books.

Rampell, C. (2010, February 6). Women now a majority in American workplaces. *New York Times,* p. A10.

Read, J. (2009). A genealogy of homo-economicus: Neoliberalism and the production of subjectivity. In S. Binkley & J. Capetillo (Eds.), *A Foucault for the 21st century: Governmentality, biopolitics and discipline in the new millennium.* Newcastle, England: Cambridge Scholars, 2–15.

Reed, L., & Saukko, P. (2010). *Governing the female body: Gender, health, and networks of power.* Albany: SUNY Press.

Ridley, J. (2010, February 10). Toyota, Jet Blue, other big companies say they're sorry in major ads, spotlighting shortcomings. *New York Daily News*. Retrieved from http:// articles.nydailynews.com/2010-02-10/entertainment/27055888_1_toyotas-barbara-lippert-ads.

Rodgers, G. (1989). Precarious work in Western Europe: The state of the debate. In G. Rodgers & J Rodgers (Eds.), *Precarious jobs in labour market regulation: The growth of atypical employment in Western Europe*. Geneva: International Institute for Labour Studies, 1–16.

Rose, N. (2003). The neurochemical self and its anomalies. In R. Ericson & A. Doyle (Eds.), *Risk and morality*. Toronto: University of Toronto Press, 407–437.

Rose, N. (2007). *The politics of life itself: Biomedicine, power, and subjectivity in the twenty-first century*. Princeton, NJ: Princeton University Press.

Rothberg, P. (2009, October 30). Being a woman is not a pre-existing condition [Web log post]. *The Nation*. Retrieved from http://salsa.wiredforchange.com.

Rubin, G. (1975). The traffic in women: Notes on the "political economy" of sex. In R. R. Reiter (Ed.), *Toward an anthropology of women*. New York: Monthly Review Press, 157–210.

Savage, D.G. (2011, June 24). Supreme Court sides with pharmaceutical industry in two decisions. *Los Angeles Times*. Retrieved from http://www.latimes.com.

Schwarz, A. (2012, October 9). Attention disorder or not, pills to help in school. *New York Times*. Retrieved from http://www.nytimes.com/2012/10/09/health/attention-disorder-or-not-children-prescribed-pills-to-help-in-school.html?pagewanted=all&_r=0.

Schulte, B. (2011, April 28). More women have ADHD…or is it the stress of modern life? *Washington Post*. Retrieved from http://www.washingtonpost.com.

Shaw, A. (2008). Direct-to-consumer advertising (DTC) of pharmaceuticals. ProQuest Discovery Guides. Retrieved from http://www.csa.com/discoveryguides/discoveryguides-main.php.

Shire. (2004, month unknown). [Advertisement for Adderall], *Good Housekeeping*.

Shire. (2009a, January). [Advertisement for Vyvanse]. *Parents*.

Shire. (2009b, May). Consistent Carl [Advertisement for Vyvanse]. *Parents*.

Shire. (2010a). Intuniv. Retrieved from http://www.intuniv.com.

Shire. (2010b, February). Helped my sister [Advertisement for Vyvanse]. *Better Homes and Gardens*.

Shire. (2010c, March). [Advertisement for Vyvanse]. *Parents*.

Shire. (2010d, April). Are your child's ADHD symptoms consistently controlled even during family time? [Advertisement for Vyvanse]. *Working Mother*.

Shire. (2010e, April). Vyvanse for adults with ADHD. Shown to be effective even at 14 hours after taking [Advertisement for Vyvanse]. *Working Mother*.

Shire. (2010f, July). [Advertisement for Vyvanse]. *Better Homes and Gardens.*

Shire. (2010g, July/August/September). Fairy tale [Advertisement for Vyvanse]. *Parents.*

Shire. (2010h, August). Consistent Kevin [Advertisement for Vyvanse]. *Parents.*

Shire. (2010i, September). [Advertisement for Vyvanse]. *Parents.*

Shire. (2010j, October). [Advertisement for Vyvanse]. *Parents.*

Sieben, L. (2011, January 27). College freshmen report record-low levels of emotional health. *The Chronicle of Higher Education.* Retrieved from http://chronicle.com.

Singh, I. (2003). Boys will be boys: Fathers' perspectives on ADHD symptoms, diagnosis, and drug treatment. *Harvard Review of Psychiatry*, 11(6), 308–316.

Singh, I. (2007). Not just naughty: 50 years of stimulant drug advertising. In A. Tone & E. S. Watkins (Eds.), *Medicating modern America: Prescription drugs in history*. New York University Press, 131–155.

Smith, R.E., et al. (1979*). The subtle revolution: Women at work.* Washington, DC: Urban Institute.

Sollman, M. J., Ranseen, J. D., & Berry, T. R. (2010). Detection of feigned ADHD in college students. *Psychological Assessment*, 22(2), 325–335.

Solomon, A. (2001). *The noonday demon: An atlas of depression.* New York: Scribner.

Sommers, C. H. (2000). *The war against boys: How misguided feminism is harming our young men.* New York: Simon & Schuster.

Spake, D. F., & Mathew, J. (2007). Consumer opinion and effectiveness of direct-to-consumer advertising. *Journal of Consumer Marketing* 24(5), 283–292.

Spinoza, B. (2000). *Ethics* (G.H.R. Parkinson, Ed. & Trans.). New York: Oxford University Press. (Original work published 1678).

Steinberg, J. (2011, January 27). Pressures of high school and economy weigh on college freshmen [Web log post]. *The Choice.* Retrieved from http://thechoice.blogs.nytimes.com.

Stephen, A. (2000). A nation puts its kids on drugs. *New Statesman*, 129(4476), 20.

Stephenson, B. (Producer), & Mills, M. (Writer/Director). (2005). *Thumbsucker* [Motion picture]. United States: Sony Pictures Classics.

Stolberg, S. G. (2002, November 17). Preschool meds. *New York Times Magazine*, 59. Retrieved from http://www.nytimes.com/2002/11/17/magazine/17RITALIN.html?pagewanted=all.

Tait, G. (2001). Pathologising difference, governing personality. *Asia-Pacific Journal of Teacher Education*, 29(1), 93–102.

Tait, G. (2003, October–December). Free will, moral responsibility and ADHD. *International Journal of Inclusive Education*, 7(4), 429–446.

Tait, G. (2005). The ADHD debate and the philosophy of truth. *International Journal of Inclusive Education,* 9(1), 17–38.

Titus, J. J. (2004). Boy trouble: Rhetorical framing of boys' underachievement. *Discourse: Studies in the Cultural Politics of Education*, 25(2), 145–169.

Tone, A., & Watkins, E.S. (2007). *Medicating modern America: Prescription drugs in history*. New York: New York University Press.

Treaster, J. B. (1998, December 25). Prudential's policyholders wait and fume. *New York Times*, p. 1.

Tuchman, G. (1996). ESS presidential address, 1995—invisible differences: On the management of children in postindustrial society. *Sociological Forum*, 11(1), 3–23.

Updated: Top ten most-watched Super Bowls of all time [Web log post]. (2009, January 29). *Nielsenwire*. Retrieved from http://blog.nielsen.com/nielsenwire/media_ entertainment/top-10-most-watched-super-bowls-of-all-time/.

U.S. Bureau of Labor Statistics. (2001, January 24). *Services fueled 1990s job growth*. Washington, DC: Division of Information and Marketing Services.

U.S. Department of Health and Human Services, National Institute of Mental Health. (n.d.). The numbers count: Mental disorders in America. Retrieved from http://www.nimh.nih.gov/health/publications/the-numbers-count-mental-disorders-in-america/index.shtml#Dysthymic.

U.S. Department of Health and Human Services, National Institute of Mental Health. (2010). Attention deficit hyperactivity disorder (ADHD) (NIH Publication No. 08-3572). Retrieved from http://www.nimh.nih.gov.

U.S. Department of Justice, Drug Enforcement Administration. (2011). *Drugs of abuse*. Washington, DC: Author. Retrieved from .http://www.justice.gov/dea/drug info/concern_meth.shtml.

U.S. Food and Drug Administration (2011). Bad ad program: 2011–2012 year end report. Retrieved from http://www.fda.gov/Drugs/GuidanceComplianceRegulatory Information/Surveillance/DrugMarketingAdvertisingandCommunications/ucm25 8719.htm.

Veijola, S., & Jokinen, E. (2008, September). Towards a hostessing society? Mobile arrangements of gender and labour. *NORA—Nordic Journal of Feminist and Gender Research*, 16(3), 166–181.

Viagra, like its fans, faces old age. (2010, June 7). *Media Week*, p. 23.

Virno, P. (1996). The ambivalence of disenchantment (M. Turits, Trans.). In P. Virno & M. Hardt (Eds.), *Radical thought in Italy: A potential politics*. Minneapolis: University of Minnesota Press, 13–36.

Virno, P. (2004). *A grammar of the multitude: For an analysis of contemporary forms of life* (I. Bertoletti, J. Cascaito, & A. Casson, Trans.). Los Angeles, CA: Semiotexte.

Vlahos, J. (2008, July 12). Pill-popping pets. *New York Times Magazine*. Retrieved from http://www.nytimes.com/2008/07/13/magazine/13pets-t.html?page wanted=all.

Vosko, L. F., MacDonald, M., & Campbell, I. (2009). Introduction: Gender and the concept of precarious employment. In L. F. Vosko, M. MacDonald, & I. Campbell (Eds.), *Gender and the contours of precarious employment*. New York: Routledge, 1–25.

Waters, R. (2005, May 1). Medicating Alliah. *Mother Jones*. Retrieved from http://www.motherjones.com/politics/2005/05/medicating-aliah.

Watkins, E. (1995, Autumn–Winter). Introduction. *Social Text*, 44, 1–2.

Weber, L. J. (2006). *Profits before people?: Ethical standards and the marketing of prescription drugs*. Bloomington: Indiana University Press.

WebMD. (2010). Attention-deficit/hyperactivity disorder: Causes of ADHD. Retrieved from http://www.webmd.com/add-adhd/guide/adhd-causes.

WebMD. (2011). Attention-deficit/hyperactivity disorder: Symptoms of ADHD. Retrieved from http://www.webmd.com/add-adhd/guide/adhd-symptoms.

Weiss, J. (2000). *To have and to hold: Marriage, the baby boom, and social change*. Chicago: University of Chicago Press.

Willis, G. (1998, October 26). Deberg gets destroyed. *New York Post*, p. 79.

Wolraich, M.L., & Baumgaertel, A. (1996). The prevalence of attention deficit hyperactivity disorder based on the new DSM-IV criteria. *Peabody Journal of Education*, 71(4), 168–186.

World Bank Group. (2002). *Constructing knowledge societies: New challenges for tertiary education*. Geneva, Switzerland: World Bank, 30, 81. Retrieved from http://www.worldbank.org.

Zita, J. N. (1998). *Body talk: Philosophical reflections on sex and gender*. New York: Columbia University Press.

Žižek, S. (1994). Introduction: The spectre of ideology. In S. Žižek (Ed.), *Mapping ideology*. London, England: Verso, 1–33, 14.

INDEX

Page listings in italics refer to footnotes.

I

J

K

L

M

N

Y

Z

Toby Miller
General Editor

Popular Culture and Everyday Life (PC&EL) is the new space for critical books in cultural studies. The series innovates by stressing multiple theoretical, political, and methodological approaches to commodity culture and lived experience, borrowing from sociological, anthropological, and textual disciplines. Each PC&EL volume develops a critical understanding of a key topic in the area through a combination of a thorough literature review, original research, and a student-reader orientation. The series includes three types of books: single-authored monographs, readers of existing classic essays, and new companion volumes of papers on central topics. Likely fields covered are: fashion; sport; shopping; therapy; religion; food and drink; youth; music; cultural policy; popular literature; performance; education; queer theory; race; gender; class.

For additional information about this series or for the submission of manuscripts, please contact:

Toby Miller
Department of Media & Cultural Studies
Interdisciplinary Studies Building
University of California, Riverside
Riverside, CA 92521

To order other books in this series, please contact our Customer Service Department:

(800) 770-LANG (within the U.S.)
(212) 647-7706 (outside the U.S.)
(212) 647-7707 FAX

Or browse online by series: www.peterlang.com

www.ingramcontent.com/pod-product-compliance
Ingram Content Group UK Ltd.
Pitfield, Milton Keynes, MK11 3LW, UK
UKHW020841290926
15470UKWH00004B/1481

9 781433 110443